ILLEGAL DRUG USE IN THE UNITED KINGDOM

£39.95 NN

Illegal Drug Use in the United Kingdom

Prevention, Treatment and Enforcement

Dr Cameron Stark MPH, MRCPsych, MFPHM
Consultant in Public Health Medicine
Highland Health Board
Beechwood Park
Inverness IV2 3HG

Dr Brian A. Kidd MRCPsych
Consultant Psychiatrist (Addictions)
Community Addiction Service
Central Scotland Healthcare NHS Trust
Old Denny Road
Larbert FK5 4SD

Dr Roger A.D. Sykes MRCPsych
Consultant Psychiatrist
Ravenscraig Hospital
Inverkip Road
Greenock PA16 9HA

Ashgate
ARENA

Aldershot • Brookfield USA • Singapore • Sydney

Published by
Ashgate Publishing Limited
Gower House
Croft Road
Aldershot
Hants GU11 3HR
England

Ashgate Publishing Company
Old Post Road
Brookfield
Vermont 05036
USA

British Library Cataloguing in Publication Data
Illegal drug use in the United Kingdom : prevention,
    treatment and enforcement
    1. Drug abuse – Great Britain   2. Drug abuse – Great Britain –
    Prevention   3. Drug abuse – Treatment – Great Britain
    I. Stark, Cameron   II. Kidd, Brian   III. Sykes, Roger
    362.2'9'0941

Library of Congress Cataloging–in–Publication Data
Illegal drug use in the United Kingdom : prevention, treatment and
    enforcement / [edited by] Cameron Stark, Brian A. Kidd, Roger Sykes.
        p.   cm.
    Includes bibliographical references.
    ISBN 1–85742–431–X (hardbound)
        1. Drug abuse—Great Britain—Prevention.   2. Narcotics, Control
    of—Great Britain.   3. Drug abuse—Treatment—Great Britain.
    4. Narcotic addicts—Rehabilitation—Great Britain.   5. Narcotic
    addicts–Services for—Great Britain.   I. Stark, Cameron.
    II. Kidd, Brian.   III. Sykes, Roger.
    HV5840.G7155   1998
    362.29'0941—dc21   98–20204
                                                                      CIP

ISBN 1 85742 431 X

Typeset by Manton Typesetters, 5–7 Eastfield Road, Louth, Lincs, LN11 7AJ, UK.
Printed and bound in Great Britain by MPG Books Ltd, Bodmin, Cornwall

Contents

List of figures and tables

Figures

Tables

List of contributors

Malcolm Bruce, MB, ChB., MRCPsych. PhD is Consultant Psychiatrist in Addiction at the Community Drug Problem Service, Royal Edinburgh Hospital. He has carried out research with medical students, psychiatric trainees and general practitioners with an interest in working with drug users. As an elected executive member of the substance misuse section of the Royal College of Psychiatrists he intends to develop the definitions of service provision for patients with co-morbidity.

Niall Coggans, BA (Hons) is Senior Lecturer in Health Promotion in the Department of Pharmaceutical Sciences at the University of Strathclyde. He has been involved in drug and alcohol research for many years, taking a particular interest in the evaluation of drug education, health promotion, and alcohol and aggression. Current research interests include drug and alcohol education, and health promotion in primary care settings.

Paul Cook, BA (Hons), MSc is Independent Consultant to the European Monitoring Centre on Drugs and Drug Addiction and formerly Chief Superintendent with the Greater Manchester Police. He is a member of the Association of Chief Police Officer's Drugs Sub-Committee.

Steven Dalton, is a qualified Practice Teacher. He has worked in the drugs and alcohol field for over 14 years as a practitioner, trainer and manager. Steven is currently employed by Forth Valley Health Board as both the Substance Development Officer and the Substance Development Team Manager. Prior to taking up the post in Forth Valley, Steven managed the regional Drug and Alcohol Social Work Service in Tayside. His previous posts include drug and alcohol work in both the voluntary and statutory sector and within an urban aid funded project.

Tony Doyle joined the Merseyside Police in 1975 having been, previously, an engineer in mechanical engineering. He served in the Force Drug Squad (twice), Vice Squad, uniform and is currently the Crime Manager at South Sefton, Merseyside. He was promoted to sergeant in 1981, Inspector in 1991 and Detective Chief Inspector in 1996. He is also Home Office-trained Force Negotiator. Mr Doyle has presented many talks on organised drug crime around the world to police forces in Canada, Hungary, Norway, Scotland, Northern Ireland and Eire.

Martin Frischer, BA, PhD is Senior Lecturer in Health Services Research, Department of Medicines Management, Keele University. Dr Frischer represents the UK on the Scientific Committee of the European Monitoring Centre for Drugs and Drugs Addiction (EMCDDA).

Sally Haw, BSc (Hons) is Research Specialist (Substance Misuse) for the Health Education Board for Scotland. She has worked in the field of substance misuse research for the last 15 years with a particular focus on the prevalence of drug misuse and HIV infection. Current research interests also include the evaluation of smoking cessation interventions and the natural history of smoking cessation.

Mary Hepburn, BSc, MD, MRCGP, FRCOG is Senior Lecturer in Women's Reproductive Health in the Glasgow University Department of Obstetrics/ Gynaecology and Social Policy/Social Work and also Honorary Consultant Obstetrician and Gynaecologist, Glasgow Royal Maternity Hospital. She established and is Consultant in charge of the Glasgow Women's Reproductive Health Service for women with severe social problems including drug use. The service also provides care for women with HIV and other blood-borne infections. This reflects Dr Hepburn's academic and clinical interests which focus on effects of all aspects of women's reproductive health including pregnancy outcome, of socioeconomic deprivation and associated issues, problem drug use and other substance misuse together with HIV and other blood-borne infections. Her interests extend to appropriate service design, provision and delivery for women with special needs and she has published work on these topics in a number of textbooks and scientific journals.

J. Kennedy Roberts, formerly senior partner in Muirhouse Medical Group, a founder member of the Edinburgh Drug Addiction Study, and joint MRC

Grant Holder (1986–1992) with Dr J.R. Robertson (follow-up of a cohort of HIV infected and uninfected patients to determine behavioural change and progression to AIDS). Since 1979 working as a GP managing mainly IV Drug Misusers in a multi-disciplinary approach, initiating needle exchange, methadone and other opiates. (Prescribing both for detoxification and maintenance.) Variety of publications relating to management of drug misusers and issues related to HIV. Involved with the Scottish Prison Service since 1994, currently Senior Medical Officer, HMP&I Cornton Vale, Scotland's only women's prison.

Brian A. Kidd, MB, ChB, MRCPsych is Consultant Psychiatrist in the Community Addiction Service in Forth Valley. He is GP trained and as a psychiatrist has worked in drug treatment services throughout central Scotland and the south west of England. His main research interests are in the development of safe systems of service delivery for drug users, shared care with GPs and the measurement of treatment outcomes. He is chairman of the Scottish Drugs Specialists Committee, an executive member of the Royal College of Psychiatrists, Scottish Division, Substance Misuse Section and a member of the Forth Valley Substance Action Team.

Pat Lerpiniere, BSc (Hons), PGCE, Dip H Ed (Distinction) is Patient Services Manager, Ayrshire and Arran Community Health Care NHS Trust. He is manager of an integrated addiction service, covering treatment, prevention, research and health promotion. Pat has a background in teaching, lecturing and health promotion with over ten years working in the alcohol and drug field. Particular interests include service delivery and outcome measurement. He is a member of a number of local and national committees and working groups, including Ayrshire Alcohol and Drug Action Team and the Scottish Office DAT/AMCC Evaluation Advisory Group.

Charles Lind, MB, BS, MRCPsych, Dip. Soc. Anth. is Clinical Director of the Addictions Service of Ayrshire and Arran Community Health Care NHS Trust and a former Chairman of the Substance Misuse Section of the Scottish Division of the Royal College of Psychiatrists. He has a long-standing interest in perceptions of rural drug use and in the peculiarities of the effective delivery of drug services in rural areas.

Natalie Morel, BA (Hons) is Coordinator at BLAST. She formerly worked at Ashworth Special Hospital on the Crisis Intervention Ward before joining the Highland Health Promotion Department and then setting up the BLAST Recreational Drugs Project with the Inverness Council on Alcohol.

xii *List of contributors*

She is an experienced clubber and is currently Chairperson for the Scottish Youth and Drugs Working Group.

Moira C. Paton, Bsc (Hons) is Strategic Planning Manager for the Highland Health Board. She was formerly Research and Planning Officer for Strathclyde Regional Council and was involved in setting up the Glasgow Drop-in Centre (now Base 75) for women working as prostitutes. She has a long-standing interest in issues of violence against women.

Cameron Stark, MB, ChB, MPH. MRCPsych, MFPHM is a Consultant in Public Health Medicine with Highland Health Board. He worked in psychiatry in Glasgow before training in Public Health Medicine. Cameron has research interests in suicide and deliberate self-harm, rural health care, service evaluation and risk perception. He co-edited the textbook *Management of Violence and Aggression in Health Care*, published by Gaskell in 1995.

Roger A.D. Sykes, MB, ChB, MRCPsych is Clinical Director for Adult Mental Health Services, Inverclyde District from 1991. He has been Consultant in General Adult Psychiatry with special interest in Substance Misuse Disorders for ten years and recent past-Chairman of the Scottish Substance Misuse Section, Royal College of Psychiatry. He has published research work in general psychiatry and both alcohol and drug misuse problems. He has worked intensively with local and national voluntary agencies in the field of counselling for alcohol and drug problems.

Avril Taylor, MA, PhD is Head of Behavioural Studies, Scottish Centre for Infection and Environmental Health (SCIEH), Glasgow. Her current research interests include the effectiveness of methadone treatment and the epidemiology of hepatitis C among injecting drug users.

Jonathan Watson, PhD, MSc. BA (Hons) is Director of Research and Evaluation at the Health Education Board for Scotland in Edinburgh, having worked in public health and health promotion for 15 years. Current research interests are in men's health, the body, new paradigms in health promotion research and evaluation methodology. He has recently co-edited *The Body in Everyday Life* with Sarah Nettleton published by Routledge in 1998.

Introduction
Cameron Stark

This book is intended for anyone who has to help shape local strategy on illegal drug use, who works in drug services, or who has a professional or personal interest in drug prevention and treatment. It provides an overview of the three strands of present UK policy: prevention, treatment and enforcement. Specialist reference books exist which deal with one or other of these aspects; this does not replace such works. It is important, however, that people understand how the components fit together, and this book is intended to give an overall picture of responses to drug use. This approach will be particularly useful to people who are coming to the area for the first time, or who work in a specialised area and want to know more of how other services fit into the United Kingdom's response to drug-related problems. Members of Drug Action Teams and Drug Reference Groups should find it of interest because of its multi-sectoral, multi-disciplinary approach.

The book describes policy issues and European responses to drug use, as well as how to measure the extent of drug use. It then discusses the nature and role of components of drug prevention, enforcement and treatment services. Later chapters review services aimed at specific important groups of people who may be at risk from drug use, including pregnant women, sex workers, club goers or prisoners. A final chapter discusses the development of local strategies.

Context of the work

Prevention, enforcement and treatment services for illegal drug use in the United Kingdom are shaped by government policy. The English White

Paper, 'Tackling Drugs Together' (HM Government, 1995) provided a statement of purpose:

- To take effective action by vigorous law enforcement, accessible treatment and a new emphasis on education and prevention
- To increase the safety of communities from drug-related crime
- To reduce the acceptability and availability of drugs to young people
- To reduce the health risks and other damage related to drug misuse.

This three-stranded approach was in keeping with the earlier Scottish Ministerial Drugs Task Force Report (Ministerial Drugs Task Force 1994), and demonstrated recognition that no one agency or sector could influence drug use on its own. Both reports recommended a move to a co-ordinated response to illegal drug use.

'Tackling Drugs Together' established Drug Action Teams (DATs) which were to deliver the national strategy in local areas. These were to include senior representatives from local authorities including education and social services; the local health authority; police, prison and probation services. In addition, DATs were encouraged to include a voluntary sector representative. The DATs in turn would establish Drug Reference Groups (DRGs) which would provide local expert advice to DATs. This was a acknowledgement that, if the DAT was to consist of sufficiently senior representatives to take decisions on resource use, then DAT members were unlikely to have particular expertise in drug misuse and would require support.

DRGs were to have broad membership, including representatives from the private and voluntary sectors, drug service users, schools and general practice. Their role was:

- To assess the nature and scale of local drug misuse problems
- To advise the DAT on measures needed to tackle the problem effectively
- To provide a local forum for exchange of information about good practice and new initiatives
- To involve local communities in action to make progress on all three strands of the statement of purpose (prevention, treatment and enforcement).

Similar arrangements were included in the Scottish Ministerial Task Force Report. It is clear, therefore, that UK policy endorses a multi-sectoral response to drug misuse, and it is that approach which this book reflects.

Conclusion

The United Kingdom policy on illegal drug use requires a multi-stranded approach involving many different agencies and groups. Agencies require an understanding of how their service or agency fits into the pattern of responses to drug use, while policymakers need information on the breadth of prevention, treatment and enforcement options. This book is intended to contribute to such an understanding.

References

HM Government (1995), *Tackling Drugs Together: A Strategy for England 1995–1998*, London: HMSO.
Ministerial Drugs Task Force (1994), *Drugs in Scotland: Meeting the Challenge. Report of the Ministerial Drugs Task Force*, Edinburgh: HMSO.

1 European drug policy on supply and demand reduction

Paul Cook

Introduction

The problems of drug misuse and abuse are not new to Europe, neither are the solutions. Historically most western countries have followed the American approach to the 'war on drugs', with its emphasis on supply reduction and disruption in consumption.

Experience reveals that if there is a demand for prohibited drugs, then there is an opportunity for organised crime to make profit by supplying that demand. Those involved in the supply of illicit drugs will find ways to circumvent legal controls by resorting to bribery, corruption and violence, while the police and customs agencies are largely left to plug the holes. The international nature of the drug problem has necessitated international cooperation and action. Many Western European countries have examined their responses to illicit drug use. They have recognised that drug-related problems have multiple causes, and need multi-disciplinary responses built into properly resourced, planned and coordinated drug policies at local and European levels.

European responses to drug misuse

The creation of the European Community in 1957 provided the impetus and framework for developing and implementing European drug policies through a number of groups and European institutions. Two significant groups in relation to drug policy development were the former Trevi Group and CELAD.

1

The Trevi Group was set up by the European Council of Ministers in 1975, to provide a basis for greater European cooperation to combat terrorism. The initial brief was later expanded to tackle other organised crime such as drugs trafficking. Membership of the Trevi Group included representatives of each member state, plus others attending as observers. An early initiative was the development of a network of Drug Liaison Officers (DLOs) in drug producer and transit countries, and national drugs intelligence units in each member state – subsequently national intelligence units linked to the Europol Drugs Unit (see page 8).

CELAD was instigated in 1989 by President Mitterand of France, who wrote to the European Community heads of government and the President of the Commission, suggesting the establishment of a European Committee to Combat Drugs: CELAD. CELAD's membership was made up of government-nominated representatives and the European Commission. CELAD prepared a programme of measures including a first European Action Plan, which was approved by the European Council in Dublin, 1990. The programme included five measures:

- Inter-member coordination
- A European Drugs Monitoring Centre
- Demand reduction
- Suppression of illicit drugs trade
- International action.

The subsequent integrated pan-European Plan, aimed to develop a programme of action at both Community and member state level, and included coordination of anti drug strategies in member states and suppression of illicit trade in drugs. The Programme includes measures intended to contribute towards the reduction in demand for drugs, and created a European Observatory on Drugs. The European Action Plan has been revised twice – in 1992 and 1994 – when CELAD held its most recent meeting. The Plan recognises that prevention must be given at least as much attention as the laws and penalties relating to drugs and drug trafficking. The latest European Action Plan, covering the years 1995 to 1998, is built on three elements:

- Prevention of drug dependency
- Reduction of drug trafficking
- Action at the international level.

European framework

What follows is a brief description of drug-related organisations currently operating in Europe, both within and outside the formal framework of the European Union. Figure 1 provides a schematic description of organisations and their interrelationships, and page 14 lists useful contacts. The European Community, based on the Treaty of Rome signed in 1957 by six countries – Belgium, France, Germany, Italy, Luxembourg and the Netherlands (the United Kingdom joined in 1973) – sets out the Community's legal framework, providing flexibility and stability for close neighbours to work together to tackle common problems such as drugs.

The expansion and strengthening of the European Community was achieved through both the Single European Act (SEA) and the Treaty of European Union (TEU). SEA, established in 1986, created a European Community without internal frontiers, and expanded areas of competence into issues such as freedom of movement for people, services, goods and capital. The TEU was ratified in November 1993 and is commonly referred to as the Maastricht Treaty. It is dedicated to increasing economic integration and strengthening cooperation among its member states, and is a major expansion and amendment to the organisational framework of the Treaty of Rome. Decision making in the European Union is divided between supra-national European institutions and the governments of the member states, supported by the European Commission.

European Union and subsidiarity

Getting the right balance between European Union and national action on issues such as drugs is known as 'subsidiarity'. The Maastricht Treaty provides a framework for governments to work together in key areas outside the tight rules of the Treaty of Rome. The Maastricht Treaty is founded on three pillars of cooperation under the European Council:

Pillar I   Public Health and Trade Cooperation (based on the Treaty of Rome, Single European Act, Maastricht Treaty), where full community rules and procedures apply.

Pillar II   Common foreign and security policy (based on the Maastricht Treaty) where inter-governmental cooperation applies.

Pillar III   Justice and Home Affairs (based on the Maastricht Treaty), where inter-governmental cooperation applies between national governments and the European Commission.

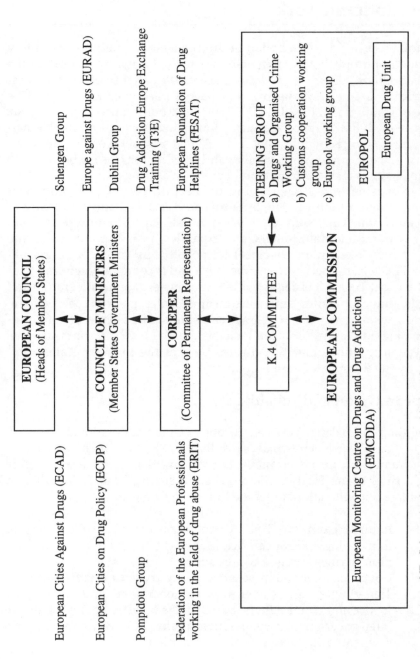

Figure 1.1 Drug-related organisations operating in Europe

NB: Schematic shows groups inside (attached) and outside (detached), the formal European Union structure

4

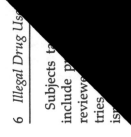

Drugs are tackled by the European Union in tw
competence', where Community institutions a:
within the framework of the Union, by 'cooperati

Community competence

Under Pillar I, powers are conferred on the
treaties which are no longer in the province of
These powers are subject to the principle of sut
that the Community shall take action only w
objectives of a proposed action cannot be sufficiently achieved by the
member states. In relation to drugs, articles within Pillar I which have
been used are:

- Articles 57 and 100A were the basis for the EU directive on preventing the use of the financial system for money laundering
- Article 113 allows the community to take steps to discourage the
  diversion of precursor chemicals for the illicit manufacture of drugs
- Article 129 relates to public health, and deals specifically with drug
  prevention
- Article 130W allows the European Community to work cooperatively
  with non-EU nations, in the field of drugs.

Cooperation between member states

Intergovernmental cooperation applies to Pillars II and Pillar III. Although
Pillar II does not refer to drugs specifically, member states have joined
together their diplomatic efforts to promote the European position: for
example, in June 1993 the European Council recognised drugs as suitable
for common action under the Common Foreign and Security Policy.

Pillar III, Title VI, Article K.1, is relevant to the drugs issue. Article K.1,
provisions 7, 8 and 9, cover drug trafficking, and provision 4, drug prevention. All Pillar III work is supervised by the Justice and Home Affairs
Council made up of government ministers of member states, supported by
the Committee of Permanent Representatives (COREPER), and a committee
of senior officials known as the K.4 committee, who coordinate all activities. Working to K.4 are three steering groups covering immigration and
asylum (Steering Group I), police and customs cooperation (Steering Group
II), and judicial cooperation (Steering Group III), each with a number of
specialist working groups; for example, the Drugs and Organised Crime
Working Group, involves agencies/representatives from all member states,
and reports to the European Council.

...ckled by the Drugs and Organised Crime Working Group ...roduction of an annual report on drug trafficking. They have ...d a wide range of issues including drug trafficking in Latin coun- ...Turkey and the Central and Eastern European Countries; drug tour- ...; domestic cultivation and production of drugs; controlled deliveries; police/Customs agreements; money laundering; synthetic drugs; chemical profiling; exchange and secondment of law enforcement officers and undercover agents.

The Customs Cooperation Working Group involves customs personnel from all member states, and addresses drug-related issues including: improving external border control; control of container traffic; cooperation on controlled deliveries; trafficking on European routes; information exchange between member states' DLOs and cross-border coordination between customs and law enforcement.

European institutions

The five most important institutions within the European Union are:

- The European Council, involving heads of state as well as the President of the European Commission. The European Council's role is to set political priorities for the EU at its twice-yearly meetings
- The Council of Ministers is made up of ministers of heads of state, and concerned with the adoption of EU legislation
- The democratically elected European Parliament is primarily involved with influencing EU policy through consultation and cooperation
- A central function is provided by the European Commission, which makes draft legislation/policy suggestions, upholds the Treaties and manages the European Union's international trade relationships
- The European Court of Justice serves as the final arbiter in matters of legal disputes among EU members and institutions.

In addition to the five primary European Union institutions, two new drug-related European institutions have been established: the European Monitoring Centre (EMCDDA), and the European Police Office (Europol).

EMCDDA was established in Lisbon in 1994, and provides the Community and its member states with objective, reliable and comparable European information concerning drugs, drug addiction and their consequences. It has five priority areas:

- Reduction of the demand for drugs
- National and community drug strategies and policies, including in-

ternational, bilateral and community policies, action plans, legislation, activities and agreements
● International cooperation and geopolitics of supply (with special emphasis on cooperation programmes and information on producer and
transit countries)
● Control of trade in narcotic drugs, psychotropic substances and pre-
cursors
● And work on the drugs economy, particularly small- and medium-
scale drug trafficking, and laundering of drug money.

Supporting the work of EMCDDA is a network of 15 National Focal Points
set up across Europe, and one at the European Commission, within the
European Information Network on Drugs and Drug Addiction (Reitox).
Reitox facilitates and coordinates activities related to EMCDDA, and acts as
a conduit to and from member states and the Monitoring Centre. The
EMCDDA should add value to the available information and drug statistics
by producing annual European-wide reports on drugs. The National Focal
Points for the United Kingdom are based at the Institute for the Study of
Drug Dependence (ISDD), which seeks to advance knowledge, understanding and policy making about drugs through research and by collecting and
disseminating information, and the Department of Health, which is responsible for health promotion including drug prevention and treatment, and
has a general brief for cross-government drugs publicity and information.
Europol was agreed in the Maastricht Treaty within Article K.3 (2c –
provision of a convention), and Article K.1 (9). Subsequently, the Europol
convention was signed in 1995 by representatives of all member states'
governments, recommended for adoption within their respective constitu-
tional requirements, and the way cleared for ratification by the European
Council in June 1996 (UK has ratified the Europol convention). The base for
Europol is The Hague. The Europol convention aims to 'improve police
cooperation in the field of terrorism, unlawful drug trafficking and other
serious forms of international crime through constant confidential and intensive exchange of information between Europol and member states'
national units'. These forms of bilateral and multilateral cooperation are
not affected by the Treaty. Principle tasks which Europol undertakes are to:

● Facilitate exchange of information between member states
● Notify the competent authorities within member states of informa-
tion pertinent to them and criminal offences
● Aid investigations in member states by provision of relevant informa-
tion to the national units
● Disseminate good practice in investigative procedures

- Provide an EU wide central and operational analysis
- Be a centre of excellence
- Give technical and linguistic support.

The Europol Drugs Unit (EDU) has been established within Europol since 1994, and is functional within The Hague. It is staffed by police and customs officers from member states of the European Union. The EDU is not an operational unit rather concentrating on criminal intelligence gathering on drug trafficking and money laundering. Intelligence is shared with national drug intelligence units in every member state, and other police and customs sources.

Each member state has an intelligence unit and liaison officers (drawn from police and customs), who provide a link between national police and customs services, and the EDU. In the UK the liaison officers are based in the police National Criminal Intelligence Service (NCIS), and HM Customs and Excise.

Since the EDU began, its remit has been extended to include the illegal trade in radioactive and nuclear materials, illegal immigration networks, vehicle trafficking and trafficking in human beings. EDU has seen a steady rise in requests for its services as more practitioners become aware of its existence and potential.

Consultation

A feature of European Union policy developments is the influence of pan-European consultation. Two committees (Committee of the Regions and the Economic and Social Committee) provide an important consultation facility on drugs issues.

The Committee of the Regions has representatives drawn from local authorities across member states. Its principal aim is to involve European citizens more directly in the legislative process. The Committee is consulted by the European Council of Ministers and the European Commission (the UK contact is the Local Government International Bureau).

The Economic and Social Committee (ECOSOC) has members from all member states and, uniquely, representatives from groups such as employers, employees, small business, the professions, family organisations, and so on. The Committee produces Opinions on community issues referred to it by the European Council or Commission, and also has the right to create Opinions on its own initiative on any matter of community interest.

European groups and networks

Action against drugs occurs across both the European Union framework and the rest of Europe. Some of the groups and networks operating independently in Europe are listed below.

Pompidou Group

The European Group to Combat Drug Abuse and Illicit Trafficking, referred to as the Pompidou Group, was set up in 1971 by the European Council, supported by President George Pompidou. It aims to examine, from a multidisciplinary point of view, the problems of drug abuse and illicit trafficking. The Group is wider in its membership than the current European Union, and includes representatives from Central and Eastern European countries. It operates within the framework of the European Council and undertakes valuable work in four broad areas:

- An examination of 'Criminal Justice' responses to the problems of drug misusers
- Exploration of ways to combat drug traffickers by tracing and confiscating their financial assets
- The collection and evaluation of data for policy formulation in the drug field
- The investigation of educational initiatives.

The Pompidou Group's demand reduction staff training programme is carried out with the support of the PHARE multi-country programme for the fight against drugs (supported by the European Commission), and in cooperation with the International Labour Organisation (ILO), United Nations International Drug Control Programme (UNDCP) and the World Health Organisation (WHO). The programme's objectives are to provide participants with skills and knowledge in order to lay the foundations for the development and implementation of nationally based professional training relevant to demand reduction initiatives (prevention, treatment and rehabilitation). It supplements and reinforces existing demand reduction activities at national level in the participating countries.

Dublin Group

The Dublin Group is a flexible, informal consultation and coordination mechanism for global, regional and country specific problems of drug production, trafficking and demand. Its participants cooperate closely on international drugs policy, taking into account in particular the UN conventions on narcotic drugs of 1961, 1971 and 1988, the United Nations Global Action Plan and the work being done on the basis of these instruments by other groups or organisations. Members of the Dublin Group includes representatives of all European Union States, the United States, Canada, Norway, Australia, Japan, European Commission, and the UNDCP. The Group operates at central, regional and local levels. Central meetings are attended by all members to deal with matters of fundamental significance requiring joint discussion and coordination. Regional meetings are attended by those with an interest in the region, while local meetings are attended by heads of mission of participants or their representatives and DLOs, who work together to produce local situation reports and implement orientations from the regional group.

Schengen Group

The Schengen Group was established in June 1985 by Belgium, France, Germany, Luxembourg and the Netherlands, who signed an agreement to abolish frontier controls and harmonise cross-border procedures for goods and persons. In practice the Group examined and discussed obstacles to the free movement of goods and persons, notably border controls. Many other member states have signed up to the Schengen Agreement, but the UK has not. The work of one of Schengen's working groups, known as STUP (stupefacients or drugs), became a forerunner to more recent legislation introduced under the European Union, and the work of Europol and the European Drugs Unit.

STUP examined the work being carried out by other organisations in the drugs field, and worked to address incompatibilities across Europe. For example, there are similarities of national drug legislation across Europe, but implementation and emphasis can vary, as with the Dutch and German approach to the sale of soft drugs, particularly cannabis. As a result of Schengen discussions, Dutch enforcement actions were modified in relation to the sale of soft drugs in coffee shops.

Article 71 of the Schengen Convention provides for the harmonisation of drugs legislation and the regulation of narcotic substances by means of criminal law, and calls for a commitment from members to take all necessary measures towards the reduction in supply of drugs.

European Cities on Drug Policy (ECDP)

Members of ECDP are cities in Europe which subscribe to the Frankfurt Resolution launched in 1990. The Frankfurt Resolution promulgates a liberal approach to drug problems including that possession of cannabis no longer constitutes a penal offence, and that drug-using offenders are offered and provided with treatment services. ECDP produces a newsletter and mounts seminars and conferences which provide the opportunity for a network of cities to exchange information and experience.

European Cities Against Drugs (ECAD)

ECAD, born out of issues raised by ECDP, involves cities which support the Stockholm Resolution, and is against legalisation of drugs, but supportive of drug prevention and treatment programmes. ECAD publishes a twice-yearly newsletter and organises conferences and seminars for mayors of affiliated cities.

Europe Against Drugs (EURAD)

EURAD, based in Ireland, is a grass roots movement of European parents, youth and other concerned citizens, cooperating in the field of drug abuse since 1989. EURAD works closely with scientists and experts in the field of drug abuse, and its aims are:

- To promote humane restrictive drug policies of prevention and intervention against drug abuse in order to prevent further damage to individuals and society
- To prevent any form of legalisation of drugs
- To promote the education of parents, youth and other concerned citizens about all matters concerning drug abuse through accurate, relevant and up-to-date information and research findings.

European Foundation of Drug Helplines (FESAT)

FESAT started informally in the early 1990s, was formally constituted in 1993 and is supported by the European Community as an information network. FESAT has produced a number of publications including a directory of services. The UK national drugs helpline is a member of FESAT.

Federation of European Professionals Working in the Field of Drug Abuse (ERIT)

ERIT is an umbrella organisation for professional national organisations in the field of drug prevention, treatment and rehabilitation. It takes a particular stance to promote the civil rights of drug users.

Drug Addiction Europe Exchange Training (T3E)

This pan-European federation was set up in 1991, and works towards the development and enhancement of a coordinated network of drug-related exchange training and research schemes in Europe. T3E runs an exchange programme, training seminars, summer university and produces publications.

Conclusion

Post-war Europe has seen rapid growth in cooperation at all levels from the political arena to grass roots activities. In particular, the European Union has provided a stable platform for tackling common problems such as drug abuse and trafficking. This is important because the all-pervasive nature of drugs respects no individual country's borders or groups of people. Opening borders throughout the world, social mobility, improved international transportation and communication systems play an important role not only in the internationalisation of trade and economy, but also in that of crime. Drug traffickers are flexible, they respond to changing markets affected by enforcement interventions, political and legislative changes, patterns of drug use, and transport developments which change the viability of countries as transit routes. For example, Central and Eastern European countries, traditionally transit routes for drug trafficking, are increasingly becoming consumer routes as their political and legislative structure prohibits trafficking, and cooperation through programmes like PHARE, take effect. New routes, such as those through the Balkan countries, are opened up to replace these old routes.

Europe's response to the drug menace has, since the establishment of the Community, been driven through three successive European Drug Action Plans. The Plans focus on supply and demand reduction, and delivery of activities is supported by new institutions such as the European Monitoring Centre, Europol and the EDU, and legislative changes. A European early warning system to identify new synthetic drugs was developed by the EMCDDA and began in January 1998. The system will aim to reliably identify new trends in use (epidemiology) and in supply availability (law enforcement and forensic analysis), in close cooperation with prevention and public health structures (demand reduction) and with good access to the expertise on health effects (pharmacology and toxicology). New networks have proliferated, which join together people across Europe with similar political views, drug services or information networks to tackle the drugs problem.

Millennium and beyond

A fourth European Action Plan will take us into the millennium and beyond, and will inevitably have an even more comprehensive approach to tackling drugs supply and demand than the previous arrangements. Enhanced existing European administrative structures will help to coordinate the policies of national ministries (horizontal coordination) and the national and regional administrations (vertical coordination).

Specific drugs issues which are likely to be developed as we go into the next century include drug supply reduction and the establishment and expansion of international information systems. A reduction in the bureaucracy of international police cooperation is likely, aided by the establishment of a central European police authority. Europol, when ratified by all member states, will become an operational arm (following ratification of the draft Amsterdam Treaty), supporting enforcement activities of member states through the provision of information and circulation of good practice. There is likely to be harmonisation of criminal law and procedure across the European Union, starting with establishing minimum rules relating to constituent elements of the criminal justice system and penalties. This will enable enforcement agencies to maximise their efforts and achieve greater results. Harmonisation of technical standards and structure within Europe will enable officers from enforcement agencies to work in partnership and cooperate at the same level. Strengthened cooperation with and between Central and East European (CEEC) countries can be expected, along with closer cooperation between police, customs and Europol.

Balancing this work on supply reduction, many workers in European Agencies expect an integrated and coordinated plan for drugs prevention involving all local, national and the European Community levels. The plan would focus on, for example, adequately resourced treatment, rehabilitation and education programmes targeted towards those who might be/are inclined to consume illicit drugs, and enhanced multi-agency rehabilitation initiatives to reintegrate addicts socially and economically, with specific measures for high-risk groups. More integrated European networks in both voluntary and statutory services can be expected, together with simultaneous education and awareness campaigns on drugs across Europe.

From early beginnings, Europe is, through cooperation and action, responding to the threat of international drug supply and the corresponding internal demand. Inevitably programmes are long-term, but the foundations of a coordinated and effective response have been laid.

Drug-related institutions and groups: contacts

Drugs and Organised Crime Working Group, Action Against Drugs Unit, Home Office. Drugs Branch, tel: 0171 273 2324.

Dublin Group, UK contact: Head of Organised and International Crime, Home Office, tel: 0171 273 2830.

Europe Against Drugs (EURAD), based in Ireland, tel: 00 353 1284 1164.

European Cities Against Drugs (ECAD), based in Sweden, tel: 00 46 8 785 93 62.

European Cities on Drug Policy (ECDP), based in Frankfurt, Germany. Coordination Bureau, tel: 0049 (069) 233 013.

European Monitoring Centre for Drugs and Drug Addiction (EMCDDA), based in Lisbon, Portugal, tel: 00351 1 811.

European Police Office (EUROPOL), based in The Hague, The Netherlands, tel: 0031 70 302 53 02.

Federation of European Drug Helplines (FESAT), c/o ADFAM National, tel: 0171 638 3700.

Federation of European Professionals Working in the Field of Drug Abuse (ERIT). UK contact: Standing Conference on Drug Abuse (SCODA), tel: 0171 928 9500.

Institute for the Study of Drug Dependence (ISDD), tel : 0171 928 1211.

Pompidou Group, Strasbourg, tel: 03 8841 2000.

2 UK policy

Brian A. Kidd and Roger A.D. Sykes

Introduction

Many diverse factors have influenced the evolution of policy regarding the treatment of people with drug-related problems in the UK. In recent years, three main 'models' of drug-related problems and their development have come to the fore. These models often share a number of features, but generally can be classified as follows:

1   *Society's model*   The impression of the extent of drug use and the problems associated with it which is informed by (often sensationalist) media reporting, the views of religious groups and other sub-groups of society with a particular perspective on abstinence, harm reduction, legalisation of cannabis or other contentious issues. These groups may be dominated by a particular dogma or philosophical view such as support for abstinence as opposed to harm reduction. They may be driven by personal tragedy and claim to represent the friends or family of those who have suffered as a result of their drug use. Society's model may support a relatively simplistic view of drug problems and the means by which these problems may be tackled. Consequently it may challenge aspects of the other models.
2   *Psychological models*   A number of different psychological theories have been applied to the development of drug addiction and drug-related problems. For example, the development of addiction can be seen as a learned or operantly conditioned behaviour (Schuster and Thompson, 1969), with secondary social factors influencing this process through so-called 'social learning'. These psychological theories have formed the

backbone of forms of 'counselling' offered to drug users. Their application to counselling is covered in more detail in Chapter 5.

3 *Medical (disease) models* Biological processes seem to have an influence on the development of addictions (Nestler, 1997) and a 'disease model' does have strong support from the field of genetics. These models have influenced the development of new drug regimes in such areas as detoxification and maintained abstinence (Resnick *et al*. 1979).

Tensions have always existed in this area with those supporting different theories often being unable to accept the validity of another. This reflects the fundamental differing belief systems as to the root cause of the problem. For example, a society which embraces a prohibitionist view of drug use has difficulty accepting that individuals with drug use problems may be deserving of understanding and (expensive) medical treatments. They may prefer to follow a policy of enforcement and punishment. In such a society drug users are readily labelled as having some weakness or inadequacy which can be used to conveniently explain their problems. On the other hand, a medical view may see a problem drug user as having underlying biological determinants which would in turn drive a move towards the use of appropriate medical treatments. This confusion is further compounded by a lack of objective evidence to support these models and in turn the policies driven by them.

Factual medical evidence is relatively hard to obtain. Even those treatments which are recognised as 'good practice' – such as methadone replacement prescribing – are supported by few objective randomised controlled studies – the scientific standard medical interventions all hope to achieve (Ward, Mattick and Hall, 1992). Statistics, however, are available from the customs, police and criminal justice system with relative ease. Numbers of arrests, drug-related crimes and seizures of supply are readily accessible (HMSO, 1995) and the availability of this evidence may reflect the relative power of enforcement strategies in government policy. Paradoxically, at the same time, other approaches, supported by a relatively thin body of evidence still attract considerable funding. For example, health promotion in the addictions and HIV/AIDS has received massive increases in funding over the last ten years. Publicity campaigns using 'shock' images and political campaigns preaching an abstinence message continue to be supported by governments of all persuasions in spite of little evidence of their effectiveness. This has been most evident in Scotland in recent months with the 'Scotland Against Drugs' (SAD) campaign. This may reflect the desire of society to espouse a 'safe' philosophy of prevention and avoidance rather than treatment and implied acceptance of the drug problem.

On the face of it policy often gives the appearance of being the result of a 'knee-jerk' reaction to medical, legal or social crises. This is reflected by funding tending to follow the short-term populist strategies formed in response to high profile issues such as HIV/AIDS (Cooper, 1981) or an increase in reported drug deaths (Greenwood *et al.*, 1997). The issue can be further complicated by professional empire building or the influence of dogma within different professional groupings. Treatment approaches are influenced by what is available, acceptable or fashionable – a process which tends to go in cycles. This can result in piecemeal developments, unpredictability of funding and poor coordination of services with local differences in approach evident from area to area.

It is beyond the scope of this chapter to give a detailed history of all aspects of UK drug policy. These are comprehensively covered in other texts (Berridge, 1989; Spear, 1994). It is helpful, however, to examine those factors which have influenced recent policy changes with regard to treatment services especially from the mid 1970s, when important developments occurred and the 'modern' approach to the treatment of drug-related problems began in earnest.

Recent history

1 1900–1961: The British system and opiate addiction defined as a medical problem

Dangerous Drugs Act (1920)

Opiate dependence was first seen as a problem in the UK at the turn of the century. Prior to this time there had been little evidence of morphine or heroin dependence, with opiates readily available in medications used to relieve pain or promote sleep. Across the Atlantic, however, America was pursuing a prohibitionist approach to a perceived drug abuse problem and, under its influence, Britain signed the first Opium Convention in The Hague in 1912, obliging the British government to prepare legislation to control drugs. The result was the first Dangerous Drugs Act of 1920. The Act allowed doctors to dispense opiates, but only 'so far as may be necessary for the exercise of his profession'. The vagueness of this statement, however, did not restrict doctors from treating opiate-dependent individuals with prescribed drugs.

Rolleston Committee (1926)

The Rolleston Committee of 1926 examined this issue of replacement prescribing and ruled that the prescribing of heroin and morphine could be seen as 'legitimate medical treatment' in the following situations:

> Those who are undergoing treament for the cure of addiction by the gradual withdrawal method. Persons for whom, after every effort has been made for the cure of addiction, the drug cannot be completely withdrawn, either because a) complete withdrawal produces symptoms which cannot be satisfactorily treated under the ordinary conditions of private practice; or b) the patient, while capable of leading a useful and fairly normal life so long as he takes a certain non-progressive quantity, usually small, of the drug of addiction, ceases to be able to do so when the regular allowance is withdrawn.

Though the Rolleston report was without statutory power, it removed from doctors the risk of prosecution should they continue to prescribe replacement opiates under this 'British System'. It also clearly defined opiate addiction as a medical problem. This situation allowed the relatively small numbers of opiate addicts in the UK to be managed by doctors in this way until the 1960s.

2   1961–1982: Escalating drug use – restriction to specialist treatments

First Brain Committee (1961)

In the early 1960s concern over the use of illicit drugs led to the sitting of an interdepartmental committee under the chairmanship of Sir Russell Brain. The First Brain Committee reported in 1961 and stated that the extent of the British drug problem was of little concern at that time, implying that there was no need to alter practice. However, during the 1960s the number of known addicts increased considerably. There were only 62 addicts known in 1958. By 1964 the number had risen to 342, and by 1968 the figure was 2 782. Young people seemed to be becoming more involved and were using drugs for pleasure and not as treatment for an existing addiction. No opiate addict under 20 years of age was known before 1960. By 1968 there were 764 under 20, the majority of whom were opiate addicts (Royal College of Psychiatrists, 1987).

Second Brain Committee (1965)

The Brain Committee was therefore reconvened and reported in 1965. It was accepted that a new group of younger, unstable addicts, who were not using for therapeutic reasons, had appeared along with associated overprescribing by doctors. The committee made three main recommendations:

- There should be compulsory notification of heroin and cocaine addicts to a central register
- Specialist treatment centres, staffed by specialist doctors with a special interest in addiction should be set up
- The prescribing of heroin and cocaine should be restricted to specialist licensed doctors.

Following the report of the Second Brain Committee the government responded with a battery of legislation.

Dangerous Drugs Act (1967)

The recommendations of the Second Brain Committee formed the basis of the Dangerous Drugs Act of 1967. Drug Dependence Units (DDUs) were set up between 1968 and 1970, mainly around the London area. These units treated the majority of drug users who were conveniently concentrated in the inner city areas. GPs could continue to use opiates to treat symptoms, but could not prescribe heroin or cocaine.

The Misuse of Drugs Act (1971)

This act established the Advisory Council on the Misuse of Drugs (ACMD). Its terms of reference were, 'to keep under review the situation in the United Kingdom with respect to drugs which are being or appear to them likely to be misused and of which the misuse is having or appears to them capable of having harmful effects sufficient to constitute a social problem', and to advise ministers accordingly. Its membership includes academics and clinicians in the area with a number of working groups which produce authoritative reports on drug problems and associated areas.

The Act also introduced controlled status to the manufacture, supply and possession of drugs deemed liable to be misused. Drugs were divided into classes A, B and C, with penalties graded according to the harmfulness attributable to the drug if it was misused. The strictest regulations related to those drugs with little or no medical use. The groups are as follows:

- Group A includes: alfentanil, cocaine, dextromoramide, diamorphine (heroin), dipipanone, lysergide (LSD), methadone, morphine, opium, pethidine, phencyclidine and class B substances when prepared for injection.
- Group B includes: oral amphetamines, barbiturates, cannabis, cannabis resin, codeine, ethylmorphine, glutethimide, pentazocine, phenmetrazine and pholcodine.
- Group C includes: drugs related to the amphetamines including benzphetamine and chlorphentermine, buprenorphine, diethylpropion, mazindol, meprobamate, pemoline, pipradrol, most benzodiazepines, androgenic and anabolic steroids, clenbuterol, chorionic gonadotrophin, somatotropin, somatrem and somatropin.

Misuse of Drugs (Notification of and Supply to Addicts) Regulations (1973)

These regulations require that any doctor attending a person and having reasonable grounds to consider that he is addicted to one of 14 drugs (Table 2.1), shall notify the Chief Medical Officer. They also state that only those doctors who hold a special license may prescribe diamorphine, dipipanone or cocaine to addicts.

Table 2.1   Drugs requiring notification

Cocaine	Methadone
Dextromoramide	Morphine
Diamorphine	Opium
Dipipanone	Oxycodone
Hydrocodone	Pethidine
Hydromorphone	Phenazocine
Levorphanol	Piritramide

Despite these initiatives, the number of drug addicts in the UK continued to rise, and by the late 1970s approximately 5 000 were known – double the number prior to the introduction of the Misuse of Drugs Act (1971). The policy of allowing only specialist services to prescribe while GPs were not permitted to do so, seemed to be failing. The issue was addressed by a report of the ACMD in 1982.

3   1982–1998: Involvement of general practitioners is encouraged

ACMD: Treatment and Rehabilitation (1982)

This report (ACMD, 1982) essentially reversed the previous policy. It acknowledged that drug use was becoming geographically more widespread and that the range of drugs used was increasing. The report saw a 'possible role for some doctors outside the specialist services to play a role in the treatment of problem drug takers, but with strict safeguards'.

The need for guidance to ensure safe practice resulted in the production of the first clinical practice guidelines on the treatment of drug misuse.

ACMD: Medical Working Group on Drug Dependence – guidelines for good clinical practice in the treatment of drug misuse (1984)

This working group consisted of representatives from the General Medical Council, the Royal College of Psychiatrists, the Royal College of General Practitioners, the Joint Consultants' Committee of the BMA, the BMA General Services Committee and the Association of Independent Doctors in Addiction. Its thrust was to encourage GPs to treat drug misusers, outlining their role and responsibilities in this process (see ACMD, 1984).

Misuse of Drugs Regulations (1985)

These regulations sought to exert further restrictions over 'controlled drugs' in the UK. The regulations divide controlled drugs into five schedules, each of which has specific requirements governing import and export, production, supply, possession, prescribing and the record keeping associated with these activities. A summary of the schedules is listed below:

- *Schedule 1*   Includes cannabis and lysergide which are not used medicinally. Possession and supply are prohibited without Home Office Authority
- *Schedule 2*   Includes diamorphine, morphine pethidine, quinalbarbitone, glutethimide, amphetamine and cocaine, and are subject to the full controlled drug requirements relating to prescriptions, safe custody (except quinalbarbitone) and the keeping of registers
- *Schedule 3*   Includes all other barbiturates, buprenorphine, diethylpropion, mazindol, meprobamate, pentazocine, phentermine and temazepam. These are subject to special prescribing requirements (except for phenobarbitone and temazepam), but not those requiring

safe custody (except buprenorphine, diethylpropion and temazepam) nor the need to keep registers. There are requirements to keep invoices for two years
- *Schedule 4*   Includes, in Part II, 33 benzodiazepines and pemoline, which are all subject to minimal control. Part I includes anabolic and androgenic steroids, clenbuterol, chorionic gonadotrophin, somatotrophin, somatrem and somatropin. Controlled drug prescribing requirements do not apply, nor do those for safe custody
- *Schedule 5*   Includes those drugs which, because of their strength, are exempt from controlled drug requirements other than retention of invoices for two years.

By the mid 1980s HIV and AIDS were beginning to cause public health concern. In Scotland the McLelland Committee Report (SHHD, 1986) highlighted the need to develop needle exchange services to improve the availability of clean injecting equipment and reduce the spread of HIV via contaminated needles. In spite of attempts to involve GPs in the care of drug misusers, only a minority were taking part. Issues such as item of service payments and improvement of back-up services, in the form of community-based drug services, were considered to improve the extent of GP involvement (Glanz and Taylor, 1986).

ACMD: Aids and Drug Misuse Part 1 (1988)

This report first acknowledged that the spread of HIV was a greater potential danger than drug misuse itself. It highlighted the need to reduce the spread of HIV in the drug-using population and encouraged the development of more community-based drug teams with the aim of having one in each health district in England and Wales. The subsequent report, ACMD: AIDS and Drug Misuse Part 2 (1989), started to address practically how to increase GP involvement, with the suggestion of a working party to look at specific issues such as remuneration and specialist training for GPs.

UK Action on Drug Misuse: The Government's Strategy (1990)

This medically based approach became incorporated into a more wideranging strategy in the 1990 UK Action on Drug Misuse. This document brought together strategies to control imports (through improved international cooperation and increased effectiveness of the police and HM Customs), maintain effective domestic deterrents, improve prevention and education as well as improve treatment and rehabilitation. In the setting of an NHS dominated by internal markets and purchaser–provider splits, the treatment strategy emphasised the development of a range of services, including abstinence and harm reduction approaches, provided by a range of statutory and independent providers.

Drug Misuse and Dependence: Guidelines on Clinical Management (1991)

Advice to doctors in the 1984 good clinical practice document was updated in 1991 (SHHD). This 'orange book' placed GPs firmly in the front line with regard to replacement prescribing for drug users. The guidelines state that it is the 'responsibility of all doctors to provide care' (for drug users) and that the 'average doctor'should offer the 'more straightforward treatments' such as 'the prescribing of oral methadone for patients dependent on opioids'. The guideline included, for the first time, extensive practical advice about safe and effective prescribing, including dose regimes and advice about specific clinical areas such as the management of withdrawal. It also described how prescribing GPs should relate to specialist back-up services, emphasising that prescribing was not a treatment in itself but should be delivered with counselling support.

The 'orange book' is currently being revised. Meanwhile, in the light of GP maintenance prescribing becoming more commonplace, the Scottish Office Department of Health has issued a detailed guide for doctors (SODH, 1996). This guide is clearly aimed at GPs and outlines aspects of good practice including drugs of choice for doctors, the use of daily supervised dispensing of methadone, as well as advice regarding treatment regimes, dealing with pregnant drug users and managing detoxification.

Tackling Drugs Together (1995) and The Task Force to Review Services for Drug Misusers (1996) – England & Wales

Meeting the Challenge: Report of Ministerial Drugs Task Force (1994) – Scotland

In England and Wales the White Paper 'Tackling Drugs Together' (HMSO, 1995) continues the new, more coordinated approach for services dealing with drug-related problems which had been evident in UK Action on Drug Misuse. The document gives an update of all of the components of services for dealing with drug problems – education, harm reduction, treatment and criminal justice – as well as focussing on community safety and enforcement strategies. It also announces an 'Effectiveness Review' of services and current practice in England and Wales – The Task Force to Review Services for Drug Misusers. This Review is an extensive document which describes the variation of services currently in place in England and Wales. It acknowledges the diversity of practice in such areas as replacement prescribing and makes firm recommendations – for example, regarding the need to prevent the prescribing of methadone tablets for drug users. However, it also acknowledges that some treatment regimes – so far untested in scientific terms – may have a place. Examples include replacement prescribing of amphetamines. The review makes a number of recommendations including:

- the development of 'shared care' with GPs
- continuity of services in prisons
- improved needle exchange services
- availability of a range of services (including counselling) with low waiting times and improved availability (opening times etc.)
- development of measures of treatment, outcome and organisation.

The comparable Scottish Office document – 'Drugs in Scotland: Meeting the Challenge' (SHHD, 1994) – contains elements similar to both, but with some specific differences such as clear messages about drugs seen as appropriate for replacement prescribing in the Scottish context.

These documents have heavily influenced the way services are coordinated and delivered locally, with a view to all areas achieving a similar minimum standard. 'Tackling Drugs Together' and 'Meeting the Challenge' propose the setting up of Drug Action Teams (DATs). These are groupings of senior representatives from the police, health service and local authority (education, social work, criminal justice) in an area. The aim is to have representatives who are senior enough to be able to make decisions regarding developments which may have funding implications. Each DAT covers a health board or health authority area and is served by a Drug Development Officer (DDO). A forum of other interested parties feeds into the DAT, giving an input from those dealing with drug problems on a day-to-day basis.

The main target areas include prevention, community safety and reducing health risks associated with drug use. Methods of monitoring the progress of these teams are outlined along with improved lines of communication between local policy makers and central government. The sense is of a move towards acceptance of the variation in opinion regarding approaches which may help those with drug misuse problems and cooperation between those agencies who will plan and deliver them. Services are beginning to be planned proactively, and the use of standards and outcome measures is being encouraged.

Conclusions

This chapter has attempted to give a flavour of the direction of government policy with regard to drug misuse in recent years. It is not comprehensive but does cover those seminal documents, recommendations and guidelines which influence those professionals dealing with drug misusers in the front line.

We have seen a relatively short period of history during which the use of drugs and the hazards associated with their use have been seen to escalate. In response, successive governments have taken specialist advice – usually from doctors – and have legislated in response to the perceived acute problem of the day – to avoid hedonistic drug use in the 1960s, to reduce harm and curb HIV spread in the 1980s. The 1990s have seen a more coordinated and proactive approach with more emphasis on multi-agency, multi-disciplinary working. The most recent policy documents have a place for a wide range of professionals from statutory and voluntary sectors with improved structures, to allow joint commissioning and planning at a local level while maintaining a national overview of standards and quality.

But new threats are developing. Abstinence based groups seem to have the ear of the politicians, resulting in the flourishing SAD campaign with its £2m Scottish Office budget and a director who openly criticises harm reduction. The government has changed and a senior police officer has been appointed as 'drug Tsar'. Methadone-related deaths are increasing and are becoming the focus of negative media publicity (Greenwood, 1997), while payment to pharmacists for the supervision of methadone consumption is becoming the subject of local negotiation. GPs have stated that they will not include the care of drug misusers as a 'core' service for primary care, while specialist services are experiencing ever greater demand and trying to involve more GPs in 'shared care' arrangements.

The development of Drug Action Teams has the potential to improve the coordination of services and to increase their range and quality for all areas. Only time will tell if this policy of cooperation and inter-agency working will remain in place.

References

Advisory Council on the Misuse of Drugs (1982), *Treatment and Rehabilitation*, London: HMSO.
Advisory Council on the Misuse of Drugs (1984), *Prevention*, London: HMSO.
Advisory Council on the Misuse of Drugs (1988), *AIDS and Drug Misuse Part 1*, London: HMSO.

Advisory Council on the Misuse of Drugs (1989), *AIDS and Drug Misuse Part 2*, London: HMSO.

Berridge V. (1989), 'Historical Issues', in S. MacGregor (ed.) *Drugs and British Society*, London: Routledge.

Cooper J.R. (1981), 'HIV', *New England Journal of Medicine*.

Department of Health, Scottish Office Home & Health Department, Welsh Office (1991), *Drug Misuse and Dependence: Guidelines on Clinical Management*, London: HMSO.

Glanz, A., Taylor, C. (1986), 'Findings of a National Survey of the Role of General Practitioners in the Treatment of Opiate Misuse', *British Medical Journal*, **293**, 543–5.

Greenwood, J., Zealley, H., Gorman, D., Fineron, P., Squires, T. (1997), 'Deaths Related to Methadone have Doubled in Lothian', *British Medical Journal*, **314**, 1763.

HMSO (1990), *UK Action on Drug Misuse: The Government's Strategy*, London: HMSO.

HMSO (1995), *Tackling Drugs Together. A Strategy for England*, London: HMSO.

Nestler, E. (1997), 'Basic Neurobiology of Opiate Addiction', in Stine, S. and Kosten, T. (eds), *New Treatments for Opiate Dependence*, New York: Guilford.

Resnick, R., Schuyten-Resnick, E. and Washton, A.M. (1979), 'Narcotic Antagonists in the Treatment of Opioid Dependence: Review and Commentary', *Comprehensive Psychiatry*, **20**, 116–25.

Royal College of Psychiatrists (1987), 'Drug Scenes', London: Gaskell.

Schuster, C.R. and Thompson, T. (1969), 'Self-administration of and Behavioural Dependence on Drugs', *Annual Review of Pharmacology*, **9**, 483–502.

Scottish Home and Health Department (1986), *HIV Infection in Scotland. Report of the Scottish Committee on HIV Infection and Intravenous Drug Use*, Edinburgh: Scottish Office.

Scottish Office Department of Health (1996), *Good Practice in Substitute Prescribing*, Edinburgh: Scottish Office.

Scottish Office Home and Health Department (1994), *Drugs in Scotland: Meeting the Challenge. Report of Ministerial Drugs Task Force*, Edinburgh: Scottish Office.

Spear, B. (1994), 'The Early Years of the "British System" in Practice' in J. Strang and M. Gossop (eds), *Heroin Addiction and Drug Policy. The British System*, Oxford: Oxford University Press.

The Task Force to Review Services for Drug Misusers. Report of an Independent Review of Drug Treatment Services in England (1996), London: Department of Health.

Ward, J., Mattick, R. and Hall, W. (1992), *Key Issues in Methadone Maintenance Treatment*, New South Wales: New South Wales University Press Ltd.

3 Education and drug misuse: school interventions

Niall Coggans, Sally Haw and Jonathan Watson

Introduction

The purpose of this chapter is to review some of the key issues in drug education with particular reference to school-based interventions, including approaches to drug education and prevention in schools, and some of the theoretical and practical issues informing such approaches. These include meeting the psychological and social needs of young people in the wider context of personal and social development in schools. In addressing these topics the importance of assessing effectiveness with the use of realistic evaluation criteria will also be considered. Also, drawing from the literature on the evaluation of drug education, good practice in drug education will be highlighted.

Concern over the growing number of young people who report using drugs and the need for school-based education and prevention programmes is reflected by government policy (Scottish Office, 1994; HMSO, 1998) and national education strategy documents (ACMD, 1993; DFE, 1995) and by the development of various initiatives to address drug education and drug misuse in the context of school curricula (personal and social development/education programmes, and pastoral care systems). In addition, the government's ten-year strategy for drug misuse emphasises the role of life skills education, starting in primary school, and the importance of integrating such programmes within personal, social and health education (PSHE) in schools (HMSO, 1998).

A range of interventions have been implemented in schools, including drugs education through curriculum subjects, through special programmes and through the ethos of the school. Evidence from evaluations of drug education interventions (in the UK and elsewhere) indicates that success has been limited, although there are a number of issues that should be taken into account, including how best to measure impact and outcomes. Furthermore, evidence from prevalence studies in the UK indicates that experimentation and recreational use of illicit drugs continues to rise among young people (e.g., Miller and Plant, 1996). This underlines the need to develop and implement more effective drug education programmes. There are, however, some significant methodological problems associated with the evaluation of drug education programmes. There is also a need to have realistic expectations of what drug education can achieve. Nonetheless, it is possible to identify the characteristics of drug education programmes that have a positive effect.

Drug education and prevention

How can drug education contribute to a prevention strategy? The Advisory Council on the Misuse of Drugs reporting on drug education in schools (ACMD, 1993) stated that a range of objectives should be addressed, including prevention or delay of onset of drug use as well as minimising riskier forms of drug use. However, in a recent review of substance misuse service provision for young people, the NHS Health Advisory Service recognised that drug education and drug prevention are two complementary fields of activity and drew a clear distinction between them. In relation to young people and drugs, education was defined as having the 'overall aim of preventing people from harming themselves by the use of substances', while prevention was defined as 'prevention of dependent forms of substance misuse and prevention of physical and psychiatric disorders that may be related to substance use and misuse' (NHS HAS, 1996). These definitions reflect the view that the goal of minimal incidence of drug-related harm is a more practical goal than one of no drug use whatsoever, and educational strategies have an important role to play. This position also recognises that experience of drugs among young people will vary according to a range of factors, including age, social and cultural circumstances, developmental stage and area of residence. Programme content and objectives, therefore, will need to be tailored to the needs of the specific target group.

However, while minimal incidence of drug-related harm is a more practical goal than eradicating drug use, drug-related harm varies in kind and degree. It would seem appropriate to include within a definition of harm-reduction all aspects of drug use that could detract from the ability of people to achieve their potential or aspirations: a hierarchy of risk reduction objectives, prioritising those that pose the greatest risk to young people.

Given the importance of working with a culture instead of against it, to promote health and well-being more effectively (Backett and Davison, 1992), it seems likely that the goal of reducing drug-related harm is more realistic than the goal of primary prevention for some groups of young people. From the perspective of many young people, use of illicit drugs is perceived to be part of youth culture, irrespective of whether they use themselves. Adults' reactions to drugs are often seen by young people as being out of touch with the reality of young people's lives (Hirst and McCamley-Finney, 1994). For important drug-related health messages to be seen as relevant to young people will require that young people can believe that these messages come from a source that understands what drugs mean to young people.

Approaches to drug education

The different approaches to drug education have been categorised as follows (Coggans and Watson, 1995; Dorn and Murji, 1992):

1   Information-based approaches (fear arousal, factual information, harm-reduction).
2   Life skills-based approaches (values and skills, personal and social competencies, social influences).
3   Resistance training approaches focused largely on resistance to peer pressure (such as Project DARE).
4   Alternatives-based approaches (usually in community settings to improve the social environment with opportunities for leisure or work-related activities).
5   Peer-based approaches.

Sometimes a combination of approaches is used within a coordinated framework. For example, a community-based initiative might include an information component using mass media and/or educational programmes for parents, as well as a life skills and social influences component delivered through schools (e.g., Pentz et al., 1989). The effectiveness of the different approaches to drug education has been reviewed in detail in other publications (Tobler and Stratton, 1997; Coggans and Watson, 1995; Dorn and Murji, 1992). Relevant findings from these reviews are discussed below in relation to the forms of drug education with most relevance for schools.

Drug education in schools

Two of the above approaches, information- and life skills-based approaches, have been employed in schools, and an extensive literature has accumulated on their effectiveness. Enhancing understanding of drugs and their effects, and facilitating development of personal and social competencies are particularly relevant approaches for schools, as these are tasks in which teachers are skilled. While alternatives-based approaches to drug use might seem to be beyond the remit of schools, there may be opportunities for schools to be a resource for a community-based project which seeks to provide activities for young people. Schools can also provide a variety of opportunities for young people to engage in pursuits, such as physical education, outdoor education and extra-curricular activities of various sorts, that can be catalysts for the communication of health education messages: a form of proactive alternatives approach (Kaley et al., 1992). Peer-based approaches to drug education could also be incorporated into school-based programmes, although the nature and extent of impact of peer-based drug education is unclear. While increasingly popular, peer-based education has been described as atheoretical and the roles of peer educators are not always clear (Milburn, 1995). Nonetheless, given that co-learning methods are employed widely in many areas of education, there would appear to be a role for peer-based approaches to be employed in drug education.

In broad terms, development of drug education strategies reflects growing awareness of the need to base drug education programmes on sound theoretical models of psychosocial development and, in particular, development of risk-taking behaviour. Early drug education programmes reflected the view that deterring substance misuse would be achieved by heightening awareness of the adverse consequences of smoking, drinking alcohol, and using cannabis or other illicit drugs – a view not supported by research evidence. However, more recent drug education programmes are designed with an emphasis on psychological and social factors which can influence development of drug misuse. Drug education in schools involves development of awareness of drugs and their effects, and frequently the emphasis is on development of personal and social competencies considered necessary to equip young people to resist influences which may encourage drug use. Standard materials are widely used in schools, which provide teachers with course content and methods, often derived from life skills approaches to drug education. A recent review and meta-analysis of 120 school-based drug prevention programmes (Tobler and Stratton, 1997) concluded that whereas non-interactive (i.e., didactic) programmes affected only knowledge, interactive (i.e., participative) programmes were more likely to influence knowledge, attitudes and drug use. Although the effect sizes of the drug education interventions reviewed by Tobler and Stratton are small (that is, the difference in levels of reported drug use between intervention and control groups attributed to the intervention is small), the lesson that may be drawn from this particular study is that drug education programmes which emphasise life skills and employ participative learning methods are more likely to have positive impact. While it would not be appropriate to assume that the American and Canadian drug education programmes that gave rise to these findings would produce the same results in the context of the UK, given the cultural differences, this study indicates that didactic methods are less effective than participative methods.

Information-based approaches

Information-based approaches range from fear arousal, in which the negative effects of drugs are emphasised and may not reflect objective indices of actual risk, through factual or non-evaluative information programmes, to harm-reduction programmes, in which factual information is presented on how to minimise harm associated with drug use. The aim of early fear arousal interventions was to prevent onset of drug use by generating anxiety in the target audience. Factual information programmes aim to deter drug use by presenting a balanced perspective on the effects of drugs, assuming that heightened knowledge will lead to disinclination to use drugs.

Information-based programmes have a reputation, based on empirical findings, of not preventing drug use, which may be seen as reason for not using such approaches. However, because information-based programmes have not prevented drug use does not mean that there is no place for this type of drug education. Instead, it suggests that the success of information-based drug education requires to be defined primarily in terms of knowledge acquisition, with account taken of the extent to which this knowledge influences behaviour, and not defining success only in terms of the prevention of drug use. For example, if the aim of an information-based programme is to reduce risks associated with, say, ecstasy use, then the success of that programme should be evaluated primarily in terms of acquisition of the key messages, with account also taken of the extent to which knowledge acquisition informs decision-making and risk reduction in behaviour. After all, if young people acquire reliable risk reduction knowledge they may still use drugs, but do so in a way which places themselves at lower risk.

The issue of abstinence versus safer use notwithstanding, a key difference between factual and harm-reduction approaches lies in evaluation criteria. Whereas fear arousal and factual approaches have usually been evaluated in terms of primary prevention, appropriate evaluation criteria for harm-reduction approaches are knowledge gain and safer drug use behaviour.

Drug education materials for schools which take a harm-reduction approach as opposed to a primary prevention approach have been developed (Cohen, Clements and Kay, 1990) and are increasingly used in some areas (Tierney, 1997). While there is a need to evaluate harm-reduction approaches to drug education, proponents of this approach argue that setting drug education's sights lower than prevention of all use is more likely to lead to effective communication of important drug-related information (Cohen, 1996). The harm-reduction approach should be evaluated to determine its effectiveness in imparting drug-related knowledge, as well as in promoting less frequent and/or safer use.

The knowledge content of an information-based approach to drug education, i.e. the nature and amount of drug-related information, should vary according to the age group targeted and the particular drug(s) covered by the intervention. The guiding criterion for which aspects of drug-related information should be covered would ideally be a reflection of the knowledge needed by young people to make informed choices about drug use. For example, the information needs of younger groups (e.g., pre-adolescents) will be biased towards learning about the beneficial role of over-the-counter and prescribed drugs in society as well as the nature and degree of harm associated with so-called 'gateway' drugs (alcohol, tobacco and cannabis). Older groups (e.g., adolescents to final year pupils) could expand their knowledge of commonly used substances as well as learning more about substances such as heroin and cocaine. Ideally, the content of any information-based initiative should be based on an assessment of the knowledge and drug-related experience, if any, of the target group. The implication of this is that teachers, or others involved in drug education, need an up-to-date understanding of patterns of drug use in their own area, in order to supplement basic core material where appropriate.

In addition to drug information provision being age-appropriate, there is also a need to ensure that drug information is balanced in terms of the risks and attractions of specific drugs, as a balanced view is more likely to be seen as understanding the part that drugs play in youth culture. In order to maximise the potential for important prevention messages to be credible to young people, it is essential for that information be perceived as coming from an 'understanding' as opposed to 'hostile' source (Dalgarno and Shewan, 1996). As some, albeit a minority, of those who experiment with drugs, or who use recreationally, progress to drugs such as heroin, there is a need to ensure that young people understand the difficulties that people frequently get into when they experiment with 'hard drugs'. While the inferred dichotomy between 'soft' and 'hard' drugs only crudely relates to associated harms, the fact remains that heroin, for example, can be a hard drug to manage and many who experiment with it or use it recreationally develop problematic patterns of use. In order that such messages are perceived as salient by those at risk of developing problematic patterns of drug use, it may be necessary for the drug educator to demonstrate that they understand the attractions of drugs as well as being knowledgeable about the negative effects.

Many teachers will be uncomfortable when involved in drug education which takes a less than hard line against drugs. To overcome this requires endorsement (e.g., by the senior management team) of the chosen approaches to drug education within a supportive educational framework. In practice this means that there should be a (whole-school) drug education ethos which is characterised by non-dogmatic attitudes to drug education, which is focused on what can be achieved in school settings, and which is well-informed about the lessons learned from rigorous evaluations of drug education. In essence, schools and teachers involved in drug education need to base their practice on evidence about effectiveness. In practical terms this means that institutions and individuals who deliver drug education require to have a critical understanding of the likely impact of different approaches to drug education and the appropriateness of the teaching and learning methods to be employed. Claims that particular programmes are 'the answer' should be treated with great caution.

While unsubtle fear arousal messages have largely been eschewed in formalised drug education programmes in the UK in recent years, there remains the likelihood that teachers could implicitly or explicitly communicate messages that are perceived as being essentially moralistic or intended to arouse fear. Teachers are after all *in loco parentis* and, in many cases, will perceive expectations on the part of parents, schools or school boards that clear anti-drug messages are required above all else. To the extent that it is possible to establish an understanding, non-hostile approach to drugs – which is not the same as condoning or adopting a *laissez-faire* approach to drug use, rather it is more a matter of creating an educational environment that is conducive to effective learning – there is a need to ensure that such an approach is established. Moreover, selective use of messages about various aspects of drug-related harm that present a biased view are likely to be seen as just that by young people sooner or later. Specific messages about drug-related harm will be more readily accepted and, hopefully, perceived as relevant to the individual when these messages are communicated in the context of an accurate account of the costs and benefits of drug use. Skilled teachers can and do help young people to be aware of the dangers of drug use without resorting to moralistic or fear arousal tactics. Such teachers are more likely to be perceived as understanding and therefore more credible. Establishing a drug education ethos that supports teachers with realistic expectations will require a strong lead from senior management in schools and the support of school boards/governors.

Life skills and social influences approaches to drug education

In broad terms, life skills approaches assume that there is a range of inter-personal and intrapersonal factors which increase the likelihood of young people taking drugs. These approaches are based on theoretical models which explain young people's drug use as arising 'because' of a lack of self-esteem, poor decision-making skills, inappropriate moral values, or a lack of social skills such as communication and assertiveness skills. Therefore, interventions based on these assumptions attempt to remedy such deficits.

Drug education programmes that tackle social and psychological factors believed to influence onset of gateway drug use were originally developed in the 1970s (Botvin and Dusenbury, 1989; De Haes and Schuurman, 1975). Since then a number of programmes have been developed and implemented that demonstrate different ways of tackling psychological and social risk factors. While there have been many interventions that fall within this category, there are particular characteristics that distinguish programmes that have had some limited success in prevention of gateway drug use from programmes that appear to be less effective. The pattern of results from evaluations of life skills-based approaches indicates that few life skills programmes have produced positive results (Tobler and Stratton, 1997; Schaps et al., 1981; Hawkins et al., 1985; Glynn, 1983). Some reviewers have concluded that this type of approach is not effective in stopping young people experimenting, although it may be effective in inhibiting a move to harder drugs (Dorn and Murji, 1992). Nonetheless, the type of drug education which has shown most promise, relatively speaking, are interventions which aim to develop personal and social competencies, based on life skills and social influences models (e.g., Botvin et al., 1995; Pentz et al., 1989; Pentz, 1993).

In the context of the UK, the impact of a life-skills approach, the basis for a drug education pack widely used in secondary schools throughout Scotland, was found to have had no impact on drug-related attitudes or behaviour, although there was a very marginal increase in drug-related knowledge (Coggans et al., 1991). While the drug education programme in question utilised a range of participative learning methods, considered to be an essential element (Tobler and Stratton, 1997), it may not have matched the limited impact of some of its American counterparts for a variety of reasons, perhaps, for example, because it lacked 'booster' sessions. (Booster sessions are follow-up sessions usually some months or years later, the aim of which is to reinforce the original sessions.) However, this is conjecture and there are many reasons why an intervention developed and implemented elsewhere would not work in a different cultural and social setting, even if the underlying theoretical constructs are valid. More recently, evaluation of Project Charlie (Huery and Lloyd, 1997) indicated that this life-skills-based programme had a positive impact on primary schools pupils. However, the sample of young people involved was very small and more research is needed before it will be possible to draw firm conclusions about this programme's usefulness with the wider population of young people.

Two points are important here, concerning the theoretical underpinnings of life skills programmes and the nature of the relationship between risk factors and drug use. First, the origins of life skills approaches lie in developmental theories of delinquency (also known as problem behaviours), in particular problem behaviour theory (Jessor et al., 1973; Jessor and Jessor, 1977; Donovan and Jessor, 1978) and the social learning approach (Burgess and Akers, 1966; Akers, 1977; Akers et al., 1979), based on social learning theory (Bandura, 1977). Problem behaviour theory accounts for adolescent problems (drug misuse, precocious sex, delinquency of various forms) in terms of these behaviours being functional for the person concerned; for example, coping with personal or social shortcomings or to attain personal goals such as social status. In other words, an individual's motivation to use drugs is based on a cost-benefit analysis that favours drug use and any attempt to prevent drug use will have to counter possibly strong motivation to use drugs by tipping the balance between perceived benefits and costs in favour of costs outweighing benefits.

Second, it should be noted that risk factors, such as those described above, are usually identified as characteristics of people who use drugs, based on particular populations that are probably not representative of the general population of young people. Moreover, such characteristics are associated with drug use and are therefore not necessarily causal. In some cases problems in intrapersonal and interpersonal functioning may be more consequences than causes of drug misuse. Nonetheless, the literature on development of problem behaviours does indicate that features of early socialisation (e.g., in the family setting) which give rise to risk factors such as poor personal and social competencies are prior events which increase the likelihood of problem behaviours arising (Coggans and Watson, 1995).

The relevance of the above points for school-based interventions based on life skills approaches is that standard programmes which are designed to remedy supposed deficits may not meet the needs of most young people, because young people participating in these programmes may not lack the skills that are the focus of the intervention. It can be useful to distinguish between more and less problematic patterns of drug use: despite levels of lifetime prevalence for 15- and 16-year-olds – who reported ever using any illicit drug – in Scotland being 50 per cent and 60 per cent for girls and boys respectively (Miller and Plant, 1996), relatively few of them will progress to dysfunctional patterns of drug misuse. (Comparable figures from the same study for other parts of the UK are: Northern Ireland 18 per cent and 39 per cent, Wales 32 per cent and 35 per cent, England 40 per cent and 44 per cent.) This means that the majority of those who experiment with drugs or use recreationally will not develop a 'drug problem'. The explanation for most people's drug use will have less to do with personal inadequacies than with perceived positive goal attainment, such as valuing the drug experience for relaxation, stimulation, socialising, or other qualities. It is unlikely, probably even untenable, that all or most young people who experiment with drugs or who use recreationally do so because of a lack of personal or social competencies, such as low self-esteem or inability to resist 'peer pressure' (Schroeder et al., 1993; Coggans and McKellar, 1994). Thus, a 'one size fits all' life skills approach that emphasises deficits is both off target and takes up valuable curricular space which could be utilised by more appropriate approaches to developing personal and social competencies and/or other forms of drug education. Drug educators should ensure that the target group is clearly defined in terms of their specific needs. This requires that the drug-related knowledge, attitudes, behaviour and motivations of the target group are taken into account in the development and implementation of drug education programmes.

It is also important to ensure that drug education in schools is integrated with other aspects of health education and health promotion, at the level of the whole school (Coggans and McKellar, 1995). Especially in relation to the development of personal and social competencies, schools should strive to ensure that all aspects of school life coherently facilitate development of positive self-regard and good social skills. Most schools have some sort of personal and social education/development (PSE/PSD) programme, very often the context within which drug education takes place. In many respects PSE is a proactive form of health promotion, addressing psychological and social development. One aim of PSE, and especially of pastoral support systems, is to contribute to the prevention of dysfunctional behaviour; the origins of which are significantly influenced by the family setting, where early socialisation has an important influence on development of problem behaviours (Kandel, 1980). The personal and social competencies required to cope with the temptations and problems of life including drugs can and should be fostered by all aspects of school life.

DARE (Drug Abuse Resistance Education)

Finally, in relation to life skills and social influences approaches to drug education, one of the most highly publicised drug education programmes in the USA is Drug Abuse Resistance Education, more often known by its acronym DARE. Despite considerable enthusiasm for this programme it is of doubtful effectiveness. For example, recent studies have concluded that DARE had no lasting impact (Ennet et al., 1994); that DARE had only limited effects in a five-year follow-up study (Clayton et al., 1996); and that DARE had significantly less effect than life skills and social influences programmes which employed more participative methods than DARE (Tobler and Stratton, 1997). Given that only very small effect sizes were demonstrated for the life skills and social influences programmes found to be more effective than DARE in the Tobler and Stratton (1997) study, the accumulated evidence indicates that there is a significant question mark over the effectiveness of DARE.

DARE has been deployed in the UK, spearheaded by Nottinghamshire Police in 1994 (Keene and Williams, 1996) and since taken up in other areas. Whelan and Culver (1997) evaluated the impact of the DARE programme on a group of young people in Nottinghamshire and concluded that it did not prepare them 'for the reality of drug offer situations'. In the light of this and other limitations of the programme, Whelan and Culver (1997) also concluded that there are 'opportunity costs' which should be considered by schools which use the DARE package. In other words, in a crowded curriculum it is all the more important that the time that can be allocated to drug education is used to good effect. This underlines the importance of assessing the usefulness and relevance of different drug education programmes by looking at research evidence.

Assessing effectiveness

Drug education programmes have become more sophisticated in recent years and the importance of rigorous evaluation as an integral part of any initiative has also been recognised. While some drug education interventions appear to be moving in the right direction, in terms of having a firmer theoretical and empirical base, it is widely recognised that there is much still to be done to develop interventions that are more effective.

Generally speaking, drug education interventions have not met expectations, although it is likely that expectations of drug education as primary prevention have been – and still are – unrealistically high. While most drug education interventions, of whatever sort, are widely seen as having failed to deliver, this conclusion is largely based on the primary prevention criterion of preventing young people from using drugs. There is a need to develop more differentiated ways of assessing whether drug education works, linking assessment procedures more closely with educational aims, not only with the goal of primary prevention. Realistic evaluation criteria for drug education will help to focus efforts on what can be achieved, particularly in school settings, and on developing more effective ways of achieving realistic goals. From an educational perspective, a useful step in the process of developing more effective interventions would be to integrate drug education more coherently with other aspects of health education and education about hazardous behaviours, reflecting one of the principal underpinnings of life skills education; that is, problem behaviour theory which conceives of drug misuse as one of a range of problem behaviours.

The critical question with any drug education intervention is 'does it work?' In attempting to answer this seemingly simple question, however, a range of issues require to be addressed, not least of which is the need to define what sort of impact should be expected from drug education interventions. There is a need to consider effectiveness in terms of the nature of input and resources, implementation processes, short-term impact and longer-term outcomes. Moreover, there is a need to identify appropriate evaluation criteria, which may or may not give priority to drug use measures. It might seem odd to suggest that drug use measures are not necessarily the most appropriate indicators of a drug education programme's success, but the issue here is to measure what is likely to be influenced by a particular drug education intervention. When assessing effectiveness, evaluation criteria (impact indicators, process and/or outcome measures) should be derived from programme objectives. Unrealistic objectives have been set in the past which have led to a focus on drug use measures. Nevertheless, patterns and prevalence of drug use should be measured when evaluating drug education programmes, although not necessarily as primary outcome measures. For example, drug education which aims to reduce drug-related harm may reduce drug-related harm by positively influencing how, when and how often people use drugs, even if broad prevalence measures do not show a decrease. Thus, while school-based drug education programmes aspire to the over-arching aim of preventing drug use, the learning objectives are more likely to be couched in less ambitious terms. Given the multifactorial nature of causes/reasons for drug use it is wise for programme evaluators to employ evaluation criteria which relate directly to an intervention's content and procedures.

Good practice in drug education

The Health Education Board for Scotland recently produced guidelines for planning drug education, based on the lessons from the literature on the evaluation of drug education and an extensive consultation exercise (Howie, 1997). Good practice in drug education (see Table 3.1) starts with specifying the needs of the target group, taking account of their drug-related knowledge, attitudes and behaviour, as well as their social, cultural and material circumstances. Once needs are specified, clear and realistic aims and objectives for a drug education intervention can be defined; with the choice of drug education approach being compatible with these aims and objectives. The chosen approach should also be feasible in relation to available resources. Key stakeholders should be identified and consulted in order to clarify expectations and support. An appropriate evaluation strategy should be developed for an intervention, which ideally would assess resourcing and other input, the processes utilised in the initiative, its immediate and short-term impact, and the outcomes of the intervention in the longer term.

Those responsible for drug education in schools face a number of challenges including coordination of school-based drug education within a

Table 3.1   Good practice in drug education

- Identify needs in terms of drug-related knowledge, attitudes and behaviour
- Identify local patterns and prevalence of drug use
- Identify a range of clear and realistic intervention objectives which relate to individual and community needs
- Identify a drug education approach/programme which is compatible with needs and intervention objectives as well as being feasible in relation to resources
- Clarify expectations of and support from stakeholders in the organisation and wider community
- Ensure that senior management and school ethos support realistic interventions
- Employ appropriate teaching and learning methods such as interactive and participative processes and avoid over-reliance on didactic approaches
- Ensure interventions are appropriate for developmental stage and are culturally sensitive
- Evaluate using realistic evaluation criteria that relate to realistic programme objectives.

network of community-based responses, and greater integration within health and social education in schools (Ives and Clements, 1996). Schools can only work within the constraints imposed by the social, cultural and material circumstances of the communities in which they are located. By building on educational methods that have the potential to deliver positive results, and by having realistic objectives, such as are found in other areas of health education, there is every reason to believe that progress can be made towards fewer drug-related problems.

The views expressed here are those of the authors and not necessarily those of the Health Education Board for Scotland.

References

Advisory Council on the Misuse of Drugs (1993), *Drug Education in Schools: The Need for New Impetus*, London: HMSO.
Akers, R.L. (1977), *Deviant Behaviour: Social Learning Approach*, Belmont, Cali.: Wadsworth.
Akers, R.L., Krohn, M.D., Lanza-Kaduce, L. and Radosevich, M. (1979), 'Social Learning and Deviant Behaviour: A Specific Test of a General Theory', *American Sociological Review* **44**, 636–55.
Backett, K. and Davidson, C. (1992), 'Rational or Reasonable? Perceptions of Health at Different Stages of the Lifecourse', *Health Education Journal*, **51**, 55–9.
Bandura, A. (1977), *Social Learning Theory*, Englewood Cliffs, NJ: Prentice-Hall.
Botvin, G.J., Baker, E., Dusenbury, L., Botvin, E.M. and Diaz, T. (1995), 'Long-term Follow-up Results of a Randomized Drug Abuse Prevention Trial in a White Middle-class Population', *Journal of the American Medical Association*, **273**, (14), 1106–12.
Botvin, G.J. and Dusenbury, L. (1989), 'Substance Abuse Prevention and the Promotion of Competence', in L.A.Bond and B.E. Compas (eds), *Primary Prevention and Promotion in Schools*, Newbury Park, Ca.: Sage.
Burgess, R.L. and Akers, R.L. (1966) 'A Differential Association-Reinforcement Theory of Criminal Behaviour', *Social Problems*, **14**, 128–47.
Clayton, R.R., Cattarello, A.M. and Johnstone, B.M. (1996), 'The Effectiveness of Drug Abuse Resistance Education (Project DARE): Five Year Follow Up Results', *Preventive Medicine*, **25**, 307–18.
Coggans, N. and McKellar, S. (1994), 'Drug Use Amongst Peers: Peer Pressure or Peer Preference?', *Drugs: Education, Prevention and Policy*, **1**, 15–26.
Coggans, N. and McKellar, S. (1995), *Health-Promoting Schools*, London: The Portman Group.
Coggans, N., Shewan, D., Henderson, M. and Davies, J.B. (1991), 'National Evaluation of Drug Education In Scotland', London: ISDD Research Monograph Four.
Coggans, N. and Watson, J. (1995), 'Drug Education: Approaches, Effectiveness and Delivery', *Drugs: Education, Prevention and Policy*, **2**, (3), 211–24.

Cohen, J. (1996), 'Drugs in the Classroom: Politics, Propaganda and Censorship', *Druglink*, **11**, (2), 12–14.
Cohen, J., Clements, I. and Kay, J. (1990), 'Taking Drugs Seriously: a Manual of Harm Reduction Education on Drugs', Liverpool: Healthwise.
Dalgarno, P. and Shewan, D. (1996), 'Predicting Risk-taking Behaviour Amongst Ecstasy Users: a Pilot Study', Final Report to Chief Scientist Office, Edinburgh.
De Haes, W. and Schuurman, J. (1975), 'Results of an Evaluation Study of Three Drug Education Methods', *International Journal of Health Education*, **18**, 1–16.
DFE (1995) *Drug Prevention and Schools*, London: HMSO.
Donovan, J.E. and Jessor, R. (1978), 'Adolescent Problem Drinking – Psychosocial Correlates in a National Sample Study', *Journal of Studies in Alcohol*, **39**, 1506–24.
Dorn, N. and Murji, K. (1992), 'Drug Prevention: a Review of the English Language Literature', London: ISDD Research Monograph 5.
Ennet, S.T., Rosenbaum, D.P., Flewelling, R.L., Bieler, G.S., Ringwalt, C.L. and Bailey, S.L. (1994), 'Long-Term Evaluation of Drug Abuse Resistance Education', *Addictive Behaviours*, **19**, 113–25.
Glynn, T. (ed.) (1983), *Drug Abuse: Prevention Research*, Rockville, MD: NIDA.
Hawkins, J.D., Lishner, D. and Catalano, R. (1985), 'Childhood Predictors and the Prevention of Adolescent Substance Abuse, in C. Jones and R. Battjes (eds), *Etiology of Drug Abuse: Implications for Prevention*, NIDA Research Monograph 56, Rockville, MD: NIDA.
Hirst, J. and McCamley-Finney, A. (1994), 'The Place and Meaning of Drugs in the Lives of Young People', Sheffield Hallam University, Health Research Institute Report Number 7.
HMSO (1995), *Tackling Drugs Together*, London: HMSO.
HMSO (1998), *Tackling Drugs to Build a Better Britain*, London: HMSO.
Howie, A. (1997), *Guidelines for Planning and Evaluating Drug Education*, Edinburgh: Health Education Board for Scotland.
Hurry, J. and Lloyd, C. (1997), *A Follow-up Evaluation of Project Charlie*, Central Drugs Prevention Unit, Home Office, London: HMSO.
Ives, R. and Clements, I. (1996), 'Drug Education in Schools: a Review', *Children and Society*, **10**, 14–27.
Jessor, R. and Jessor, S.L. (1977), *Problem Behaviour and Psychosocial Development – A Longitudinal Study of Youth*, NY: Academic.
Jessor, R., Jessor, S.L. and Finney, J. (1973), 'A Social Psychology of Marijuana Use: Longitudinal Studies of High School and College Youth', *Journal of Personality and Social Psychology*, **26**, 1–15.
Kaley, F., Allan, K. and Coggans, N. (1992), 'Evaluation of the Quality of Life Project', Report to the European Commission, Number 91CCVE1254-0.
Kandel, D.B. (1980), 'Drug and Drinking Behaviour Among Youth', *Annual Review of Sociology*, **6**, 235–85.
Keene, J. and Williams, M. (1996), 'Who DARES wins? Drug Prevention and the Police in Schools', *Druglink*, **11** (2), 16–18.
Milburn, K.C. (1995), 'A Critical Review of Peer Education with Young People with Special Reference to Sexual Health: a Critical Review', *Health Education Research: Theory and Practice*, **10** (4), 407–20.
Miller, P. and Plant, M. (1996), 'Drinking, Smoking, and Illicit Drug Use Among 15 and 16-year-olds in the United Kingdom', *British Medical Journal*, **313**, 394–397.
NHS Health Advisory Service (1996), *Children and Young People: Substance Misuse Services*, London: HMSO.

Pentz, M.A. (1993), 'Comparative Effects of Community-based Drug Abuse Prevention', in G.A. Baer, J.S. Marlatt and R.J. McMahon (eds), *Addictive Behaviours Across the Life Span: Prevention, Treatment and Policy Issues*, London: Sage.

Pentz, M.A., Dwyer, J.H., MacKinnon, D.P., Flay, B.R., Hansen, W.B., Wang, E.Y. and Johnson, C.A. (1989), 'A Multicommunity Trial for Primary Prevention of Adolescent Drug Abuse', *Journal of the American Medical Association*, **261**, (22), 3259–66.

Schaps, E., DiBartolo, R., Moskowitz, J., Palley, C.S. and Churgin, S. (1981), 'A Review of 127 Drug Abuse Prevention Program Evaluations', *Journal of Drug Issues*, **11**, 17–43.

Schroeder, D.S., Laflin, M.T. and Weis, D.L. (1993), 'Is There a Relationship between Self-Esteem and Drug Use?, Methodological and Statistical Limitations of the Research', *Journal of Drug Issues*, 645–65.

Scottish Office Home and Health Department (1994), *Drugs in Scotland: Meeting the Challenge, Report of the Ministerial Drugs Task Force*, Edinburgh: HMSO.

Tierney, J. (1997), 'Disseminating Harm Reducing Drug Education in the North West of England', Paper presented at the 8th International Conference on the Reduction of Drug Related Harm, Paris.

Tobler, N.S. and Stratton, H.H. (1997), 'Effectiveness of school-based drug prevention programs: a meta-analysis of the research', *Journal of Primary Prevention*, **18**, (1), 71–128.

Whelan, S. and Culver, J. (1997), 'Don't say "No", say "DARE"?', Kirkby-in-Ashfield: North Nottinghamshire Health Promotion.

4 Operational policing issues
Tony Doyle

Introduction

Government policy recognises enforcement as one of the three planks of drug misuse strategy. European cooperation on supply reduction has been reviewed in Chapter 1. This chapter concentrates on the challenges of day-to-day police work and describes the changes in operational policing of drug-related crimes over the last 15 years. While much of the detail is drawn from experience of working in Merseyside, the description reflects changes in police work throughout the United Kingdom.

The 1980s

Merseyside Police 'F' Division includes Toxteth, Dingle, Aigburth, Garston, Halewood and Speke, and then inwards to Wavertree, Allerton, Belle Vale, Woolton, Calderstones and Netherley. Of these, Allerton, Calderstones, Aigburth and Woolton are comparatively affluent, while the others share the problems of many metropolitan inner-city areas.

Toxteth and Dingle are adjacent districts of Liverpool, situated at the southern end of the city. The populations of each contain large numbers of African-Caribbean, Asian, Western European and Irish immigrants. Traditionally poor housing has recently been upgraded. Toxteth encompasses the 'red-light' area of the city, with prostitutes operating in the shadow of the Anglican cathedral to support both drug addiction and young families. The once derelict Mersey waterfront now boasts fine examples of land reclamation including tourist attractions and technology parks.

The Wavertree area is a typical inner-city area with high unemployment, particularly among the younger generation, a multi-racial population and run-down housing stocks. In contrast it also boasts one of the most success-ful technology parks in the North West of England. Netherley and Belle Vale encapsulated all that was wrong with city planning during the fifties, being subjected to the building of high- and mid-rise developments con-nected by so-called 'spine blocks' – four-tier elongated housing strips, join-ing the blocks together. Ultimately the council were to demolish these sites and embark on a programme of low-rise redevelopment. Unfortunately, however, the area remains high on the league tables regarding illicit drug trafficking and general crime.

Further along the river, Speke and Halewood have also undergone facelifts – though Speke remains grey and anonymous. This area hosts the new airport development and incorporates the gigantic Ford Motor Company which provides a lifeline of employment to the region. Drug misuse re-mains high in the area, with users and dealers able to be hidden by row upon row of terraced housing.

In 1983 heroin was more prevalent in the Toxteth and Dingle areas, so police efforts were concentrated there. Much of the information used was gleaned from local prostitutes who were often drug addicts. Police officers would quickly identify these women and follow them to their supplier. After she had visited the dealer the woman would be stopped and detained for the purpose of a drug search to confirm that drugs had been obtained. With this confirmation police officers would watch the house the following night. Observation would confirm high numbers of visitors – often up to eighty in one night. In other cases, members of the public would provide tip-offs to the police, allowing observation to begin. A search warrant would then be sworn and the house would be raided on a subsequent night when there was similar activity. A sledgehammer would be used to break down the door, enabling the police to enter and secure the premises before com-mencing the search.

The findings were virtually always the same, small wraps of heroin in paper envelopes usually cut from a writing pad or similar. The drug squad officers would search for the pieces of paper from which the envelope had been cut in order to match them. Silver foil was often found at the scene with heavy burn marks where the dealer had been smoking their own drugs. At this time, the sound of the sledgehammer on the door would often cause the residents to freeze in shock for long enough for the first police officer to reach the suspected dealer and so prevent destruction of evidence.

It was unusual to lose a case in these early days. The first important change to this pattern was when it was decided that the words spoken by drug users to police officers who answered the door when the users were calling at the home of a suspected drug dealer, were inadmissable. The case of *R. v. Kearley* (1992) redefined such words as hearsay. In addition, drug dealers realised that they were making things easier for the police by keeping their drugs, money, wrapping paper and workings in the one premises. It was commonplace when a house was raided by police to find large amounts of cash, 'wraps' (wrapping paper folded in the form of a mini-envelope), pieces of scrap paper containing lists of names with cash figures next to them (e.g., 'Tony £50', 'Bill £30', etc.) as well as rough calculations where the suspect had clearly been reckoning up how much he was either owed or stood to make. These calculations were often damning as the suspect was usually unable to properly explain them to a jury at a trial.

On the streets, it was harder for the police to detect, particularly if the dealer employed another person to hold the drugs on their behalf. That way, the dealer would be 'clean' and in return he would pay his 'grafter' for taking the risk for him. This was an effective strategy and it became more difficult for officers to capture the main dealer in a hands-on situation. The police responded by using more static and mobile surveillance so that a picture could be built up for the Courts, of the relationship between the dealer and the 'grafter'. The surveillance often resulted in the identification of the dealer's safe house, where they stored their drugs. If the dealer could be recorded going to the safe house and a working relationship could be shown between the two players, then the conspiracy could be proved and a conviction secured.

The 1990s

The cartwheel conspiracy

The increased use of surveillance caused dealers to change tactics again (see Figure 4.1). The main dealer is represented by the central or inner circle. This is the main dealer who secures the services of a person to order a number of mobile telephones on their behalf, but not in the dealer's name. Any subsequent telephone billings will be paid by this person on behalf of the dealer, and in return they will be paid a cash bonus each month. The mobile telephones are then distributed, first to the person who is going to run the 'mail-order' side of the business, by simply answering the incoming calls, taking orders and then directing the buyers to particular places around the dealer's patch. That telephone number will, of course, have been circulated around the dealer's customers. The delivery man is next, and in addition to a

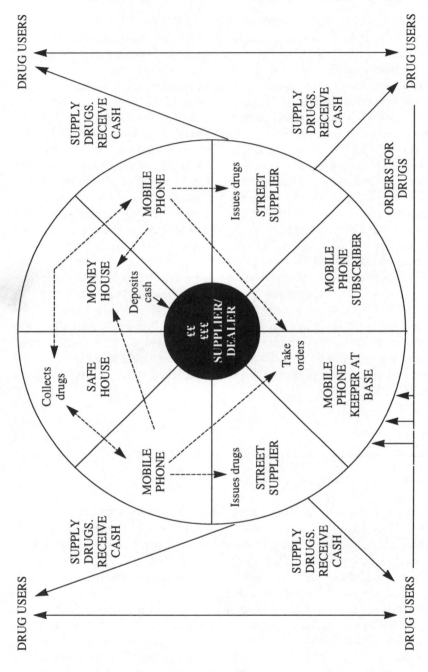

Figure 4.1 The cartwheel conspiracy

46

mobile phone, they are provided with a vehicle, usually a good second-hand high-powered model, in order to make the deliveries on the dealers behalf. It is they who will be actually employed by the dealer and who will be given hours of business throughout which they are expected to operate. This delivery driver, however, will engage the services of someone else, whose task it is to actually carry the controlled drugs on his person in small quantities so that, if they are stopped by the police and have no time to swallow the drugs, all that is revealed are two or three small wraps of heroin or cocaine to which the holder will say, 'They are mine, for my own use'.

When the wraps have been delivered, then the delivery man will go to the safe house where the drugs are stored. A few more small wraps will be collected and distributed accordingly and, when the money is collected in sufficient amounts, it is delivered to the money house, a separate premises to the others. It is here where the cash is kept until such time that the dealer calls to collect.

This arrangement presents enormous challenges to the police. If officers raid the premises where the orders are taken, all they seize is a mobile telephone with a whole number of names and locations, which does not in itself allow any offence to be identified. Should they raid the premises of the person who orders the mobile telephones for the dealer, all they will seize is a possible list of telephone demands, again resulting in no prosecutions. If officers raid the money house and find the money, they have to return it because it is not an offence merely to possess money. If the drug safe house is raided, the drug store will be discovered, but cannot be tied to the main dealer. The keeper of the drugs will probably go to prison, and in most cases this is usually someone without much prospect of a job, with little cash, who has been asked to mind a parcel without asking questions. The difficulties are completed when police arrest the buyer, the addict, with a small wrap of heroin. In isolation they will be fined and the matter recorded as another drug statistic.

The difficulties, therefore, in bringing a successful prosecution against a dealer are enormous. To be successful, it will entail countless hours of detective work, looking at associations of all the constituent members of the cartwheel, days and even weeks of static and mobile surveillance, as well as the tasking of registered informants.

The use of informants is, under properly controlled circumstances, one of the most productive areas of intelligence gathering. The Merseyside force places great importance on informant handling issues, and lays down strict codes of conduct to ensure that both the informant and informant handler (the police officer) are protected.

A great deal of time and effort can go into the development of an informant and, if successful, they can earn significant amounts of money. They are involved in a dangerous game as the criminals are aware of their existence and would pay dearly to have them identified, thus reducing their own risk of arrest and prosecution. Within the police force it is recognised that a good informant is worth weeks of observation. They are a very cost-effective resource and should be protected at all costs.

Most informants do their work for basic reasons. They may simply wish to earn more money, to reduce a potential sentence associated with a case against them or exact revenge upon another. Often, this may be an estranged partner, wishing to get even for violent treatment in the past or wishing to stop some activity seen as 'unacceptable' – such as using children as dealers or couriers. In Merseyside, registered informants are closely supervised. The handling officer will usually be accompanied by another. Both will report to a controlling officer who will scrutinise the intelligence report and any payments to the informant. This system is highly confidential.

Even where all the players can be identified and the case against them proved, it may well be the case that the dealer is only one member of an organised crime team which comprises ten or more similar players. This often causes the public much concern, and they feel it must be possible to arrest the local villains from the estate – after all they are 'driving nice cars, dripping in jewellery and always have plenty of money; they must be dealing in drugs'. The police have to explain that it is not so easy.

The police service was pleased to see the implementation of both the Drug Trafficking Offences Act, 1986 and the Drug Trafficking Act, 1994. Prior to these two pieces of legislation, officers were able to seize any monies in the possession of drug traffickers, including those items such as motor vehicles, jewellery and other expensive items as well as drug paraphernalia (electronic scales, etc.). With the appearance of Drug Trafficking legislation dealers became frightened to make deposits of drug cash into banks or other financial institutions. The legislation gave law enforcement officers the authority to enquire into the means of any person charged with a drug trafficking offence, to establish the extent to which a suspect has benefited financially.

In so doing, officers could apply to the courts for production orders which in turn would be served upon financial institutions, ordering the production of accounts and relevant documentation. If they failed to comply they would be liable to a term of imprisonment. Once an account has been traced and it is considered worthwhile to apply for confiscation, a separate order can be applied for which effectively freezes the suspect's account until the outcome of a court case is known. If the suspect is convicted of drug trafficking, the court will establish the benefit made and will make a confiscation order accordingly.

Section 52 of the 1994 Act also made it an offence for a person to fail to disclose their suspicions about potential trafficking. If a person opened a new account and started making regular cash deposits, it became the duty of the relevant officer of the bank to inform the National Criminal Intelligence Service. Failure to do so could result in imprisonment. Both Trafficking Offence Acts may appear somewhat draconian. However, as they are aligned with International Cooperation Treaties, they permit enforcement officers to apply for confiscation orders relating to money or property throughout the world.

Clubland conspiracy

The Police Service now face a similar problem when dealing with drug investigations in the club scene (Figure 4.2). Reports are made to the area plain-clothes departments, or indeed to the central drug squad, to the effect that drug dealing is taking place on the dance floor area of the club, or anywhere else within the club premises. Usually, the police are told that small-time dealers are selling Ecstasy in small numbers, but a preliminary examination of the premises quickly reveals that as many as eight or ten dealers are found to be working for one club doorman, or bouncer. In some

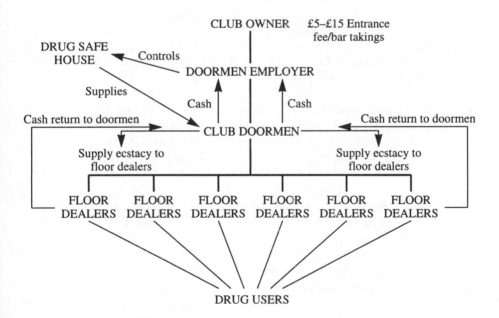

Figure 4.2 The clubland Ecstacy conspiracy

of the larger clubs where drugs are being sold, there could be as many as 20 club doormen, most of whom are employing their own dealers to work on their behalf. So, within a small period of time, it is possible to find a major network of distribution taking place in those premises. Everybody associated with the premises may know that the dealing is taking place, often including the person who has the contract for the door security – in other words, the man who employs the doormen. My own experience indicates that it is they who control the drugs flowing into the premises through their own contact, and obviously it is they who control the doormen. So a sizeable but unlawful profit is available to them if they decide to permit the drug distribution to take place.

The club owner may be aware of the drug dealing. If they have the right club with the right reputation, they will receive their profits from money taken at the door as well as the money made behind the bar. So we find ourselves in a most demanding situation in trying to deal with the overall conspiracy taking place within that club. If the low-level floor dealers are arrested, then, unless it can be proved that a supply of drugs took place to another person by that dealer, all they will face is a charge of simple possession for perhaps five or six ecstasy tablets found on their person. Similarly, if the supply by the doormen to the dealers cannot be shown, then the police struggle to find the necessary evidence against them. And how are the police to deal with the main man who engages all the door staff? The answer is similar to the police approach to the cartwheel conspiracy, with experienced drug squad detectives engaging in hours of painstaking investigations, surveillance, both static and mobile and the deployment of officers working undercover.

The deployment of such officers is not taken lightly, but is a tactic which has been very successful over the years. The criminals know that they are used. Some club owners are warned in advance, but still persist in allowing drug dealing to take place. A young officer will make purchases and then ask for a price for 'buying in bulk'. The dealer often goes straight back to their doorman and brings them into the negotiations. The rest is fairly straightforward. Continued negotiations which take account of the issues surrounding the use of *agent provocateur*, will normally result in the arrest of entire teams of dealers in a club. Doormen realise how the police work in these situations, but fall into the trap time and time again.

The issues around the use of *agent provocateur* (or 'entrapment' as it is sometimes known) are closely considered at all stages of such an operation. Home Office guidelines dictate that undercover officers or informants who take part in crime must only play a minor role in its commission. The offence must already have been planned and the officer must have no part in that process. It is likely that the offence would have been committed anyway, and the use of an agent was necessary to frustrate the offence or apprehend the offenders afterwards. One can see, therefore, the degree to which 'Clubland Conspiracy' operations must be planned, while ensuring that the ruling of *R.* v. *Bryce* (1995) – i.e. the need to ensure the corroboration of evidence – is strictly applied.

It would, however, be inappropriate to assume that all door staff in the club scene are involved in unlawful drug trafficking. That is simply not the case, and many conduct themselves with a good deal of professionalism and restraint.

Preparation of the court file

When people have been arrested and charged with Conspiracy to Supply Controlled Drugs, usually Class A type such as heroin, crack cocaine and ecstasy, much work is involved in the preparation of the file for court. Usually, an officer from the team is nominated as the 'team leader' who will take day-to-day control of the operation. They will dictate the pace, direct their colleagues as to what is required of them and take control of the arrest situation on 'strike day'. But it is the file which takes the time, sometimes countless weeks of organising exhibits, attending case conferences with counsel and, more demanding, dealing with requests for information by defence counsel. An example of this demand is best illustrated when the Liverpool team arrested 14 members of an organised crime team in Liverpool for offences ranging from Conspiracy to Supply to Unlawful Possession of Firearms. The officer dealing with the file was fully engaged in the project for just over twelve months, the time it took for the case to go to the Crown Court, and during this time there were numerous requests for information from defence solicitors which consumed a great deal of resources.

The officer in question applied for leave of the Court to allow for the undercover officers to give evidence behind screens and to use a pseudonym in order to both protect their own identity and the integrity of other ongoing investigations in which they were involved. The stipendiary magistrate rejected this and ordered that the officers should identify themselves. An appeal was immediately launched to the Queen's Bench Division, which invariably meant a delay of some months for the trial. Solicitors for the defence applied for bail for the defendants, who had been remanded in custody for very serious offences indeed involving Class A drugs and firearms, and the magistrate agreed to the applications. In the ruling *DPP* v. *Liverpool City Magistrates* (1996), The Appeal Court judges overruled the decision not to allow the officers anonymity, and were scathing in respect of the decision to award those defendants bail for offences which appeared to them to be clearly made out (i.e., when based upon the evidence placed before the court, the suspects are clearly guilty). This all resulted in substantial delays.

The trial itself also presents problems for the police. In the more high-profile cases, involving defendants who face substantial terms of imprisonment, the police have to face up to the threat of intimidation to both the jury and independent witnesses. It is becoming more common now for large groups of males to turn up at the trial and simply stare at the jury throughout the entire time they are in court. Even as the Court ends, these men will go and stand outside and wait for the jury members to leave the Court building, where all that will happen is that they will stare at them. Sometimes this intimidates the jury, and others try the same tactics. There is no possible police response to this at present, as no offence has been committed.

Drug support teams

Under the leadership of Derek O'Connell, former drug squad officer, Merseyside adopted a multi-agency approach to drug misuse some years ago. Since the introduction of the Government White Paper 'Tackling Drugs Together', every police force within England and Wales is now obliged to demonstrate that they are approaching the drug problem with consistency. Merseyside has pioneered some of these approaches and has supported other forces in adopting similar policies and practice.

When the Drug Squad was merged into the Major Crime Unit at Merseyside, looking at organised crime throughout the county, the Chief Constable insisted that a drug support team remain in order to deal with those issues stemming from work within the Drug Reference Groups. This ensured that a team of officers was available to liaise with school teachers and school drug education coordinators, as well as providing a point of contact for the five police districts of Merseyside Police for the provision of specialist advice and support. This support often comes in the form of providing young officers who work long hours, usually without pay, purporting to be drug users purchasing drugs from the street dealers and bringing back evidence to the small team of drug support staff. When we believe there is sufficient evidence to organise arrests and searches, teams are organised and the policing plans are implemented.

Conclusion

Enforcement in drug misuse has changed greatly in the last 20 years. Criminals have responded to police efforts by providing compartmentalised schemes which make evidence-gathering more difficult. Enforcement methods will have to continue to develop to meet new demands.

5 Counselling for drug misuse

Pat Lerpiniere

Introduction

Counselling for drug problems has not had a long history in the UK. It is, however, an area of rapid expansion with a large number of counselling agencies having been established over the last 10–15 years. This fairly recent development of services is not surprising as counselling itself has a relatively short history of around 40–50 years. Over this period a huge variety of theories and models in the field of counselling has arisen, many of which have been applied to the field of drug misuse, accompanied by a significant increase in illegal drug use.

Counselling for drug misuse problems is probably the most fundamental of the range of treatment options available to clients seeking help. Once a client becomes engaged in the network of care that is on offer from statutory or voluntary services it would be almost impossible for them not to be offered counselling.

Although the word counselling is used frequently, there is little guarantee of a common meaning or even agreement over the approach being taken. This underlines a major current difficulty. What actually constitutes the process of counselling for drug misuse problems? This chapter attempts to address a range of questions in this area including:

- Defining the meaning and process of counselling
- Defining the purpose and process of counselling drug misusers
- The increasing professionalisation and standard setting of counsellor's work.

Within the drug field there has been heated debate over which approach to take with drug problem clients. The two major treatment philosophies of abstinence or harm reduction/maintenance programmes seem to have become polarised into treatment options, instead of the complementary or linked processes they often are.

Matching client needs to treatment options

Even if a client has the luxury of choice over which service to use, they will often find it difficult to match their needs to the best treatment programme. Choice, however, in this field is usually controlled by purchasers and providers of services who are swayed by a variety of beliefs and evidence. The available evidence is still often buried within the academic and research world and can be confusing for practitioners to translate into clear decisions regarding service delivery. It can be difficult for such information to hold sway against powerful belief systems about the right way to treat people with drug problems. Such belief systems also have the potential to carry strong moralistic overtones and judgements. In the context of working with drug users this is understandable, but issues can become clouded, using up time and energy in unhelpful debate over treatment philosophy. The recent controversy over the approaches of local Drug Action Teams and Scotland Against Drugs is an excellent example of this.

The nature of drug use

To further complicate the picture, patterns of drug misuse are complex, the spectrum of users ranging from those dependent on prescribed drugs (e.g., benzodiazepines) and trying to come off; those on prescribed drugs and intending to stay on (e.g., methadone programmes); and users of a whole range of illicit drugs. Individuals can be involved in using drugs in many ways, with wide variation in: the type of drug used, method of use (smoking/ingesting/injecting) and frequency/style of use (occasional/recreational/experimental/dependent). Consequently, diverse demands are placed on drug treatment agencies. Often the response is to set up further subdivisions of counselling provision for each of these groupings (Armstrong, 1996). Many workers are, for instance, ambivalent about some of the issues surrounding counselling clients taking prescribed medication, with opinions being at times strongly divided.

Project Match

Whether clients can be properly matched to a particular treatment regime is a question that Project Match (1997), an extremely comprehensive research programme carried out in the USA, has attempted to answer. This study evaluated the success of three treatment modalities and the possibility of matching clients' needs to the most appropriate treatment. Early results indicate that outcome is most successfully predicted by analysis of client parameters, and that for most clients the actual form of treatment is less important. The only significant variable appears to be the level of psychiatric illnesss. This has indicated that 12 step facilitation may be more effective than cognitive behavioural techniques for those with less severe psychiatric disorders using abstinence oriented programmes. The 12 step facilitation approach is based on the Alcoholics/Narcotics Anonymous philosophy, but does not necessarily rely on the same spiritual basis. This approach is widespread although less popular in certain areas. Uptake appears to be very much linked to the views of professionals and the philosophy of related services available locally. The spiritual, prayer and meditation focus of many UK 12 step programmes does not, however, seem to be a significant cause of dropout from the programme (Polkinghorne Report, 1996).

It would be too simplistic merely to translate these findings to the UK context since cultural and belief systems radically affect the nature of service delivery. In particular, much depends on whether drug use is conceptualised as a medical condition or a behavioural problem. In the USA, the bias towards a medical approach has resulted in a much greater prominence of abstinence-focused treatments using standard and routine techniques, with an emphasis on continuous lifetime support and acceptance of a drug-using status which must be controlled.

Implications for service delivery

The above factors have significant implications for service funders and providers – not least in resisting increasing pressure to go for the cheapest service option. The differences in cultural and belief systems mean that solutions do not automatically translate from one country to another. The variety of needs that clients present with is complex, ranging from minimal intervention to detoxification through to intensive residential support. This is further complicated by the other circumstances of the client, e.g., do they have home support, secure employment, a positive social network and good physical and psychological health. Clients clearly want a wide range of treatment options and will gain benefit from those they find most useful and acceptable. Even with the work of Project Match, it does not look as if we are at a point where we can confidently measure client needs and relate these to a clear treatment programme based on rational objective evidence. Until such a methodology exists we will require to offer a comprehensive range of services.

Model of drug and alcohol use

One specific difficulty for staff working in this field lies in tolerating their clients' deviant activities (Lanarkshire Health Board, 1996). From a societal point there is a mixed reaction to drug use, particularly if contrasted with alcohol. We seem to categorise those using alcohol or other drugs with the same labels but apply them differentially. The following model of accept-ability attempts to describe these differing viewpoints.

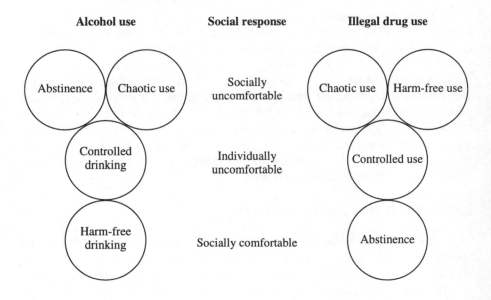

Figure 5.1   Acceptability of drug and alcohol use

This model links the classic descriptions of the ways in which individuals use alcohol or other drugs to the most typical social or individual (drug user) response.

Abstinence

Abstinence from illicit drug taking is the preferred goal of most treatment agencies and reflects the current majority view of funders. Support for prevention and treatment work is underpinned by the intention of moving clients and society to a drug-free state. There has already been a lot written to demonstrate that the position on the acceptability of drug and alcohol use in society has changed dramatically over the last century. Alcohol is generally accepted, to the point where those who choose to abstain are often thought of as slightly odd, or killjoys, when others are drinking and wishing to experience the disinhibiting effect of alcohol.

Controlled use/drinking

Controlled use (prescribed drugs under medical supervision such as methadone programmes) is generally tolerated for the common good but may not always be viewed positively. The public tends to consider such programmes to be condoning or even encouraging drug use, while those receiving the drug are sometimes unhappy to be dependent on the clinic or GP as provider. Additionally, prescribed drugs (purposely) do not produce the same intoxicating effects as illicit ones, such as heroin, and clients who are not well motivated to change can promote a sense of dissatisfaction with prescribing programmes. Controlled drinking has a less intense but equally negative reaction from many. In social situations, many people are uncomfortable with those either not drinking or limiting their drinking, as this does not fit with the disinhibition usually associated with alcohol use. For those chosing controlled drinking as their goal, there is the discomfort of remaining in a state of cognitive vigilance in all drinking situations.

Chaotic use

Those who use drugs or alcohol chaotically are normally viewed negatively. Often, for the individual, this is accompanied by an inability to see the possibility of any change or improvement in their circumstances. Socially the individuals and the behaviours associated with such chaotic use are usually strongly criticised.

Harm-free use

The other real contrast shown by the model is in the concept of harm-free use. While this is seen as acceptable by the majority of the population in relation to alcohol, it is not so acceptable for illicit drugs: aside from any legal considerations, it is anathema to many to even suggest that drugs might be taken harmlessly. Currently the main debate in this area seems to be on the use and acceptability of cannabis.

Application of the model

Reaction to this model will also be affected by the age group (with younger people tending to have more tolerant and accepting attitudes towards illegal drugs) or the specific type of drug (cannabis tending to create a more mixed response than heroin or cocaine). The reaction to tobacco is also changing with a clear majority accepting abstinence as the only acceptable goal, with both harm-free and controlled use being ruled out on health grounds. These attitudes over acceptability impact significantly on the culture and direction of service delivery which includes defensiveness when undertaking a harm reduction approach.

Harm reduction

The harm reduction concept has been misunderstood or misinterpreted by many as an approach that supports or condones drug use. It is essentially, however, a pragmatic way of working with people rather than any deeply held ethical viewpoint about drug use. There is a simple recognition that, although the ultimate goal for drug users may be to become drug-free, for many this is an unrealistic short-term goal. By making smaller changes clients can move towards a drug-free state with each change improving their situation. The large numbers of agencies using this approach acknowledge that this can be a slow process and that clients often 'stick' at certain points for long periods before moving on. As a way of working, the harm reduction approach has been adopted by the majority of statutory bodies, but with the recognition that the client's choice will determine the extent of their cooperation.

In the USA these options are sometimes referred to as the 'high threshold route' (abstinence) and the 'low threshold route' (harm reduction) with both options attempting to help clients overcome their problems and become drug free.

Counselling service delivery

There are many beliefs regarding who is best placed to deliver services to clients. The main providers are social services, health services, churches, trained voluntary agency staff or untrained community groups with life experience to offer. Often these community groups are the starting points for activities that go on to become funded professional agencies. This can create difficulties for the original group in separating the advocating and lobbying role from the service delivery component. The group can find themselves in the position of receiving funding from those who they have initially criticised and becoming subject to service delivery agreements that limit their action in relation to commenting on policy and service provision.

There is also debate concerning who will make the most effective drug counsellors from within the three following groupings normally involved:

- Specialist or generic workers
- Paid and/or voluntary staff
- Ex-drug users as counsellors (often the most contentious issue).

It is worth reiterating that we are dealing with a relatively new way of counselling, just beginning to carve out its own professional niche. This is, in turn, being applied to a relatively new set of drug-related problems that are in themselves often ill-defined. There are numerous modes of thinking and much confusing debate, often of a contradictory nature but this is perhaps understandable in such new areas of work. Currently there is a lack of clear consensus over the aim of counselling interventions: are we condemning or condoning drug use, stopping drug use or stopping the damage and despair it brings to individuals, their families and local communities and, finally, are we trying to blame or understand the user? In the meantime, the use of all kinds of drugs is on the increase (with accompanying moves towards tacit acceptance of such use) throughout all socio-demographic classes, and particularly among teenagers and women.

For many workers and organisations there are issues in recognising the difference between using counselling skills and counselling. This can extend into confusion in distinguishing between the various ways of helping people. Often activities described as counselling would be better termed advice, guidance, mediation or befriending. Conversely, activities that can be considered as counselling are often not referred to as such (e.g., the work of the Samaritans is described as befriending but contains many of the competences of counselling).

Definitions of helping activities

To put some framework around this a description is given of some of the recent theoretical and practical thinking from the worlds of counselling, behaviour change and drug use, and how these interrelate to help clients with a range of presenting problems. This traditionally means beginning with a definition – one of the most useful modern descriptions being that produced by the Advice, Guidance, Counselling and Psychotherapy Lead Body (AGC&PLB). This has produced a set of working definitions that not only describes these discrete activities but also draws useful boundaries between them (Russell, Dexter and Bond, 1992). Thus it establishes counselling within a set of other helping activities (including befriending) in a non-hierarchical way.

The AGC&PLB definition for counselling is:

> An activity freely entered into by the person seeking help. A relationship that has its boundaries clearly defined and is clearly and explicitly contracted. It offers the opportunity for the client themselves to identify things that are troubling or perplexing and is a process designed to help self exploration and understanding. The thoughts, emotions and behaviours once accessed may offer the client greater opportunities for a greater sense of personal resources and self determined change.

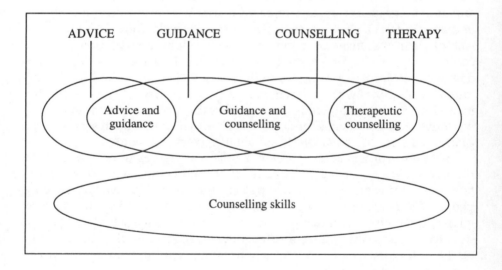

Figure 5.2   Chain of activities

This model reinforces the specific nature of helping activities and their relationship with each other, but carefully avoids describing any activity as more important. It is possible within this description for workers to be more comfortable in taking on roles other than counselling without feeling they are carrying out less 'specialist or complex' tasks. It also describes therapy as a separate activity that uses counselling skills but is not a 'better' intervention for clients.

Applying these principles to the field of drug counselling, clearly much that is described as counselling would be more appropriately considered as advice and guidance. Those activities described in the Polkinghorne Report as 'the giving of information and support to help clients manage the consequences of their drug misuse' would clearly fall into this category. They also highlight the significance of the mental health issues that complicate the lives of many clients (recent estimates by Rorstad indicate that anything up to 40 per cent of specific groups may exhibit co-morbidity [Rorstad and Checinski, 1996]). For these clients in particular, counselling needs should be built in as part of an overall care package that may well contain aspects of more intense therapeutic intervention. Counselling will, of course, also form part of a large number of the treatments offered to clients – e.g., needle exchanges, detoxification and day-care services all use counselling as part of the programme.

Models and theories of counselling

These have principally involved a move away from the psychoanalytic techniques of Freud, common until the late 1950s, to the client/person-centred approaches developed by Rogers (1964). Over the last decade there has been a noticeable introduction of cognitive-behavioural techniques into the area of drug counselling. There has been a slowly growing consensus as to which counselling techniques and skills are effective with clients, although not an agreement over basic philosophy or models. As these changes in preferred models have taken place no methods have been dropped, so that there is now a wide-ranging mix of favoured approaches, models and styles adopted by service providers. This can be a confusing picture for those seeking help who naturally search for the most appropriate treatment or method to deal with their problem.

According to the psychoanalytic model, an individual's drug use is related to their personal history and intra-personal conflict. The technique is non-directive and uses these internal strengths and conflicts to create change. This form of therapy can take many sessions, sometimes stretching over years, to achieve change (Morea,1990).

This model gave way to the patient-centred theories of Carl Rogers in the early 1960s in which more attention was given to a client's present situation. More critically it is a less directive approach that accepts, as a core principle, that clients are able to make their own decisions. The major shift in thinking introduced by Rogers was the importance of a relationship in which workers would use empathy, acceptance and genuineness as the main qualities in working with patients to create change. The role of the counsellor within this model is to bring themselves into the relationship but allow clients the control and responsibility of decision-making (Mearns and Thorne, 1988). As the nature of our thinking about drug problems became further 'demedicalised' this slowly shifted to a person-centred approach. After so many years this is still the favoured approach of most statutory providers and purchasers of services.

Newer models and developments of the person-centred, psychodynamic and cognitive-behavioural approaches have also had their influence. It is not the function of this chapter to give detailed explanations of these models, already well described elsewhere. For the sake of clarity a very brief overview of the most important models and their impact on drug counselling is provided: the range includes personal construct counselling from George Kelly, rational-emotive therapy from the work of Albert Ellis, transactional analysis from the work of Eric Berne and, probably of most direct influence, cognitive-behavioural counselling from the work of Aaron Beck.

Personal construct therapy

This refers to a frame of mind based on the way we perceive and construct our understanding of the world. It assists clients in reconstructing the way in which they view the world using a set of skills in a three-stage process (similar to Egan's exploring, understanding and acting described further on in this chapter) which take clients from a perception of themselves as helpless and worthless to seeing themselves as they would like to be (Fransella and Dalton, 1990).

Rational-emotive behaviour therapy

This was originally described as rational-emotive therapy but Ellis has recently added in the behavioural component. It uses a person-centred approach and makes the common-sense link that our thinking, feelings and behaviour are inextricably interlinked. This linking, however, is not straightforward, and if any of these are not in sympathy with each other then we are disturbed at some level. It is the function of REBT to work to bring these elements back to a level of harmony that allows clients to function without distress. If our way of thinking is altered we will feel and act differently. Like cognitive-behavioural therapy it sits very well with our understanding and use of the model of change of Prochaska and DiClemente (as described in a later section in this chapter).

Transactional analysis

This way of understanding interactions between people uses the notion of 'ego states' to describe communication between two individuals, from the work of Eric Berne who proposed that each of us can adopt any of three ego states (parent, adult or child) when we communicate (Berne, 1968). If these communications are effective he refers to them as 'complementary transactions'. He also developed the idea of 'ulterior transactions' in which one thing is said but another meaning is contained in the message. It was this observation that led Berne to introduce the concept of 'games' which he described as life positions which people adopt, some of these being regarded as deep-seated and enduring. Within the field of addiction two particularly powerful games were recognised: the 'alcoholic' and the 'helpless addict'. It was postulated that people adopted these roles as dominant life positions and would resist making any changes because they gained reinforcement from using the role. The ideas are still in common usage, at least in framing many workers' view of a client's situation. The worker's role is to challenge clients to see that they are making decisions to stay in a role that is more comfortable than any alternative. Once this is accepted the task is to work with clients to find other ways of living that provide the means to make new decisions for themselves.

Cognitive-behavioural therapy (CBT)

As we move to shorter, evidence-based interventions there has been an accompanying shift to adopt cognitive-behavioural techniques, which fit well into the change of emphasis from disease to behavioural model of drug use. This model is based on the premise that it is our perception and interpretation of a problem rather than the problem itself that is of most significance. The technique uses a three stage ABC process (Activating event, Beliefs and Consequences), but emphasises the importance of the three core conditions of the person-centred approach (Trower, Casey and Dryden, 1988).

One application of CBT is in dealing with clients' practical problems including legal, health, employment, family, community and wider social problems. Counselling has to deal with the belief system that creates the consequences for clients. These can range from the perceived power of the substance over the individual, their own feelings of self-esteem and self-worth, the helplessness of their current position and fatalism. The beliefs can also focus around unhelpful positive ideas about drugs. These include views such as 'drugs are causing no problems' (usually meaning something else is, e.g., other people or lack of money) or drugs do not really cause any harm.

Problem management

Underpinning much current thinking is also the work of Gerard Egan, who has developed a three-stage problem management technique for the application of helping skills (Egan, 1994). These stages have been summarised as: Exploring (reviewing problem situations and unused opportunities in the client's life); Understanding (developing the preferred scenario) and Action (determining how to get there). This methodology fits well with the kinds of situations many drug users find themselves in and so has been adopted as a framework by many workers. It also allows workers to borrow from a range of models and approaches to find a way of working that best fits their own style and meets the needs of the client.

Currently the majority of workers and agencies seem to favour such an eclectic approach. This involves using a variety of ideas and techniques from a range of models. Each client is counselled in an individual, but clearly thought through, way with the counsellor drawing on whichever skills and techniques are appropriate for the presenting situation (Norcross and Tomcho, 1993).

Other related helping techniques

Three ways of working, closely related to counselling, are worth describing. These are motivational interviewing, solution focused brief therapy and critical incident debriefing. As with the models of counselling it is not intended to describe in detail ways of working that are well explained elsewhere, but simply to highlight how these techniques impact on drug counselling.

Motivational interviewing

This method developed by Walter Miller has become almost synonymous with drug counselling and involves using a set of skills and questioning techniques to move people on in the process of change (Miller and Rollnick, 1991). These changes (either behavioural or psychological) are selected by the client as ones they wish to make and feel able to achieve. There is an underlying relationship between this technique and the model of change, with part of the strategy being the identification of the stage of change that each individual has reached. The counsellor then uses positive reinforcement to encourage and empower clients to move on to the next stage.

Solution-focussed brief therapy

This is a more recently developed technique which recognises that within any client's current or past life there will be areas which they have been able to cope with. Based on work by de Shazer it focuses on these areas and builds on these positive feelings and coping strategies. At its most extreme, workers will ignore problem aspects of a client's life and will not undertake any complete exploration of lifestyle (essential components for those using Egan's model or any personal construct techniques). Attention is given to getting clients to identify a life in which things are going well for them. A scaling technique (from 1–10) is used by clients to rate themselves on relevant areas (these are not set but develop as part of the interaction). The sessions often involve the use of the 'miracle question' ('If you woke up in the morning and all your troubles had gone how would you know?'), followed by examining in minute detail the way in which clients know they are feeling better. These areas can then be used by clients to recognise their own strengths and abilities and from this be able to control and feel better about their life.

Critical incident debriefing

There is a growing use of this technique for certain clients who have been through some trauma (even some time in the past). It is an associated way of working developed by Dyregov and Mitchell, which they argue has been effective in reducing the complications and intensity of post-traumatic stress disorder. It is a very defined and sequential process that takes individuals through their feelings and actions leading up to and during the traumatic incident, and can be helpful for those clients who may be using drugs to cover up or cope with an event from the past, for example child abuse, rape or being involved in some disaster. Currently some doubt is being expressed about the validity of this approach although it is not certain if this relates to the nature of the intervention or the difficulties of establishing which clients may benefit from this approach.

Model of Change

The cognitive-behavioural approach sits neatly with the most recent thinking in the understanding of how people move through a process of change.

This work, developed by Prochaska and DiClemente as the model of change, has been adopted by most workers as the framework for their work with drug users. It is based on original work carried out on smoking cessation, but it relates well to most behaviour change situations (Prochaska and DiClemente, 1983). Again it has been endorsed by the Polkinghorne Report as a useful guide.

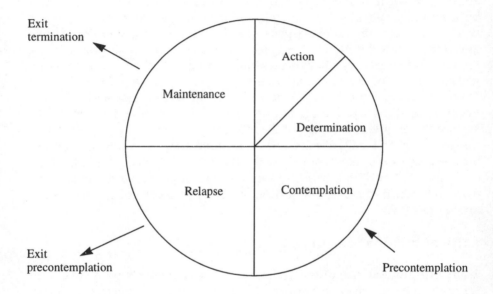

Figure 5.3   States of change

Precontemplation

If people are not experiencing or recognising any problems with their behaviour, they are said to be in 'precontemplation', in which state they will be happy to carry on as they are. This is the situation for a number of clients and even more people who do not come near counselling services.

Contemplation

When people begin to experience some level of concern (social, physical or psychological) they are moving into 'contemplation', in which state they have a growing discomfort over their situation and are beginning to think about making changes. It is important to recognise that at this stage people are not ready to actually make any change. If rushed into action at this point many individuals will feel resentful and unprepared and the likelihood of the change lasting is not high. The task for workers at this stage is to increase cognitive dissonance and to encourage clients to move to a position where they feel ready to make a change.

Determination

Once this happens, clients are in the 'determination' stage and can then be encouraged to plan how they will make the change. This essential step is often missed out which again can cause clients to fail in their attempt to change. Clients who plan how they will make the change, often considering in great detail how this will be accomplished, are more likely to succeed. An essential component is to have coping strategies and alternatives for when things do not go as planned.

Action

Having prepared as thoroughly as possible the 'action' stage is obviously when clients make the change. It is better for the timing and place of this to be decided in advance with support (both physical and emotional) available. Again it is sensible for clients to have contingency plans for when things do not turn out as planned. The action stage does not usually last for long (3–6 months) and is generally characterised by enthusiasm, excitement, energy and commitment.

Maintenance

As this wears off clients enter the 'maintenance' stage, which is often a time of great difficulty as the benefits of making the change seem less important and the attraction of the original lifestyle seems great. Often support is less at this stage as families and friends tend to believe the worst is over and that people should be getting on with their new life. During this period people are in a constant state of awareness referred to as cognitive vigilance. This state can last for extended periods of time (typically over the period during which someone refers to themselves as an 'ex-addict', etc.).

Relapse

This frequently means that people return to previous behaviour patterns, particularly when they face stressful events or conversely when they feel very good about themselves ('I deserve it' or 'I can handle it' or 'I can't cope' or 'I'm useless' are rationalisations often used at this stage). It is argued that some people even test out their resolve by putting themselves at risk. For these various reasons it is highly likely that people will relapse. Clients also need to realise that returning to drugs is not necessarily repeating the same old behaviour patterns. It could simply be a one-off event and, if it can be perceived in this way, they can move back into the maintenance stage having experienced a lapse rather than a relapse. If it is a full relapse then clients can either give up and move back into precontemplation (sometimes feeling worse than they did before they tried to give up) or they can move back round the cycle of change, usually more quickly and realistically. Many clients find themselves going around the cycle a number of times before permanently making a behaviour change.

Termination

If a permanent change takes place then most clients slowly become less conscious of the change and less likely to consider themselves an 'ex'. At this point they are considered to be in 'termination' and to have moved out of the cycle.

This model has been developed and refined over the years but has recently been challenged as incomplete by Farkas et al., who proposed an alternative addiction model which identifies that there are more effective predictors of change outcomes for clients than those described by the work of Prochaska and DiClemente (Farkas et al., 1996).

The counselling relationship

There is currently some doubt surrounding the concept of counselling being 'an activity freely entered into...'. This is clearly not the case for a large number of drug clients for whom counselling forms part of a compulsory package of care. The most obvious examples are those on any form of diversion from prosecution/sentencing, or disciplinary employment referral. Drug courts, a recent development from the USA, have been the focus of interest among several police forces and drug agencies over the last couple of years. Under this type of scheme, first-time offenders with no history of violence may be offered the opportunity of attending a treatment centre with an immediate referral system from a specially established court. Those who are referred to such schemes will have continued contact with the court and may also be offered a college course. Evidence from pilot schemes in Florida has demonstrated that such schemes have resulted in fewer court appearances and longer periods of time between such appearances (Cooper and Bartlett, 1996). The element of coercion on a client to attend for counselling is, however, much less obvious. Even those self-referring will often have had family or other pressure placed upon them to attend. Recent evidence suggests that clients have better outcomes if they are under some form of coercion. It has been argued that this is an obvious conclusion since alternatives to not attending and doing well could be job loss or imprisonment, both strong motivators. This presents some counsellors with ethical problems, working with clients who have been 'sent' for counselling.

A critical matter in dealing with such a 'coercive' referral is how the counsellor deals with the 'here and now' relationship with their client. This involves them in allowing clients to make genuine decisions, within the limits of possibility, about their situation and the choices they wish to make. It is this setting of limits and boundaries on choice that creates the tension between much current practice and the pure person-centred approach. This latter approach allows clients to carry on in a destructive and chaotic lifestyle if they choose to do so in a rational and well-considered way. Even when counsellors resolve these issues for themselves they are often driven by the imperatives and demands of employing organisations who require to see changes and improvements in directions they have determined. These are generally in terms of reduced drug use, reduction in crime, less family or social harm and an increase in social functioning and stability and health gain. Juggling with these issues can involve very real ethical conflict for counsellors using the person-centred approach. As has been commented upon by Tyndall and others, the principles of Rogerian therapy have been applied too rigidly in some cases, particularly such maxims as never giving advice or direction to clients.

Process of drug counselling

A major recent development has been the introduction of 'contracting' for a limited number of sessions, following which the client's progress is reviewed. This obviously has the potential to reduce the amount of contact for clients. It also has implications for the type of counselling model used: for instance, the traditional psychodynamic approach is incompatible with a limit on the number of sessions. Similarly, strict limitation of sessions would clearly be inappropriate in providing the necessary support and supervision to clients on methadone maintenance programmes, for whom continued contact is a prerequisite for prescribing of the drug.

Working within the frameworks described above there has developed a fairly standard routine to working with clients in most mainstream drug counselling services. This is a process which includes the following activities:

- Establishing the relationship
- Assessment of the problem
- Assessment of the client's life
- Goal setting
- Problem solving
- Decision making
- Maintenance of change
- Relapse management
- Ending the relationship.

These processes have their roots in work by Egan who discusses three processes, firstly exploring the client's situation, leading to understanding and consequent action. These ideas have been developed to include some of the more important practical tasks. Velleman outlines six stages very similar to the ones described above, although he uses the term 'empowering into action' rather than decision making which perhaps more clearly links the process to the stages of change model (Velleman, 1992).

Ideally, clients would progress through such a process in a predictable and orderly fashion. For most, however, the process involves revisiting a number of stages, sometimes repeatedly. This is particularly the case with goal setting, problem solving and relapse management as clients encounter and confront newly-discovered problems requiring further change and the development of new goals. Such goals may be more realistic or more challenging as, during the course of treatment, greater strength, confidence and empowerment are achieved.

As a framework within which these processes can take place, counselling is often considered as a relationship with three stages – beginning, middle and end – during which particular skills are applied and ways of relating to clients are refined (see Table 5.1).

It is worth examining these essential processes in a little more detail in order to highlight the essential features and the range of skills and techniques used.

Building the relationship

It is important for clients to understand the nature and purpose of the counselling relationship and to realise what they can and cannot expect

Table 5.1 A working model of practice

	PROCESS	WAYS OF BEING	WAYS OF DOING

B E G I N N I N G S	Coming together
	
	Establishing the
	    relationship
	Exploring the issues
	Acknowledging fears
	    and anxieties
	Assessing
	Negotiating the
	    contract including:
	    – setting the
	        boundaries
	    – clarifying the
	        expectations
		Empathy ⎤
		Acceptance ⎬ the core
		Genuineness ⎦ conditions
		Trust
		Openness
			Receptive attentive
			    listening
			Observing and sensing
			Appropriate accurate
			    responding:
			    – reflecting back
			    – paraphrasing
			    – summarising
			Facilitating
			Information seeking
			Exploring
			Identifying strengths
			Acknowledging
			    difficulties

M I D D L E S	Working together
	
	Deepening and using
	    the relationship
	Exploring significant
	    issues and feelings
	Holding boundaries
	Insight and
	    understanding
	Making connections
	Reworking
		All of the above *plus*:
		
		Advanced empathy
		Listening to and using
		    self
		Monitoring client's
		    use of counsellor
			All of the above *plus*:
			
			Being specific
			Being concrete
			Focusing
			Challenge
			Use of here and now
			Linking
			Interpreting

E N D I N G S	Separating
	
	Recognition of change
	    and no-change in
	    relation to:
	    – self
	    – significant others
	    – counsellor
	    – context
	Separation and loss
		All of the above *plus*:
		
		Acknowledging work
		    done
		Equality of regard
		Looking to the future
		Letting go
			All of the above *plus*:
			
			Reviewing work done
			    and not done
			Saying goodbye

Source: Adapted from Confederation of Scottish Counselling Agencies (1992, p. 15).

from the counsellor. Clients rarely come to counselling in a neutral, accepting frame of mind; often there is anxiety and concern. Drug clients, in particular, may be suspicious and antagonistic. This can be heightened if the agency is seen as part of a statutory organisation and even more so if the client has been sent by a court order or some employer referral scheme. Under the expressed feelings there may also be other negative emotions (e.g., anger or despair) and perhaps some positive feelings (e.g., hope and relief). It is important for counsellors to recognise and acknowledge the mixed emotions brought by clients to the start of a counselling relationship. There is a need to work through any negative emotions, strengthen the positive ones and ensure that the client is aware of the extent and limits of the relationship. Many clients understandably come with expectations that their problems will be resolved by the counsellor. Accepting that the relationship is more subtle than this, with the counsellor acting to allow the client to work through their problems and come to their own decisions, can be extremely frustrating for clients. Some do not accept this form of help and do not return. This in turn can be difficult for counsellors who may feel that they have failed their clients. Provided that departing clients are aware of alternative helping agencies, the counsellor should consider their responsibilities to have been discharged.

Within the limits of the information-giving, exploration of feelings and contract-setting taking place in the first stage of counselling, it is also the counsellor's task to begin giving responsibility to the client. The counsellor should remain in control of the process, while the client is responsible for the direction and decision making. Such shifting balance of power and control is integral to the developing relationship. Although at the beginning it seems that all the responsibility is in the hands of the counsellor, by the end it should have substantially transferred to the client. The counsellor has the task of drawing the relationship to a close once the client has indicated their intention to do so. As mentioned earlier some 'purists' can hold on to power by refusing to move out of the strict letter of the person-centred approach, resulting in their being unable or unwilling to share relevant information and guidance with clients for fear of distorting the counselling relationship. This can be an unproductive way of working with drug clients who may be required to attend for counselling and for whom other alternatives are either extremely limited or non-existent.

Assessment

A wide range of techniques is used to investigate clients' life circumstances, including the extent and consequences of their drug use. These include physical measures such as drug testing, the use of validated and objective assessment tools such as the Severity Of Drug Dependence Checklist or Opiate Treatment Index, as well as local assessment procedures. Less frequently, interviewing is carried out in a free-ranging manner without the use of any systematic tool. Previously this was much more common, counsellors working entirely with the clients' choice of material content. Currently there are considerable pressures on agencies to gather much more consistent and defined information from clients, for a number of reasons including national and local pressures to collect data on prevalence and trends of drug use and to provide baseline measures of clients' problems in order to measure outcomes. The latter may be of interest in assessing the agency's effectiveness. These fairly recent pressures should be monitored to ensure that the drive for consistency and data collection is not allowed to interfere with the delivery of flexible counselling services which are appropriate to clients' specific needs.

The actual process of assessment involves exploring with a client a whole range of aspects of their life in order to formulate an understanding of the pertinent issues affecting them, and to tailor an approach to their frame of reference. Generally this exploratory process will involve a great deal of uncertainty: the client's feelings must be appreciated and respected while essential information is sought in a sensitive manner. Counsellors particularly look for any feelings of dissonance and contradictions at this point (not to be used to trip clients up, but as a way of helping them to work through current issues and perhaps clarify some mixed feelings to help establish treatment goals).

The specific information needed includes the client's use of all types of drugs along with an estimate of frequency, amount and method of use. In the event of polydrug use it is helpful to know how organised or – more likely – chaotic is the style of use, e.g., using randomly whatever drugs are available or planned use of drugs by type, to get high, for dancing or to 'come down'. Relevant information also includes an individual's history of drug use, i.e., how long (months/years) drugs have been used and increases and changes in use over the years (in amounts, types and methods of use, particularly as these relate to the development of dependence). Often clients can be extremely knowledgeable and may have a comprehensive understanding of the ways to use and the impact of drugs. It is important, however, not to assume full knowledge (even in those who sound most impressive), as it may be that they do not fully understand the risks inherent in what they are doing, particularly if much of their information has been gathered from their own network of friends. In addition to information about drug use other areas to be explored are the client's relationships: do they live alone, have a partner, children or other close family and friends. This history should also establish the quality of the relationships, e.g., whether important others are critical, supportive or even involved in the client's drug use.

How the client fills his/her time provides a better understanding of their social networks, whether they are in, or seeking employment or in some form of education. If not, there are obviously greater difficulties for the counsellor in helping the client to build a structured, stable lifestyle, which is predictive of more successful outcome for coming off drugs.

Finance is an equally important area for assessment. Supporting a drug habit is an extremely expensive business that can cost several hundred pounds a week – generally supported by criminal activity. Much petty crime, including shoplifting and housebreaking, is carried out simply to provide the money for drugs, and drug users may become involved in dealing at various levels to finance their own drug habit. Avoiding the risks of prosecution for such crimes may be a useful motivator for change.

It is important to attempt to discover a client's reasons for coming forward for counselling, without automatically assuming that a self-referral has not involved some source of external pressure. Sorting out the internal from the external motivating factors is an important first step in moving clients forward to the goal setting and decision making stages.

A client's previous successes (as well as what is working well now) can give an indication of areas of strength. It is essential not to emphasise episodes of perceived failure. Further, when exploring current drug-related problems it is helpful to consider practical issues rather than get locked into any feelings of helplessness and hopelessness.

To elicit this amount of information, counsellors have to work in a detailed and questioning way with clients. To avoid an atmosphere of interrogation it is more appropriate for the counselling process to use the 'funnelling' technique. This starts by asking broad-based open questions that focus down into specific areas. It is also useful to remember that not all the information has to be gathered in the first session. Indeed, for understanding of the client to become a truly 'global holistic assessment', it requires to be an ongoing process. It would be naive to think that assessment takes place at the beginning of the relationship and then ceases. Effective counsellors continuously gather new information and understanding about their clients as the working relationship progresses.

Goal setting

Once clients have reached a clearer understanding of their position, including an awareness of their own internal conflicts and dissonance, they are usually ready to begin the process of goal setting. This is essentially a behaviourally-focussed exercise that encourages identification of desired changes, based on taking their broader aims and selecting small actions and changes that will be both meaningful and manageable. It links very closely with the techniques of problem solving and decision making to move clients on through the process of change.

The selection of goals is significant since their achievement has the potential to empower and improve the client's situation. They must be chosen by the client so that success is attributed to them and not the counsellor. The role of the counsellor is to work with the client to pick out of their current problems those things they would most wish to change. From these, more specific tasks are selected, often of a deliberately simple and practical nature especially for depressed or disempowered clients who may feel unable to make any change at all. Examples of such small goals might be: having one less argument with a partner, going out for a 20-minute walk twice over the next week, or to stop sharing spoons when mixing drugs for injecting. Each of these tasks, no matter how small, has the potential to engender feelings of success or failure and, for this reason, it is important not to allow selection of overly complex or ambitious goals. Longer-term projects will become feasible as smaller goals, seen as steps on the way, are reached.

It is helpful to have the client consider the obstacles standing in the way of their achieving a particular goal. This needs to be done thoroughly since clients may not realise, or tend to gloss over any obstacles. During goal setting counsellors need to be encouraging and supportive but also require to bring the task to a focussed end without demoralising the client.

Problem solving

Much has been said about the importance to clients of developing coping strategies. To do so effectively requires the application of problem solving techniques, a process which should be led, created and decided upon by the client, since they are in the best position to know the specific problems in their life that they wish to tackle. Client ownership of this process is crucial. The counsellor's task is to encourage clients into 'lateral thinking' about their problems and to make best use of their inner resources. Often some triggering or brainstorming needs to be generated by the counsellor since clients at this point are often unable to see any way out for themselves or any real possibility of change.

There is usually little difficulty in establishing the problem areas. The challenge often arises in making these specific, e.g., moving from 'a problem with drugs' to 'I am at risk of losing my job because my time keeping is poor due to my taking ecstasy and heroin at the weekends.' Clients can then better identify the most important issues and look with the counsellor at alternative ways of dealing with them. In the initial stages the counsellor may have to provide information in order for clients to recognise problems (particularly in relation to their drug use) of which they were unaware.

Decision making

This fairly simple-sounding procedure can be a major step for clients, being the point at which determination has to give way to action and therefore potentially threatening. Often the reluctance shown at this stage is due to ambivalence about the unknown benefits of future lifestyle choices set against the known benefits of past ones. At this point, motivational interviewing techniques can be effective in encouraging clients to make a difficult transition, the emphasis being on the gains of the new lifestyle weighed against the losses of the old.

These steps obviously need to be undertaken with care, given the potential for the client to manipulate. It is imperative, therefore, for counsellors to have established a trusting and sound working relationship with their client.

Maintaining the change

Some clients get 'stuck' in the middle of a counselling relationship and, after making some initial changes, seem content or concerned and so find it difficult to move on. Such reluctance to accept further change may be for very similar reasons in both contented and concerned clients. They may find it more comfortable to hold on to the relationship with their counsellor (in which they feel valued and respected) as it stands and/or they may be anxious about making further changes in their life. This is especially so when it involves having to work out and make their own decisions about the substance that has been so central to helping them cope with, or enjoy, life. These are potentially threatening situations and it is perhaps not surprising that many clients relapse, fail to make progress and feel unsettled during the middle phases of counselling. It is worth commenting about clients on methadone maintenance programmes for whom the 'middle' period of counselling may last for several years. Often clients in this position feel despondent even though it may appear that they are at least getting treatment. It seems that even those clients who opt for maintenance rather than reducing doses of methadone will, sooner or later, become tired of this middling lifestyle and choose to come off or reduce their level of medication, although it may take up to 7–10 years to reach this stage.

Relapse management

This technique is based mainly on the work of Marlatt and Gordon, who stressed that discussing relapse as a preventative measure could be effective (Marlatt and Gordon, 1985). The task is to work with clients to create confidence and prepare psychological and behavioural strategies to deal with risky situations. The model suggests that clients benefit from recognising that a lapse into one episode of taking drugs after deciding not to does not inevitably lead to further drug taking. The option not to take more drugs, in effect, is still available and it is clearly important for the counsellor to help the client become aware of this possibility, allowing plans to be prepared for dealing with such an eventuality. Traditionally, relapse was not discussed in case it triggered the event, but it is now becoming recognised that including relapse management as part of the preparation for action can actually reduce the likelihood of a relapse occurring and reduce its intensity, at least in the short-term.

Within this process, the counsellor's role is to identify with the client occasions when they are most at risk and clarify effective coping strategies for these. Brief therapy techniques may be useful in this regard.

Ending the relationship

In a logical, linear process there would be a clear end point to counselling. Many factors, however, conspire to prevent this. The cyclical nature of the change process may, for many clients, obscure the fact that they have accomplished a great deal, perhaps all that counselling in itself has to offer. Some contractual arrangements place specific requirements on counsellors regarding when to terminate therapy, which they may consider to be premature and leaving important issues unaddressed. (Clients may of course not always share this viewpoint.) At the end of the counselling relationship, the counsellor has the task of tying up any loose ends, working with the client to establish how much has been accomplished and leave the option open for further contact in the future, if required.

For some clients there is an immediate or increasing realisation that counselling is not the appropriate intervention so they end the contact (often without explanation).

Another influence on the effective closing of the process is the development of dependence in the relationship between the client and counsellor which may affect either party, with the possibility of contact lingering on inappropriately. These two issues for counsellors should be worked through in supervision.

Counsellor competence

The issue of counsellor competence is creating great debate currently. There is a clearly emerging trend towards professionalism within the field, which is being driven by organisations, academic institutions and the government (Baron, 1996). While this is welcomed by many, there are concerns expressed (particularly from the independent sector) that this professionalisation will create barriers between client and counsellor, possibly reducing the effectiveness and quality of therapeutic relationships. Evidence is lacking as to whether such concerns are well-founded but, as the drive towards qualifications appears inexorable, may be available over the next few years.

The drive for professionalism is also apparent within counselling circles, probably because of the perception that more opportunity for self-regulation will follow. External pressure is growing for more easily measurable standards of practice and a clearer understanding of the purpose and process of counselling. There are, however, natural concerns as to the practicability of establishing standards in this way. It has, for instance, been argued that counselling is a complex process which defies reduction to a set of simple task descriptions, with outcome depending to a large degree on intangible qualities of the counselling relationship. In the opinion of Rogers (1964) the essential nature of counselling prevents its description in terms of a set of technical functions. Inherent difficulties such as assessment by observation are only now being addressed.

There are currently various options for those seeking training. These range from a number of short courses (from a day to several weeks) with no consistent guarantees of quality, through to the vocational courses provided by national charities. Of these the most relevant would be the training programmes offered by Alcohol Concern – the Volunteer Alcohol Counselling Training Scheme (VACTS) or the Scottish Council On Alcohol. Both of these train volunteers to work specifically within alcohol counselling agencies. There appear to be no direct equivalents within the drug field. More academically-based training is provided by a number of universities, colleges and foundations providing certificate (120 hours) and diplomas (450 hours) in counselling. The newest qualifications in the field are those being produced by the AGC and PLB, who will be releasing a Level 3 Scottish or National Vocational Qualification (S/NVQ) in counselling in late 1997, followed by a specialist Level 4 S/NVQ in Addictions in 1998. The Polkinghorne Report recognises these as useful additions. S/NVQs differ in that they are competence-based measures and not achieved through attending training courses.

Clearly few drug counselling services currently achieve an acceptable standard in respect of training and level of staff qualifications. The Compass Survey indicated that only three out of 18 agencies surveyed were able to reach BAC criteria and that 25 per cent of staff stated that they needed counselling training.

Supervision

Throughout the counselling process counsellors should ensure they have adequate supervision, affording the opportunity to review skills and the extent to which they are correctly identifying and responding to the behaviour and feelings of their clients. Supervisors will also discuss whether they are adopting appropriate strategies with clients; also whether they may be holding on to or discharging clients inappropriately (perhaps because of unrecognised personal prejudices). Problems such as over-involvement in the client's situation and any issues of transference or counter-transference can also be identified and remedied.

Supervision should be a requirement for counsellors as part of their personal development. It is not intended as a means of control but as an opportunity for learning, growth and reflection. Supervisors should, however, challenge the practice of counsellors and work to a code of ethics (usually the BAC Code) which carries the responsibility to raise with counsellors any concerns about over-involvement with clients, sexual harassment or neglect.

Supervision may be carried out independently of management functions but, in some instances, is linked into performance monitoring which has the potential to create considerable anxieties for the counsellor.

A useful framework for supervision identifies six modes of supervision:

1 Reflection on content of the counselling session.
2 Strategies and interventions used by the counsellor.
3 Counselling process and relationship.
4 Counselling counter-transference.
5 'Here and now' process as a mirror of the 'there and then' process.
6 Supervisor's counter-transference.

Summary and conclusion

The degree of reliance placed on counselling within many agencies throughout the country suggests that drug counselling has a secure future as an integral part of the range of treatments for problem drug users.

Within the field, however, there are unresolved areas of concern over the delivery of care. To ensure greatest effectiveness, services need to be clearer about all aspects of their activities. A framework of definitions is currently being prepared for use in the field of counselling which should prove helpful in establishing a sounder knowledge base for agencies. Clear recruitment and in-service training programmes should also be instituted to ensure that staff are professionally trained, qualified and competent both in counselling and knowledge of drugs.

It appears that an eclectic model is being most widely adopted, which draws on the experience and theories from a wide range of schools and models of counselling. Some of these counselling models encompass such divergent viewpoints that it is impossible for any consensus to emerge. Most drugs agencies now use the 'model of change' as a framework for understanding and working with clients in relation to their drug use. Evidence for the effectiveness of counselling as an intervention is far from complete and there remains a pressing need for agreement over better outcome measures.

References and bibliography

Advice, Guidance, Counselling and Psychotherapy Lead Body (1996), *Occupational Standards in Advice, Guidance and Counselling*, Ments: AGC and PLB.

Armstrong, P. (1996), 'Counselling and Mind-altering Medications', *Counselling*, 7, (3), November.

Baron, J. (1996), 'The Emergence of Counselling as a Profession', in R. Bayne, I. Horton and J. Bimrose (eds), *New Directions in Counselling*, London: Routledge.

Berne, E. (1968), *Games People Play*, London: Penguin Books.

British Association of Counselling (1988), *Code of Ethics and Practice for the Supervision of Counsellors*, Rugby: BAC.

British Association of Counselling (1993), *Code of Ethics and Practice for Counsellors*, Rugby: BAC.

British Association of Counselling (1995), *Code of Ethics and Practice for Trainers in Counselling and Counselling Skills*, Rugby: BAC.

Carroll, M. (1996), *Workplace Counselling*, London: Sage Publications.

Compass Partnership (1995), 'Review of Community Based Drug Agencies', in Polkinghorne *Report of an Independent Review of Drug Treatment Services in England. The Task Force to Review Services for Drug Misusers*, London: Department of Health.

Confederation of Scottish Counselling Agencies (1992), *Counselling Training Pack*, Stirling: COSCA.

Cooper, C.S. and Bartlett, S.R. (1996), Drug Courts: An Overview of Operational Characteristics and Implementation Issues. Volume II, BJA Drug Court Resource Centre, Washington D.C.: The American University.

Davidson, R., Rollnick, S. and MacEwan, I. (eds) (1991), on behalf of the New Directions in the Study of Alcohol Group *Counselling Problem Drinkers*, London: Routledge.

de Shazer, S. (1985), *Keys to Solution in Brief Therapy*, Norton.

Dryden, W. (1991), *Seminal papers Vol. 1*, London: Whurr Publishers.

East, P. (1995), *Counselling in Medical Settings*, Buckingham: Open University Press.

Egan, G. (1994), *The Skilled Helper: a Problem Management Approach to Helping*, California: Brooks Cole Publishing Company.

Farkas, A.J. et al. (1996), 'Addiction versus Stages of Change Model in Predicting Smoking Cessation', *Addiction*, **91**, 9, September, 1271–80.

Feltham, C. (1995), *What is Counselling: the Promise and Problem of the Talking Therapies*, London: Sage Publications.

Fransella, F. and Dalton, P. (1990), *Personal Construct Counselling in Action*, London: Sage Publications.

Hammersley, D. (1995), *Counselling People on Prescribed Drugs*, London: Sage Publications.

Heather, N., Wodak, A., Nadelmann, E. and O'Hare, P. (eds) (1993), *Psychoactive Drugs and Harm Reduction: from Faith to Science*, London: Whurr Publishers.

Heron, J. (1990), *Helping the Client – a Creative Practical Guide*, London: Sage Publications.

Lanarkshire Health Board (1996), 'Preliminary Report No. 5: Drugs', from *Lanarkshire Health and Lifestyle Survey*, Lanarkshire.

McLeod, J. (1996), 'Counsellor competence' in R. Bayne, I. Horton and J. Bimrose (eds), *New Directions in Counselling*, London: Routledge.

Marlatt, A. and Gordon, J. (eds) (1985), *Relapse Prevention*, Guilford: New York.

Mearns, D. and Thorne, B. (1988), *Person-centred Counselling in Action*, London: Sage Publications.

Miller, R. and Rollnick, S. (1991), *Motivational Interviewing*, London: Guilford Press.

Morea, P. (1990), *Personality: an Introduction to the Theories of Psychology*, London: Penguin Books.

Nelson-Jones, R. (1997), *Practical Counselling and Helping Skills*, (4th ed.), London: Cassell.

Norcross, J.C. and Tomcho, T.J., 'Choosing an Eclectic not Syncretic Psychotherapist' in W. Dryden (ed.) (1993), *Questions and Answers on Counselling in Action*, London: Sage Publications.

Palmer, S. and Dryden, W. (1995), *Counselling for Stress Problems*. London: Sage Publications.

Polkinghorne , J. (1996), *The Task Force to Review Services for Drug Misusers: Report of an Independent Review of Drug Treatment Services in England*, London: Department of Health.

Prochaska, J. and DiClemente, C. (1983), 'Stages and Processes of Self-change of Smoking, and Towards a More Integrative Model of Change', *Journal of Clinical and Consulting Psychology*, **51**, 390–5.

Project MATCH Research Group (1997), 'Matching Alcoholism Treatments to Client Heterogeneity: Project MATCH Posttreatment Drinking Outcomes', *Journal of Studies on Alcohol*, **58**, 7–29, January.

Rogers, C. (1964), *On Becoming a Person*, New York: Constable.

Rorstad, P. and Checinski, K. (1996), *Dual Diagnosis: Facing the Challenge*, Herts: Wynne Howard Publishing.

Russell, J., Dexter, G. and Bond, T. (1992), *A Report on the Differentiation between Advice, Guidance, Befriending, Counselling Skills and Counselling*, London: Department of Employment.

Saunders, C. (1996), 'Solution-focused Therapy in Practice: a Personal Experience', *Counselling* **7**, (4).

Shohet, R. and Wilmot, J. in W. Dryden and B. Thorne (eds) (1991), *Training and Supervision for Counselling in Action*, London: Sage Publications.

Trower, P., Casey, A. and Dryden, W. (1988), *Cognitive Behavioural Counselling in Action*, London: Sage Publications.

Tyndall, N. (1993), *Counselling in the voluntary sector*, Buckingham: Open University Press.

Velleman, R. (1992), *Counselling for Alcohol Problems*, London: Sage Publications.

6 Medical interventions
Brian A. Kidd and Roger A.D. Sykes

Introduction

Treatments for problem drug users which are delivered by medical staff usually involve prescribing. No other professional group can offer this key function, which has become a cornerstone of UK treatment policy in recent years (see Chapter 2 – UK policy). Medical treatments, however, are only effective as part of a combined approach which may involve various psychological and social interventions, including those falling under the broad title of 'counselling'. These areas are covered elsewhere in this book.

Medical treatments have progressed in parallel with the development of new drug regimes. There has also been a realisation that individuals with drug addiction problems may respond poorly to interventions based solely on counselling and/or advice, the nature of which may vary from area to area (McLellan et al., 1994). Research-based evidence supporting specific treatment regimes is lacking. However, a number of treatment stratagems, based on a combination of drug prescribing and 'counselling' has become popular, particularly in the treatment of opiate misuse. Evidence suggests that such approaches show improved outcomes when compared to individual therapies (Ball and Ross, 1991; Joe et al., 1991; Mattick, 1994). In the UK, much of the treatment offered to drug users is now delivered in the community, in preference to in-patient or residential units. This chapter will focus on community-based approaches for the treatment of opiate misusers.

Medical treatments can be divided into two main categories: replacement prescribing and detoxification techniques. A third area of interest involves the prescribing of medicines aimed at interfering with processes central to addiction such as habituation and relapse. This chapter will explore the historical perspective before examining these three areas in more detail.

History

Pharmacological interventions in the treatment of drug use problems have been developed and refined only relatively recently. From the early 1960s onwards a succession of position documents by UK authorities sought to consolidate the growing body of published evidence in favour of effective pharmacological treatments for drug misusers. In 1984 the Government's main standing committee, the Advisory Council on the Misuse of Drugs (ACMD), through published guidelines sent to all doctors, urged the profession to accept responsibility for treatment of all addicts' medical needs, rather than delegate exclusively to the few specialist centres which existed at the time (ACMD, 1984). The advent of spreading HIV infection amongst injecting drug addicts added further impetus to the Committee's advice, and their subsequent reports in the late 1980s stressed the need to tackle drug misuse problems as part of the effort to control HIV spread (ACMD, 1988; ACMD, 1989). More specific advice on replacement prescribing and detoxification appeared in the Department of Health document (DoH, 1991). These publications, which were widely disseminated and generally well received, can be seen in retrospect as having outlined a progressive change in emphasis towards more involvement of generalists, both in hospital and community settings, in the treatment of drug misusers. The Government's position, reflecting specialist advice, is brought up to date in the more recent recommendations of the ' Task Force' groups in both Scotland and England, derived from comprehensive reviews of existing drug treatment services. A more comprehensive review of UK policy development appears in Chapter 2.

Replacement prescribing

The supplying of replacement opiates for the treatment of opiate addiction has been practiced medically in the UK for many years. In fact it was concern over the prescribing of such drugs which led in 1926 to the formation of a committee under the chairmanship of Sir Humphrey Rolleston, President of the Royal College of Physicians. The report of the Rolleston committee saw replacement prescribing as a 'legitimate medical treatment' if opiate addicts were being gradually withdrawn in order to 'cure' their addiction or were unable to function in society without a 'certain, non-progressive quantity' of the drug of addiction. Though it had no statutory power, the Rolleston report formed the basis of good practice for the treatment of drug addicts. This approach became known as 'the British System' and replacement prescribing of opiates – mainly pethidine and morphine as well as heroin – formed the basis of treatment until the 1960s (Royal College of Psychiatrists, 1987).

In the 1960s the face of drug addiction in the UK changed, with larger numbers of young people using drugs recreationally for effect. Replacement prescribing remained a core element in the treatment approach. It was at this time that initial reports from America advocated the use of another oral opiate for the treatment of heroin addiction – methadone.

Methadone

Initial publications on the use of this drug originated from research findings in the USA. Dole and Nyswander (1965) and others enthusiastically advocated the prescription of safer opiate replacement medicines as the main plank of their treatment programmes for heroin addicts, numbers of whom had begun to increase dramatically around that time. Methadone had the advantage of being administered orally. It could be taken only once daily as it prevented symptoms of opiate withdrawal for some 24–36 hours. Dole and Nyswander felt that its use reduced craving for heroin, allowing patients to improve their social functioning and more successfully use any therapeutic services which were available to them (1967).

When a similar pattern of problems to those in the USA became apparent in the UK, a number of treatment centres were set up utilising regimes based on the American model. Refinement of these treatment approaches has taken place over the intervening thirty years or so and many more services have been deployed throughout the country, although with marked inter-regional variation in their availability and in the types of treatments offered.

Harm minimisation

The concept of 'harm minimisation' has formed a central tenet of replacement programmes, especially since the importance of intravenous drug users ('IVDUs') in the spread of HIV was recognised (Cooper, 1989). There is an established hierarchy of treatment goals with the guiding principle being the reduction of damage from drug misuse. The aims can be summarised as follows:

- Stop or reduce use of contaminated injecting equipment
- Stop or reduce sharing of injecting equipment
- Stop or reduce drug misuse.

Various treatment strategies are outlined in the Department of Health Guidelines, including prescription of substitute oral methadone. Depending on the outcome of assessment procedures a treatment programme can be devised which aims at reducing the potential harm to the individual drug misuser and possibly those in contact with them.

Maintenance or reduction? – the evidence

Replacement prescribing programmes have therefore arisen as a pragmatic response to the clinical needs of drug-dependent individuals. Evidence for effectiveness has accumulated mainly from uncontrolled studies, but there have been a few attempts at randomised, double-blind controlled studies which tend to be fraught with methodological difficulties (Task Force Review, 1996). In short, the available research evidence in favour of clinical effectiveness of oral methadone maintenance prescribing for opiate addicts is convincing. Being on methadone maintenance has been shown to be associated with lower rates of HIV infection in opiate injectors (Des Jarlais, 1992; Blix and Gronbladh, 1988), reduced injecting drug use and reduced sharing of injecting equipment (Ball and Ross, 1991). Methadone maintenance has also been shown to reduce the death rate of heroin addicts by ¾ by virtue of a reduction in heroin overdose (Caplehorn et al., 1996). Research evidence in support of short-term use of methadone is much less convincing (Vanichseni et al., 1991; Yancovitz et al., 1991), although methadone reduction regimes (using gradually reducing doses over a period of a few months rather than weeks) have been shown to be effective in certain circumstances (Gossop et al., 1995). American reduction programmes (often without associated counselling and support and undertaken very rapidly) have been shown to have little value when compared to maintenance programmes (Simpson and Sells, 1982; Hubbard et al., 1984).

A number of factors have been identified as being of critical importance to the success of methadone prescribing (Ward et al., 1992). These include the following:

- Proper assessment procedures to ensure in particular that the individual is opiate-dependent; regular monitoring and supervisory arrangements including checks for illicit opiate intake (Ward et al., 1992)
- Drug dispensing to the individual which minimises opportunities for abuse of their prescription – almost invariably involving daily dis-

pensing, at least in the early stages, and supervised consumption (Task Force Review 1996)

- Adequate duration of treatment – results of previous studies have suggested that more than two to three years may be necessary before significant behaviour change is observed (Simpson, 1981). However, recent prospective work in the UK has shown considerable improvements in the early months after entering treatment programmes (Gossop et al., 1997)
- Utilising adequate dosage of methadone with a flexible approach to dosage levels (Ball and Ross 1991).

The use of methadone, as opposed to alternative substitute opiates or heroin (diamorphine) itself, is advised because it is longer-acting and less likely to be abused. The favoured preparation (Department of Health Guidelines, 1991) is a viscous mixture containing 1mg per 1ml. This form has the advantage of being almost impossible to inject but can easily be swallowed in adequate dosage. Methadone tablets have potential for crushing and injecting, making their use undesirable for the treatment of drug misuse. However, up to ten per cent of methadone prescriptions have been shown to be in tablet form (Task Force Review, 1996). Some centres continue to advocate the use of other opiates such as heroin, morphine, buprenorphine or dihydrocodeine as oral or intravenous substitutes for illicit heroin. Similarly, injectable methadone may be a useful alternative to the oral preparation in certain circumstances – such as those drug misusers who cannot stop injecting. The Task Force Review could not find evidence to support its use and suggested that only very experienced clinicians should consider prescribing it. However, in excess of ten per cent of methadone prescriptions in the UK are in injectable form (Task Force Review, 1996). None of these alternatives has to date been shown to have a clear benefit over oral methadone, and all carry distinct disadvantages. The prescribing of heroin to addicts requires a special licence.

Other groups of drugs and replacement prescribing

Substitute prescribing of drug classes other than opiates is much less well researched. In harm reduction terms, there ought to be potential health advantages in replacing illicit drugs with pharmaceutically pure alternatives and IV drugs with oral forms. The risk/benefit analysis with other drugs, however, is much more problematic because in most cases they are either less prone to cause physical dependence (e.g., benzodiazepines), are difficult to monitor in urine samples or both. Nevertheless some substitute prescribing of benzodiazepines (such as diazepam) is indicated where dependence tends to maintain risk-taking behaviours. Though the Task Force Review found that replacement prescribing of benzodiazepines was widespread, it acknowledged the lack of systematic research to support this approach. Similarly some practitioners will prescribe amphetamines on the basis that advantages to the patient outweigh the risks inherent in their continuing misuse of impure 'street' drugs (Fleming and Roberts, 1994). These more controversial uses of replacement prescribing tend to be restricted to specialist centres and at the moment cannot be seen as mainstream treatment.

One of the most important benefits of replacement prescribing is that the patient remains in contact with services, providing the opportunity for continuing counselling, education and advice which are crucial to bringing about long-term advantages such as adaptive changes in lifestyle and, ultimately, reduction in drug misuse or even abstinence. No other therapeutic interventions have so far been shown to confer benefits of comparable magnitude for this patient group.

Disadvantages of replacement prescribing

It is important to stress that there are significant risks attached to any form of replacement prescribing which must be balanced in every case against potential benefits. Although risks can be greatly reduced by the adoption of appropriate procedures as outlined above, it remains the case that there are considerable dangers inherent in providing drugs to addicts. Two main areas are affected:

1   The patient in receipt of the drug – for example, there are dangers in combining prescribed drugs with other 'street' drugs, about which the patient must be warned.
2   The society in which the drug user lives – for example, the risk to society arising from prescribed drugs 'leaking' into the community via poor supervision, inadequate monitoring or overprescribing.

Methadone is particularly important with respect to combination effects because of its relatively long duration of action (24–36 hours). When combined either with other opiates, sedatives or alcohol, potentially fatal respiratory depression may occur. There have been reports of an increase in drug-related deaths involving methadone as replacement prescribing has become more popular in many countries (Greenwood et al., 1997; Bentley and Busuttil, 1996; Williamson et al., 1997; Steentoft et al., 1996). Although such deaths are to some extent inevitable, the rise in methadone-related deaths has already attracted considerable adverse publicity in the media.

The issue is further complicated by the fact that what actually constitutes a 'methadone-related death' is disputed and currently signifies simply the presence of significant blood methadone concentrations at post-mortem (Merrill et al., 1996). Somewhat paradoxically, lower dose methadone may be dangerous because of the temptation to add opiates in search of euphoriant effects. With high-dose methadone maintainance, it becomes theoretically impossible to bring about euphoriant effects ('buzz' or 'hit') since all the available opiate receptors are occupied by the methadone – so-called 'narcotic blockade'. American authors advocate high-dose regimes for this reason (Dole et al., 1966).

Service delivery of replacement prescribing in the UK has so far tended to be patchy and inconsistent. A number of reasons can be identified, such as inadequate resources, lack of appropriately trained staff and a general reluctance of GPs to become involved in shared care of drug misusers. Another factor has been the rather piecemeal development of specialist drug services and a lack of coordination between agencies providing care, many of which have been within the voluntary (or 'independent') sector and may have lacked access to medical expertise. Many of these services have been reluctant to embrace so-called 'medical model' approaches, tending to rely on psychotherapeutically-based methods such as counselling or cognitive-behaviour therapy. There is now a growing recognition that all these methods are often more effective when underpinned by replacement prescribing which assists addicts in maintaining a more settled and stable lifestyle.

Multi-disciplinary working and closer collaboration between drug treatment agencies is becoming more common but much remains to be done to involve important groups such as GPs. Specific financial incentives for GPs and pharmacists are being introduced in some areas, to good effect. Much depends on health and social work authorities building in these elements when commissioning and purchasing services. It would be fair to say that, as things stand, progress has been made but a great deal remains to be done, particularly in the provision of adequate resources. The risks inherent in prescribing programmes can be substantially reduced if resources are in place to provide key-workers, proper urine screening and supervised self-administration of drugs.

Detoxification

Detoxification can be seen as the process of withdrawing drugs from a dependent individual with the minimum of discomfort (Kleber, 1981). Many methods are available, usually involving prescription of gradually reducing doses of an appropriate (opiate) drug in order to avoid or mitigate unpleasant withdrawal symptoms. Alternatives to the actual drug of abuse can be used because of the neuropharmacological phenomenon known as cross-tolerance, whereby drugs with similar actions can substitute the effects of one another on the nervous system. In this way methadone has commonly been used to detoxify heroin-tolerant individuals (Senay et al., 1981). Methadone also has the advantage of lesser withdrawal effects than heroin, due to its longer duration of action (Olsen et al., 1977). However, if untreated, methadone withdrawal symptoms peak later than heroin (4–6 days for methadone, 36–72 hours for heroin) and subside as much as seven days later (Kleber and Riordan, 1982). Users often describe detoxification from methadone as much more unpleasant than from heroin.

Individuals are said to be tolerant to the effects of a drug when increasing doses are required to produce the same effect. As tolerance develops the likelihood increases that withdrawal symptoms (sometimes referred to as an abstinence syndrome) will appear on stopping the drug. Such symptoms tend to be more severe if levels of drug in the body fall rapidly; hence the benefits of detoxification techniques which aim to control the rate at which the nervous system has to adjust to removal of the drug. Tolerance develops to most psycho-active drugs to some extent, but is more problematic with sedative classes, e.g., alcohol, benzodiazepines (such as diazepam or temazepam) and barbiturates. It occurs to the greatest extent, however, with opiates which on withdrawal cause excessive excitability, or 'overdrive' in key centres of the brain. The resulting symptoms of anxiety, restlessness, aching limbs, running nose and diarrhoea are notoriously unpleasant and are accompanied by intense psychological craving for opiates. During detoxification insomnia is often severe, and can be persistent and difficult to treat satisfactorily. The final goal is to let the patient reach a drug-free state.

Symptoms can be reduced or prevented by three main methods:

1   Gradual reduction of drug dose.
2   Introduction of other sedatives which help because of cross-tolerance.
3   Giving drugs which specifically block some of the more distressing physiological effects of withdrawal, for example, clonidine and lofexidine.

Other treatments such as opiate detoxification under anaesthesia, using opiate antagonists, are unproven to date and cannot be considered a mainstream clinical treatment (Strang et al., 1997).

Management of detoxification starts with assessment. Drug users will often approach services stating that their desire is for a 'detox.' – only for their actual drug-seeking to become apparent later. There is often a degree of ambivalence and the request may be driven by a sudden desire to 'get clean'. Such a request is unlikely to succeed if the patient's motivation and social situation (including supporting responsible adults) are not fully explored. Many users are not aware that alternatives may be available, and considerable time and effort can be wasted if the wrong treatment option is chosen. Detoxification should be seen as one treatment option which a full and comprehensive assessment will support or exclude.

Deciding whether to conduct the procedure in an in-patient, day attendance or community setting is of great importance. Environmental factors can be of crucial importance, especially in more vulnerable individuals who may require emotional support as much as medication. Availability of in-patient facilities is often extremely limited and the only option may be an open psychiatric ward, which will usually provide less than ideal surroundings and the potential for unhelpful interactions with other patients and/or staff. Special attention to training of general ward staff can help to minimise these problems. The criteria for deciding on outpatient detoxification as an option will include the willingness and motivation of the patient as well as whether or not there are adequate supports available in the form of family and appropriate accommodation. Distance from and quality of medical back-up are also important factors. The decision will inevitably be influenced by a history of any previous failed attempts at outpatient detoxification, which worsens the outlook of further such efforts. An estimate of the level of recent and current drug intake is vital since high intake is likely to lead to more troublesome withdrawal symptoms.

Methadone reduction

Methadone detoxification regimes remain a common way of attempting to achieve abstinence in opiate users who are already stabilised on replacement methadone prescriptions. Programmes have shown success rates of as much as 63 per cent (Paneptino et al., 1977). Although many writers have described different reduction regimes, they all have generally raised the same issues which influence outcome (Mintz et al., 1975; Senay et al., 1977; Paneptino et al., 1977):

- *Rate of reduction and its relation to methadone dosage* It is generally recommended that reduction should be slow and gradual, with the rate of methadone reduction slowed at some point (Kleber, 1977, Cushman, 1981). It is commonly believed that the rate should slow at around 20mg of methadone (Lowinson et al., 1976)
- *Blind or open treatment* There is no evidence to support either blind or open dose reduction schedules

- *The place of counselling* Though it is generally accepted that some form of counselling or psychotherapy is likely to assist the process of withdrawal (Milby, 1988), there is no evidence to support the case for any specific type of counselling – e.g. group or individual (Kleber, 1977).

Clonidine and lofexidine

The use of α-adrenergic agonists as opiate withdrawal agents has promised much in recent years. The antihypertensive agent clonidine suppresses many physical signs of opiate withdrawal with little effect on more subjective complaints and overall distress (Jasinski et al., 1985). This is achieved through a reduction in the adrenergic outflow at the locus coeruleus normally experienced on cessation of opiates (Gold, 1993). Clonidine has various unpleasant side effects including blurred vision, sedation and hypotension making it unlikely to be abused (Rudd and Blaschke, 1985). The severe hypotensive effect, however, precludes its use in outpatient detoxification (Bearn et al., 1996). Lofexidine is known to have far fewer worrying side effects and in particular causes less hypotension making its potential use in out-patients a safer option (Washton et al., 1983; Bearn et al., 1996).

If detoxification using lofexidine is being considered, it should be preceded by giving information regarding the symptoms expected during detoxification, their likely duration, what treatments are to be given (including any night sedation) and possible side effects of treatment. A full physical examination should be undertaken with a focus on the cardiovascular system.

Some services introduce the lofexidine alongside the opiate, which is then stopped once the patient is on an adequate dose of lofexidine to cover withdrawal symptoms. A recent paper (hampered by small numbers) suggested this can be successful (Eveleigh, 1995). However, it is more standard practice to stop the opiate, introducing the lofexidine immediately afterwards (Bearn et al., 1996). A test dose of the drug should be given under observation, with any severe hypotensive effects excluding the patient from community detoxification. In the absence of problems the detoxification can be commenced with the dosage of lofexidine being titrated to withdrawal symptoms experienced. In this way maximum effectiveness of symptom relief can be achieved, increasing the likelihood of a successful outcome. The current data sheet gives a standard treatment regime which begins with a dosage of 0.4mg on day one, increasing by 0.4mg per day to a maximum of 2.4mg. Treatment is continued for some seven to ten days. Once detoxification is completed the drug can be withdrawn over two to four days.

Polydrug use

The clinical picture may be further complicated in the case of 'polydrug' use. If, for instance, there is significant coexisting dependence on benzodiazepines, as is often the case in heroin addicts, these drugs will add to the severity and duration of withdrawal problems and will necessitate the prescription of substitute sedative medication.

Unfortunately the research evidence for the superiority of any particular management option for detoxification is scanty and generally of poor quality. Comparisons between experimental groups are complicated for many reasons, which include problems in patient selection and controlling for confounding variables, as well as the major difficulties in measuring outcomes when many patients default from follow-up. In general, in-patient detoxification tends to lead more often to patients becoming drug-free in the short-term, and usually this is achieved in a shorter time. It is not so far proven whether specialist rehab/residential units are more successful than acute in-patient units (Task Force Review, 1996).

Other medical treatments

The following section will examine two drugs which, though still not routinely used in UK services for drug users, are used elsewhere and have potential for the future – naltrexone and LAAM.

Drugs which assist in maintaining abstinence: opiate antagonists

The long-acting opiate antagonist, naltrexone, was developed from the short-acting drug naloxone, used mainly in anaesthesia to treat and reverse the actions of opiate drugs. Naltrexone can be taken orally, is relatively free from serious side effects, and remains in the body for long enough to permit dosing every few days. When given to abstinent opiate addicts, it blocks the effects of any opiate drugs taken by any route, so that no euphoria is experienced. This prevents tolerance or further physical dependence developing and thereby breaks the 'vicious cycle' of addiction. Its use in relapse prevention appears to be most successful when combined with close supervision arrangements following complete detoxification (Resnick et al., 1974).

Many studies, mainly in the USA, have looked at the effectiveness of naltrexone programmes with varying results (Bradford et al., 1975; Brahen et al., 1984). Success tends to be greatest in well-structured programmes and in highly motivated individuals of high social class – such as medical professionals or business executives. It may, however, be possible to produce a profile of patients most likely to successfully use naltrexone (Kleber, 1985). The use of naltrexone can be seen as limited in the context of UK drug treatment services as they are currently configured.

Laevo-alpha-acetyl methadol (LAAM)

This drug is a long-acting analogue of methadone which has been studied in Holland and the USA, having been granted a license in the USA in 1993. It can be administered every few days and is likely, because of this, to have uses in maintenance programmes for specific patient groups (Ling and Compton, 1997):

- Patients with transport/work schedule problems, making compliance with daily dispensed methadone consumption difficult to achieve
- Patients with a history of methadone treatment failure
- Patients with a fear of methadone treatment.

LAAM is felt to have a number of advantages for society. Patients do not require to take doses home, thus reducing diversion into the community. Also, the drug is not likely to be abused intravenously (Goldstein, 1994). These advantages may make LAAM a favoured drug in the UK in future years as concern over methadone-related deaths increases.

Conclusions

Medical treatments in drug misuse are currently the subject of intense interest from professionals, purchasers of services and the general public, primarily because of the rapid uptake of replacement prescribing programmes in many areas of the UK. There is a very real danger under these circumstances that a proper perspective is lost and that complex and poorly understood issues become over-simplified amid the scramble for resources and political pressure to be seen to be responding to the burgeoning 'drug problem'. Although there is undoubtedly a dire need for more trained personnel on the 'frontline' tackling the day-to-day problems of drug misusers, it is crucially important that we improve our knowledge of which interventions are most effective and most economical.

This chapter gives some indication of the current limitations of the available medical interventions, as well as the real potential to benefit the health of drug users. Above all, coordination of efforts and sensible policy decisions will help to deploy scarce funds to best advantage. Real incentives should be sought which encourage joint working, most particularly between specialist services, general practitioners and pharmacies. The emphasis must be on the development of services which work well in community settings and are readily accessible at relatively low cost to the majority of drug misusers.

References

Advisory Council on the Misuse of Drugs (1984), *Prevention*, London: HMSO.

Advisory Council on the Misuse of Drugs (1988), *AIDS and Drugs Misuse Part 1*, London: HMSO.

Advisory Council on the Misuse of Drugs (1989), *AIDS and Drugs Misuse Part 2*, London: HMSO.

Ball, J.C., Ross, A. (1991), *The Effectiveness of Methadone Maintenance Treatment: Patients, Programmes, Services and Outcome*, New York: Springer-Verlag.

Bearn, J., Gossop, M., Strang, J. (1996), 'Randomised Double-blind Comparison of Lofexidine and Methadone in the In-patient Treatment of Opiate Withdrawal', *Drug and Alcohol Dependence*, **43**, 87–91.

Bentley, A.J., Busuttil, A. (1996),' Deaths Among Drug Abusers in South-East Scotland (1989–1994)', *Medicine Science and the Law*, **36**, (3), 231–6.

Blix, O., Gronbladh, L. (1988) 'AIDS and IV Heroin Addicts: the Preventive Effect of Methadone Maintenance in Sweden', Paper presented to 4th International Conference on AIDS, Stockholm.

Bradford, H.A., Hurley, F.L., Golondzoeske, O., Dorrier, C. (1975), 'Interim Report on Clinical Intake and Safety Data from 17 NIDA-funded Naltrexone Centers', in D. Julius and P. Renault (eds), *Narcotic Antagonists: Naltrexone*, NIDA Research Monograph 9, pp. 163–171, Washington, DC: US Govt.

Brahen, H.S., Henderson, R.K., Capone, T., Kondal, N. (1984), 'Naltrexone Treatment in a Jail Work Release Programme', *Journal of Clinical Psychiatry*, **45**, (9), 49–52.

Caplehorn, J.R., Dalton, M.S., Haldar, F., Petrenas, A.M., Nisbet, J.G. (1996), 'Methadone Maintenance and Addicts' Risk of Fatal Heroin Overdose', *Substance Use and Misuse*, **31**, (2), 177–96.

Cooper, J.R. (1989), 'Methadone Treatment and Acquired Immunodeficiency Syndrome', *Journal of the American Medical Association*, **262**, 1664–8.

Cushman, P. (1981), 'Detoxification After Methadone Treatment', in J.H. Lowinson and P. Ruiz (eds), *Substance Abuse: Clinical Problems and Perspectives*, USA: Williams and Wilkins.

Department of Health, Scottish Office Home and Health Department, Welsh Office (1991), *Drug Misuse and Dependence: Guidelines on Clinical Management*, London: HMSO.

Des Jarlais, D.C. (1992), 'The First and Second Decades of AIDS Among Injecting Drug Users', *British Journal of Addiction*, **87**, 347–53.

Dole, V.P., Nyswander, M. (1967) 'Heroin Addiction – a Metabolic Disease', *Archives of Internal Medicine* **120**: 19–24

Dole, V.P., Nyswander, M. (1965), 'A Medical Treatment for Diacetylmorphine (Heroin) Addiction', *Journal of the American Medical Association*, **193**, 80–4.

Dole, V.P., Nyswander, M., Kreek, M.J. (1966), 'Narcotic Blockade', *Archives of Internal Medicine*, **118**, 304–309.

Eveleigh, B. (1995), 'The Use of Lofexidine in an Outpatient Methadone Detoxification Programme', *International Journal of Drug Policy*, **6**, (3), 2–3.

Fleming, P. and Roberts, D. (1994), 'Is the Prescription of Amphetamine Justified as a Harm Reduction Measure?', *Journal of the Royal Society of Health*, **114**, (3), 127–131.

Gold, M.S. (1993), 'Opiate Addiction and the Locus Coeruleus: The Clinical Utility of Clonidine, Naltrexone, Methadone and Buprenorphine', *Recent Advances in Addictive Disorders*, **16**, 61–73.

Goldstein, A. (1994), 'Addictive Tranquility: The Opiates', in A. Goldstein (ed.), *Addiction: From Biology to Drug Policy*, New York: Freeman.

Gossop, M., Marsden, J., Edwards, C., Wilson, A., Segar, G., Stewart, D., Lehman, P. (1995), 'The October Report', The National Treatment Outcome Research Study, London: DoH.

Gossop, M., Stewart, D., Lehmann, P., Edwards, C., Wilson, A., Segar, G., Marsden, J. (1997), *NTORS: The National Treatment Outcome Research Study. 2nd Bulletin*, London: Department of Health.

Greenwood, J., Zealley, H., Gorman, D., Fineron, P., Squires, T. (1997), 'Deaths Related to Methadone Have Doubled in Lothian', *British Medical Journal*, **314**, 1763.

Hubbard, R.L., Rachal, J.V., Craddock, S.G., Cavanaugh, E.R. (1984), 'Treatment Outcome Prospective Study (TOPS): Client Characteristics and Behaviours Before, During and After Treatment', in F.M. Timms and J.P. Ludford (eds), *Drug Abuse Treatment Evaluation: Strategies, Progress and Prospects*, NIDA Research Monograph 51, National Institute of Drug Addiction, USA.

Jasinski, D.R., Johnson, R.E., Kocher, T.R. (1985), 'Clonidine in Morphine Withdrawal: Differential Effects on Signs and Symptoms', *Archives of General Psychiatry*, **42**, (11), 1063–66.

Joe, G.W., Simpson, D.D., Hubbard, R.L. (1991), 'Treatment Predictors of Tenure in Methadone Maintenance', *Journal of Substance Abuse*, **3**, 73–84.

Kleber, H.D. (1977), 'Detoxification from Methadone Maintenance: the State of the Art', *International Journal of the Addictions*, **12**, 807–20.

Kleber, H.D. (1981), 'Detoxification From Narcotics', in J.H. Lowinson and P. Ruiz (eds), *Substance Abuse: Clinical Issues and Perspectives*, Baltimore: Williams and Wilkins.

Kleber, H.D. (1985), 'Naltrexone', *Journal of Substance Abuse Treatment*, **2**, 117–22.

Kleber, H.D., Riordan, C.E. (1982), 'The Treatment of Narcotic Withdrawal: a Historical Review', *Journal of Clinical Psychiatry*, **43**, (2), 30–4.

Ling, W., Compton, P. (1997), 'Opiate Maintenance Therapy with LAAM', in S.M. Stine and T.R. Kosten (eds), *New Treatments for Opiate Dependence*, New York: Guilford.

Lowinson, J., Berle, B., Langrod, J. (1976), 'Detoxification of Long-term Methadone Patients: Problems and Prospects', *International Journal of the Addictions*, **11**, 1009–1018.

McLellan, A.T., Alterman, A.I., Woody, G.E., Metzger, D., McKay, J.R., O'Brien, C.P. (1994), *Evaluating the Effectiveness of Substance Misuse Treatment*, a Report Prepared for the Ministerial Task Force, London: Department of Health.

Mattick, R.P. (1994). *Maintenance Approaches to Treating Drug Misusers: A Review of the Empirical Evidence*, a report prepared for the Ministerial Task Force, London: Department of Health.
Merrill, J., Garvey, T., Rosson, C. (1996), 'Methadone Treatment. Methadone Concentrations Taken as Indicating Deaths Due to Overdose Need to be Reviewed', *British Medical Journal*, 313, 1481.
Milby, J.B. (1988), 'Methadone Maintenance to Abstinence: How Many Make It?', *Journal of Nervous and Mental Disease*, 176, 409–22.
Mintz, J., O'Brien, C.P., O'Hare, K., Goldschmidt, J. (1975), 'Double-blind Detoxification of Methadone Maintenance Patients', *International Journal of the Addictions*, 10, 815–24.
Olsen, G.D., Wendel, H.A., Livermore, J.D., Leger, R.M., Lynn, R.K., Gerber, N. (1977), 'Clinical Effects and Pharmacokinetics of Racemic Methadone and its Optical Isomers', *Clinical Pharmacology and Therapeutics*, 21, (2), 147–57.
Paneptino, W, Arnon, D., Silver, F., Orbe, M., Kissin, B. (1977), 'Detoxification From Methadone Maintenance in a Family Orientated Programme', *British Journal of Addiction*, 72, 255–59.
Resnick, J., Volavka. J., Freedman, A., Thomas, M. (1974), 'Studies of EN-1638A (Naltrexone): A New Narcotic Antagonist, *American Journal of Psychiatry*, 131, 646–50.
Royal College of Psychiatrists (1987), 'Opiates', in *Drug Scenes*, London: Gaskell.
Rudd, T, Blaschke, T.F. (1985), 'Antihypertensive Agents and the Drug Therapy of Hypertension', in A.G. Gillman, L.S. Goodman and T.W. Rall (eds), *The Pharmacological Basis of Therapeutics (7th Edition)*, New York: Macmillan.
Scottish Office Home and Health Department (1991), *Drug Misuse and Dependence: Guidelines on Clinical Management*, Department of Health, Scottish Office Home and Health Department, Welsh Office, HMSO.
Senay, E.C., Dorus, W., Goldberg, F., Thornton, W. (1977), ' Short-term Detoxification with Methadone', *Annals of the New York Academy of Sciences*, 362, 203–16.
Senay, E.C., Dorus, W., Goldberg, F., Thornton, W. (1981), 'Withdrawal from Methadone Maintenance Rate of Withdrawal and Expectation', *Archives of General Psychiatry*, 34, 361–7.
Simpson, D.D. (1981). 'Treatment for Drug Abuse: Follow-up Outcomes and Length of Time Spent', *Archives of General Psychiatry*, 38, 875–88.
Simpson, D.D. and Sells, S.B. (1982), 'Effectiveness for Treatment of Drug Abuse: an Overview of the DARP Research Programme', *Advances in Alcohol and Substance Abuse*, 2, (1), 7–29.
Steentoft, A., Teige, B., Holmgren, P., Vuori, E., Kristinsson, J., Kaa, E., Wethe, G., Ceder, G., Pikkarainen, J., Simonsen, K.W. (1996), 'Fatal Poisonings in Young Drug Addicts in the Nordic Countries: a Comparison Between 1984–1985 and 1991', *Forensic Science International*, 78, (1), 29–37.
Strang, J., Bearn, J., Gossop, M. (1997), 'Opiate Detoxification Under Anaesthesia. Enthusiasm Must be Tempered with Caution and Scientific Scrutiny', *British Medical Journal*, 315. 1249–50.
The Task Force to Review Services for Drug Misusers. Report of an Independent Review of Drug Treatment Services in England (1996), London: HMSO.
Vanichseni, S., Wongsuwan, B., Staff of the BMA Narcotics Clinic no. 6, Choopanya, K., Wongpanich, K. (1991), 'A Controlled Trial of Methadone Maintenance in a Population of Intravenous Drug Users in Bangkok: Implications for Prevention of HIV, *International Journal of the Addictions*, 26, 1313–20.

Ward, J., Mattick, R., Hall, W. (1992), *Key Issues in Methadone Maintenance Treatment*, Kensington: New South Wales University Press.

Washton, A.M., Resnick, R.B., Geyer, G. (1983), 'Opiate Withdrawal Using Lofexidine, a Clonidine Analogue with Fewer Side Effects', *Journal of Clinical Psychiatry*, **44**, 335–37.

Williamson, P.A., Foreman, K.J., White, J.M., Anderson, G. (1997), 'Methadone-related Overdose Deaths in South Australia 1984–1994. How Safe is Methadone Prescribing?', *Australian Medical Journal*, **166**, 302–305.

Yancovitz, S.R., Des Jarlais, D.C., Peyser, N.P., Drew, E., Friedmann, P., Trigg, H.L., Robinson, J.W. (1991), 'A Randomised Trial of an Interim Methadone Maintenance Clinic', *American Journal of Public Health*, **81**, 1185–91.

7 Residential rehabilitation services

Steven Dalton

The provision of residential rehabilitative care for drug users has long been a subject for debate. Does residential placement work? If so, which type of residential provision is the most effective? Who is it most suitable for? When in a drug user's career should the residential option be sought?

It is generally accepted that it is preferable to help drug users to overcome their difficulties without separating them from their own communities and family supports. It may be argued that society and environment play an important part in shaping a person's life and behaviour, and removing these influences can create an artificial situation which may not be sustainable in the long term.

Nevertheless, there do seem to be occasions when the drug user requires 'time out' from his community, with the opportunity to focus more intensively on the difficulties they are experiencing. These may be situations in which the drug user is unable to benefit from the services based in their own community. They may already have failed in various treatment regimes and have run out of community-based options. They may have a desire to break away from their environment and the social contacts which may be sustaining involvement in the drug-using culture or increasing the risk of relapse. The majority of those attending drug treatment services are living in deprived areas and involvement in crime, violence and the effects of poor housing and unemployment are commonplace. Drug users are more likely to be suffering from psychiatric illnesses or other mental health problems, reducing their ability to cope with adversity (HMSO, 1995). Even those who are successfully treated using harm reduction strategies and replacement prescribing may be living in intolerable situations and be unable to sustain stability or progress towards abstinence. Detoxification may be unsuccessful without appropriate support and following detoxification and/or abstinence may be difficult to maintain.

In these cases – often representing a group of drug users from the 'hard end' of the spectrum (i.e. with longer, more severe and intractable problems associated with co-morbidity) – residential rehabilitation can be an invaluable resource to assist drug users in dealing with problems which may appear overwhelming when in their home environment. Under these circumstances, it is reasonable to consider referral to a residential rehabilitation facility (Gerstein and Harwood, 1990). As explained by Rosenthal (1994):

> [T]he treatment process addresses not (*only*) drug abuse itself, but the underlying problems that prompt and sustain it. In fact it may be argued that residential settings are best perceived as designed to encourage and support social learning which society itself is not.

This chapter will outline the range of residential services offered, discuss how clients may be 'matched' with an appropriate placement and examine best practice in order to increase the likelihood of success.

Characteristics of programmes – types of approach

It is important to note that the following classifications should be used as a guide rather than a definitive description of the different houses. In practice, establishments may 'borrow' from each of the models described below.

There are many different types of residential rehabilitation programmes. Recent review and guidance documentation classified the following main categories (Task Force Review, 1996; Yates, 1997; Malinowski and Preston, 1993):

- *Therapeutic communities (or 'concept houses')*   These utilise a clear hierarchical structure through which residents can progress. There is a strong emphasis on personal responsibility, and staff help individuals to confront issues, often using group therapy or encounter groups with success, allowing an increase of privileges and progress through the structure
- *'12-step' Minnesota model houses*   This model involves the use of the 12-step programme of the anonymous fellowships. These adopt a disease model of addiction and rely heavily on self-help techniques to overcome addiction and achieve abstinence. Although the length of stay is often shorter than with therapeutic communities, they tend to have strong links with AA/NA for aftercare support

- *General houses* These provide a supportive environment in which individual or group counselling can be offered. They often describe themselves as democratic communities and emphasise resident choice. The programme could be described as client-led
- *Christian houses* Christian Houses tend to use one to one counselling and house meetings rather than confrontational groups to help people change. They vary in the emphasis they place on residents accepting Christianity. The programmes are usually less intensive than concept or Minnesota method houses.

It is important to note that the categories shown all have some houses which vary in their degree of adherence to the specified model.

The 1996 Task Force Review states that there are 1 279 residential rehabilitation places situated in 70 centres throughout the UK, with the majority run by the voluntary sector. They are often set in rural out of the way places, but accept referrals from considerable catchment areas. It is stated that in excess of 50 per cent of these centres can detoxify individuals prior to or on admission. In practice, however, detoxification may be more difficult to access than this figure suggests. Residents in the main must be drug-free to enter the programmes with no psychoactive substances other than tobacco allowed on the premises. Breaking this rule will often result in exclusion.

Residential rehabilitation programmes traditionally required a considerable commitment from the drug user with programmes of 12–18-month duration being commonplace. However, in recent years, programmes have tended to reduce in length. This has been partly in response to funding difficulties experienced in some areas, with local authorities, short of resources, stopping available funding altogether or reducing the period they will be prepared to fund arbitrarily. There is no evidence to support the effectiveness (or lack of it) associated with shorter programmes. However, as in all forms of treatment, those who are successful are likely to have stayed in the programme longer (Gossop et al., 1997). Access to treatment may also be difficult if the facility for detoxification is unavailable prior to admission. It is not unusual for a valuable place to be lost as detoxification cannot be achieved in time by local community or in-patient services.

Characteristics of residents

As residential rehabilitation centres offer a more concentrated and intensive therapeutic experience than can realistically be offered in the community, they tend to deal with individuals who are more heavily dependent on illicit drugs and who have been unable to use mainstream treatments successfully.

In the National Treatment Outcome Research Study, the individuals in four treatment modalities were examined. The modalities chosen were as follows:

- In-patient units
- Residential rehabilitation programmes
- Out-patient/community-based methadone reduction programmes
- Out-patient methadone maintenance programmes.

When compared with those in the other areas of treatment, the residential rehabilitation cohort were similar in terms of age (29 years) and length of heroin-using career (9.2 years). They were, however, more likely to have used crack cocaine and amphetamines and reported the highest alcohol intake. They also showed higher co-morbidity, with more reporting psychological or physical health problems and more having a past history of psychiatric in-patient treatment. They were more likely to be unemployed, to be involved in drug-related crime and to be on probation or parole (Gossop et al., 1995).

Assessment

The major purpose of assessments is to gain knowledge and understanding of people and circumstances so as to provide and guide intervention ... ... they are never true inasmuch as they reflect the perspective of the assessor ...
(Coulshed, 1990)

Nowhere is this more important than in the assessment of drug users. In general, drug users are suspicious of 'authority figures'. A drug-using parent may have preconceptions regarding the likelihood of their children being received into care. Drug users are in the main involved in illegal activity (if only through their use of illicit drugs) and therefore can be less than candid in reporting their personal circumstances. They often have a variety of difficulties which may or may not be related to their drug use, including health, accommodation and employment problems (ISDD, 1992). This can present the worker with an individual who follows a chaotic lifestyle which, due to its complexity, can create problems in assessment (such as knowing where to start!), and can require a more time-consuming and detailed approach than may usually be the case. Given the importance attributed to the assessment process, it is essential to outline the basic factors which underpin best practice in assessment.

- *Motivation* Motivation is a term often used when referring to drug users and their ability to change harmful behaviour. Motivational techniques are often employed when drug users are being counselled regarding their options. Motivation is equally important for the workers involved in the assessment of drug users. Given the difficulties in assessment outlined above, the worker can be faced with what seems to be an insurmountable task. Workers in this area need to be aware of the support networks available to them to assist in the reduction of factors which may dampen their commitment.
- *Joint assessments* A number of agencies will often be involved with each client. Jointly agreed assessment procedures, both with other community teams and with residential workers where possible, should be adopted. This will minimise the interviews, questionnaires and forms which have to be completed. Joint assessments will also speed up the process allowing a more rapid response by the services involved. It will assist the matching process and ensure a greater understanding of the criteria to be fulfilled prior to acceptance by any residential establishment.
- *Values* The emphasis on the worker's value base may be of particular importance with regard to users of drugs and alcohol. Professional workers are not immune to the media influence operating around drug issues. It is therefore likely that the highlighted 'problems' which are a focus for media attention may influence the worker's perception of the problem. As stated earlier, the worker's own attitudes, values and beliefs may have an impact on the assessment process in general. This can be exacerbated by the societal and media 'hype' which ebbs and flows around us daily. It is therefore reasonable to assume that individual workers may have quite diverse beliefs as to what constitutes a drug problem. It follows from this that the worker's own attitudes should be closely examined both prior to and during work with drug users as they may have an impact on the therapeutic relationship.
- *Matching* The importance of accurate matching cannot be overstressed. Choosing an establishment which is inaccessible to supportive family members, when an equally suitable placement is available more locally, may lead to unnecessary stress on the user and their family. Given the high financial cost and the potential damage to the user as a result of inappropriate placement and subsequent breakdown, it is important to ensure as close a matching to the users's

needs as is possible. This requires a sophisticated assessment process on the part of the worker which must include a thorough understanding of the theoretical models and counselling techniques which are incorporated within each type of residential establishment. There are numerous permutations of this which add to the difficulties in matching the resource to the need accurately.

There is evidence from the initial findings of the American Project Match research (Allen, 1997) that the matching of alcohol clients with different treatments may be less important than the skills and abilities of the counsellors. However, the authors advise caution, in that the study 'does not address potential matching effects that possibly could appear if more diverse treatment were contrasted (inpatient vs outpatient treatments, group vs individual therapies, or pharmacological therapies vs psychosocial therapies). Nor do these findings hold for all substance abusers with varying or multiple substances of abuse, or the homeless'.

Given the complexity involved in the assessment process, it is hardly surprising that most generic workers are daunted by the task. It has been suggested that improved processes which employ clear guidelines and use specially designed assessment tools would improve the effectiveness of treatment through appropriate matching. However, a recent UK census of protocols and tools used for community assessments of drug users showed that generic tools were regularly used – leaving it up to the worker to be sure of covering appropriate areas of inquiry (Kidd and Turner, 1997). On a positive note, the skills of assessment which are possessed by the majority of care workers are readily transferable to the drug-user group. The skills employed in assessment or intervention (anti-discrimination, empowerment, acceptance) are equally valid. However, some more specialised skills may be required when dealing with the drug user – focusing on the user's attitudes to the process they are involved in, and involving an awareness of the worker's own attitudes towards the user and their problem.

Drug users may look towards the residential option as the last resort in a history of failed community options. Thoughts such as: 'I need to get out of this place to get my head together' or 'I've tried everything else, if this doesn't work nothing will' are not uncommon. This view may also be held by the worker involved in the assessment and subsequent placement. The danger inherent in this underlying assumption becomes evident should the placement breakdown. Following breakdown, what progress is possible should both the client and worker believe in this last chance scenario? Relapse is regarded by most professionals as part of the problem rather than as a failure. It follows that a client may require several attempts in residential placement (or any other treatment) before a successful outcome is achieved. It is essential to eliminate this attitude as it is an obstacle to future progress, can create an increased pressure on the client to succeed, and may preclude the possibility of relapse and subsequent re-entry to residential services.

Drug and alcohol issues cross over all client groups being represented across the age range and being associated with many coexisting problems. Therefore the boundaries between drug users and those requiring the attention of other interventions can be blurred. The co-morbidity chapter (Chapter 13) within this book provides a useful analysis of this issue.

Choice

Respect for client choice is a principle of good assessment and care management. It is both a means to a sound assessment and an end in itself in the assessment and care management process.

(Kaye and Seed, 1994)

To enable an informed choice for the drug user, the worker must have a full understanding of the models and programmes operating within each residential establishment. This information is fundamental in assisting the drug user's choice in obtaining an accurate matching of need. Without a strict matching of need, the placement's potential for a positive outcome is vastly reduced. The environment and 'feel' of an establishment are also crucial factors influencing a user's willingness to remain in what may be a stressful and uncomfortable situation. It is therefore important to provide the drug user with the opportunity to visit their choice of establishment.

People on a touring holiday will view a hotel room prior to booking an overnight stay. Why, therefore, do we expect drug users to agree to placements sometimes hundreds of miles from their home without any introductory visit? In some cases the worker's impression of the establishment is based only on a brochure or presentation rather than personal experience.

Residential care can be seen in some cases as a positive option rather than a last gasp attempt at rehabilitation. It is essential to outline the practical issues of undergoing a residential programme with the drug user prior to commencement of the placement. These include:

1 *The care plan* A care plan (which should be signed by all parties) should outline the areas which will be addressed during the placement, including the rights and responsibilities of each party. It should incorporate the review process, including frequency of reviews (Department of Health, 1991).

2   *Complaints procedure*   The procedure for complaints should be explained in detail. This will help prevent misunderstanding and should assist the drug user in seeking help to settle any problems. Such simple interventions may help maintain a placement, threatened by frustration or anger at a perceived lack of understanding.

Influences on outcome

An accurate assessment has been undertaken and the user's needs have been matched with an appropriate residential setting. The user has visited the placement and the care plan has been agreed between the residential staff, the drug user and the worker. Which factors now become crucial in determining a successful outcome?

1   *Review*
   Placements often breakdown early. The NTORS residential cohort showed 44 per cent leaving treatment in the first month (Gossop et al., 1995). A study undertaken by the University of Sussex points to a very high percentage of placement breakdowns occurring in the first three months – amounting to as much as 65 per cent (Community Health Studies Unit, 1993). The figures reduce over time, suggesting the likelihood of placement breakdown decreases as the placement continues. Research also suggests that length of time in treatment is directly related to positive outcome (Simpson and Sells, 1982). It has been suggested that those who do best stay for a least one third of the programme length (Gerstein and Harwood, 1990). It is therefore essential to review the placement early in the programme (i.e. within the first two to six weeks). Early review will help identify any problems which were not evident prior to placement and enable an early resolution of difficulties which may threaten the placement. Careful consideration should be given to the timing of subsequent reviews with the safeguard of emergency review available to all parties.

2   *Aftercare*
   The process of aftercare should begin prior to placement in residential rehabilitation. A major factor affecting successful outcome with any drug user is the support of family and friends. As Welteke states, 'The chances of success for in-patient long term therapy stand and fall with the availability of effective and co-operative follow-up care' (Welteke, 1997). This support should be encouraged before, during and after place-

ment to maintain and develop the support structures within the community. It is also crucial for the drug user to be aware of the ongoing support offered by the community agency worker involved and any follow-up support offered by the residential staff .

Outcomes

Despite the number of residential rehabilitation centres in operation nationally, there are very few studies which concentrate on the outcome for drug users on the programmes offered. As previously mentioned, the main thrust of available research points to an increased potential for positive outcome the longer the drug user remains in the programme. The NTORS study showed reduced consumption of drugs and alcohol, improved mental and physical health and reduced criminal activity at six-month follow-up for the residential cohort. These improved outcomes were maintained after leaving the residential programme (Gossop et al., 1997).

It is my contention that accurate matching of need, assessments and choice for drug users remains lacking in general. The present situation could be described as patchy at best. In a joint report commissioned by SCODA and Alcohol Concern it was stated that, following the introduction of the Community Care Act (1990), the following shortcomings were identified (Rayner, 1994):

- The quality of the assessment process varies
- Some residential care leavers are becoming homeless
- There is little consultation with users or families
- New barriers to accessing services have been created
- There is little diversification of services.

In addition to this report, the Department of Health Guidance for Health Authorities and Social Services Departments (1997) states: 'A recent SSI inspection of substance misuse services in five local authorities found that assessments were often determined mainly on the basis of the resources available, rather than being based on well informed consideration of client's needs.' Despite the introduction of Community Care this report suggests that there is little evidence of any substantial improvement in the position of drug users requiring residential rehabilitation.

Conclusion

Residential rehabilitation should seldom, if ever, be used as an alternative to community provision, but should supplement the services currently available in the community. It is not a panacea for drug problems but is a useful and, in some cases, essential treatment option.

Inadequate assessments and lack of matching will lead to inappropriate placements which have a greater chance of breakdown. Residential services are costly, both in financial terms and with regard to the client's self-esteem and mental health. It is, therefore, essential that assessors and providers alike ensure as thorough and detailed assessment and resource matching as possible. It is important to view residential placement as a positive option rather than a 'last gasp' attempt at rehabilitation. This will reduce the stress on the user which will increase the likelihood of a successful residential placement and allow for the possibility of relapse without precluding re-entry into residential services.

References

Allen, J.P. (1997), 'Matching Alcoholism Treatments to Client Heterogeneity: Project Match Post-treatment Drinking Outcomes', *Journal of Studies on Alcohol*.

Community Health Studies Unit, Phoenix House (1993), *Client profile 1992*, Trafford Centre for Medical Research: University of Sussex.

Coulshed, V. (1990), 'Assessment: the necessary skills', in *Social Work Practice: An Introduction*, London: Macmillan.

Department of Health (1991), *Care Management and Assessment: Practitioner's Guide*, London: HMSO.

Department of Health (1997), *Purchasing effective treatment and care for drug misusers*, London: HMSO.

Gerstein, D.R., Harwood, H.J. (1990) (eds), *Treating Drug Problems. Volume 1. A Study of the Evolution, Effectiveness and Financing of Public and Private Drug Treatment Systems*, Washington: National Academy Press.

Gossop, M., Marsden, J., Edwards, C., Wilson, A., Segar, G., Stewart, D., Lehmann, P. (1995), *The October Report. NTORS*, A report prepared for the Task Force Review, London: Department of Health.

Gossop, M., Stewart, D., Lehmann, P., Edwards, C., Wilson, A., Segar, G., Marsden, J. (1997), *NTORS. The National Treatment Outcome Research Study. 2nd Bulletin*, London: Department of Health.

HMSO (1995), *Tackling Drugs Together. A Strategy for England 1995–1998*, London: HMSO.

ISDD (1992), *An Introduction to Drug Services*, factsheet, London: ISDD.

Kaye, G., Seed, P. (1994), *Handbook for Assessment and Management of Care in the Community*.

Kidd, B.A., Turner, I. (1997), 'Assessment', *Journal of Substance Misuse*, (2), 105–108.

Malinowski, A., Preston, A. (1993), *The Rehab Handbook,* Dorset: CADAS.

Rayner, G. (1994), *Community Care and Residential Rehabilitation Services: The First Year*, SCODA/Alcohol Concern Joint Contracts and Community Care Project.

Rosenthal, M.S. (1994), 'Therapeutic Communities', in B. Glass (ed.), *The International Handbook of Addiction Behaviour*, London: Routledge.

Simpson, D.D., Sells, S.B. (1982), 'Effectiveness for Treatment of Drug Abuse: An Overview of the DARP Research Program', *Advances in Alcohol and Substance Abuse*, **2**, (1), 7–29.

The Task Force to Review Services for Drug Misusers. Report of an Independent Review of Drug Treatment Services in England (1996), London: HMSO.

Welteke, J. (1997), 'What Can Assist? Successful Factors of In-patient Therapy in a Therapeutic Community', *European Federation of Therapeutic Communities Newsletter*, **5**, 12.

Yates, R. (1997), 'A Guide to the Development of Services for Alcohol and Drug Misusers', Edinburgh: HMSO.

8 Drug services in rural areas

Charles Lind

It is my belief, Watson, founded upon my experience, that the lowest and vilest alleys of London do not present a more dreadful record of sin than the smiling and beautiful countryside.

Arthur Conan Doyle – 'The Copper Beeches'

Introduction

For the last two hundred years rural areas have been prone to a form of archaism in which the countryside is perceived as a peaceful and solid combination of utility and beauty. It has been seen as a uniform place where the travails and stresses of urban life do not intrude, and where tranquillity and the inexorable yet benign cycles of nature are the dominant forces. This is the caricature of the countryside as theme park which has, to varying degrees at various times, played a significant part in shaping rural policy. This fantasy's main purpose appears to have been to fulfil both the need of the urban population to have the notion of pastoral idyll close to hand when required, and the need of the rural population to appear to maintain a safe and self-sufficient haven from the more questionable practices of city life.

Unfortunately, such a landscape and the community that it is supposed to support has not existed since eighteenth-century Georgian Britain. It has been gradually eroded by a variety of circumstances, including the process of Enclosures in England and Wales, the Clearances in Scotland (in which sheep were felt to fulfil the requirement of utility much more readily than humans), and the Industrial Revolution. The first two of these produced an increasingly powerful but lessening number of landowners whose agendas began to veer towards utilitarianism and economic efficiency rather than

111

the pre-existing state of landscape husbandry. The third produced large migrations of workers into the cities and an increasingly urban concentration of national resource. Together they changed the demographic nature of the countryside irreparably. Previously distinct rural economies, with the subsequent wholesale breakage of the previously close links between places of production and places of consumption, became little more than a second-best urban economy. Inevitably this mirroring has, albeit slowly, produced precisely those problems which were previously thought to be a function only of urban environments and, in particular, those of the inner city.

Unfortunately, the desire of both city dwellers and country dwellers to maintain the shibboleth of rural peace and order has led to the difficulties that the countryside faces being continually underestimated by both groups. Unquestioning adherence to this perception, and the allied perception that rural folk are in some way more able to 'look after their own' if problems do arise, means that both groups have difficulties in even recognising that there are some worms in the apple, let alone providing some form of solution to them.

Nowhere is this more dramatically seen than in the area of drug problems. The argument (which has also posed problems in other forms of priority care service delivery such as mental health and HIV/AIDS) goes that those things that are known to be the antecedents of urban drug problems in the last two decades, such as deprivation, poverty and limited activity options, simply do not exist in rural areas and that, even if they did, living in a rural area is in some way protective against them. The recent level of nationally expressed surprise and horror (despite frequent such observations from rural drug workers over the last decade) at the revelations that there were indeed substantial levels of drug problems in some rural communities is testimony to the depth, and perhaps the national importance of that belief. This is, unfortunately, amplified by the extraordinary logistic difficulties of translating anecdote into realistic needs assessment in diverse and geographically widespread areas. To date there are very few rural areas in the UK which have an adequate or accurate assessment of the numbers of drug users, let alone any clarity of what their needs are. National databases provide little useful information as they reflect only the activity of already existing services which are predominantly urban-based. This puts such areas at some disadvantage when trying to persuade purchasers of the need to develop such services, especially when compared to the much more obviously demonstrable needs of urban services.

A further difficulty is the perception of rural communities as being homogenous. Nothing could be further from the truth. There is a profound difference between truly agrarian communities (with their overtones of residual feudalism), and those communities which began their existence as a part of heavy industry, for instance, mining villages (House of Lords, 1994). The problems that they display and the subsequently proffered solutions can be expected to be quite different. For instance, the latter began with little or no formal social infrastructure and relied instead upon the development of structures of their own devising, which depended heavily upon common work purpose. These structures had great difficulty surviving the decline of whatever heavy industry filled this core role, the subsequent sharp rises in unemployment and the movement away of significant members of the population. They are essentially industrial populations placed in the middle of the country with little left in the way of social, leisure or employment infrastructure. Options, therefore, become much more limited than those available to the same population in the middle of a city, and to constructively fill time is correspondingly difficult. For instance, the prospect of waiting indefinite periods of time for unreliable and infrequent public transport services in order to travel long distances to access a leisure centre, makes it less likely to be an attractive and viable option than accessing the same leisure centre if it were just around the corner.

The former group, on the other hand, cling to ideas of order, conservatism and self-sufficiency which heavily stigmatises any behaviour that is seen to be deviant. This stigma, combined with the high level of individual visibility in such communities, results in a disproportionately high level of difficulty for drug users seeking help, and indeed for their families and relatives in recognising and dealing with such problems

Assumptions

There are a number of commonly held assumptions with regard to the characteristics of rural communities which determine the nature of drug service provision in such areas.

Assumption one

First, it is commonly held that rural communities are more closely knit, and that people offer more mutual support and assistance than their urban counterparts. In fact there is no empirical evidence for this (Blank et al., 1995). Informal social networks can serve to support families during periods of stress, but rural families do not seem to receive either more or more efficacious forms of support than their urban counterparts (Coward and Jackson, 1983). Variables other than rural residence seem to be more powerful at determining how strong a family's or community's support network is. For instance, the psychological sense of community that has become a central concept in understanding the ways in which people derive or fail to derive satisfaction from the area in which they live (Sarason, 1972) appears to have been substantially diluted in rural Britain. This has come about partly because of the outmigration of the younger and better skilled group, leaving behind a population with a higher dependency ratio and a subsequently higher sense of community stress (Coward and Jackson, 1983). In addition, the proportion of those working in urban areas while living in rural communities has increased, which is accompanied by the impaired development of strong community ties (Fox et al., 1994).

There is absolutely no evidence to suggest that a rural community is any more skilled at dealing with problems related to drug use. In fact, it may be that their initial difficulties in accepting the problem make it more rather than less difficult to cope.

Assumption two

The second assumption is that rural people automatically have strong ties to larger population centres. Services are therefore developed around 'urban hubs'. Urban-working rural residents typically view themselves as part of the greater urban community, have more urban ties and are consequently more likely to utilise the hub-based services. Conversely, indigenous rural residents have markedly fewer integrative ties to the hub and therefore use such services less (Hill, 1988).

The service implications of such an assumption, however, are that rural drug users can reasonably be expected to attend 'hub-based' services, be they counselling, needle exchange, substitute prescribing or, indeed, any other form of service. This, despite the fact that, especially since the deregulation of bus services and the perception of rural bus services as being economically unviable, the use of public transport can be a lengthy, unreliable and ultimately frustrating business which adds yet another hurdle to those who are seeking help. In addition, formalised and reliable childcare is less readily available in rural communities, which disadvantages women and single parents still further when seeking treatment.

Yet another complication is the fact that there often exists long-standing rivalries between towns and villages which may make it difficult for a person in one town to accept services in another.

Assumption three

Third is the notion that services are being provided for a low-risk population. The relationship between the level of deprivation in an area and subsequent levels of problems relating to drug use, is by now well-established. However there has been little recognition until recently that deprivation plays any significant role in determining the needs of rural populations. Neither, as discussed above, is there anything to suggest that living in a rural area is in any way protective against the sequelae of deprivation.

Most local authority studies of deprivation levels in the rural parts of their areas show that, when using standard indices of deprivation such as the Townsend or the Carstairs scales, and simply comparing the overall level of deprivation between urban and rural communities, such levels are generally lower rurally. Strathclyde Regional Council (1991), for instance, found exactly this, but also found that there were extremely high levels of deprivation clustering in two main categories. These occurred first in areas of declining industry, where the highest levels were found in households with young children, and second in remote communities, where there were very high levels of deprivation among elderly people living alone. They also observed that the problems were much less spatially concentrated and that, therefore, as well as considering the needs of fragile communities, services needed to be targeted on individuals and households irrespective of the apparent wealth of the community in which they live.

A difficulty is that deprivation indices may well measure deprivation differently in rural and urban areas. At equivalent levels of deprivation (Reading et al., 1993) some indicators are consistently poorer in urban areas (e.g., car ownership and unemployment) and others are poorer in rural areas (e.g., overcrowding and high commodity prices). Although this weighting tends to skew towards higher measures in urban areas, it may be that it reflects the way in which transport priorities and low-paid jobs contribute more to poverty in rural areas as compared with unemployment as the main cause of poverty in urban areas.

A report from Shelter (1997) suggested that in rural Scotland homelessness had increased twice as quickly as in towns and cities, that council house waiting lists were stagnant, that there were much higher levels of housing below the official 'tolerable standard', and that homes were more likely to be damp and in poor repair.

In the last 20 years there has been a sharp decline in primary industry and manufacturing jobs, which has been offset to some extent by service sector growth (Edmonds et al., 1996). There has been a tendency towards part-time, low-paid, casual and insecure employment, especially among females, and the average income among those working in rural areas is substantially lower than those working in urban settings. Many in rural areas are very well off, but less is seen of the fact that in rural Britain 65 per cent of households exist beneath or on the poverty margin (Shucksmith, 1991).

A survey of rural communities (Shucksmith, 1994) discovered that change and powerlessness were dominant themes. A sense of belonging in society depends on the adequate functioning of four systems (Commins, 1994)

- The democratic and legal system (promoting civic integration)
- The labour market (promoting economic integration)
- The welfare state (promoting social integration)
- Family and community (promoting interpersonal integration).

The survey noted evidence for failure in three of these systems. The feeling of powerlessness and the community's perception of a large gap between local people and local policy making is indicative of failure in the first (civic) system. The labour market is restricted because of difficulties in accessing childcare and transport facilities and because of diminished opportunity. This is especially the case for younger groups and women who, in the setting of failing heavy industry and an increasingly heavily mechanised agricultural industry, often settle for low-paid jobs with little in the way of security or prospects for improvement. Agriculture, which for so long has been the traditional mainstay of rural employment, now employs far fewer people than ever before. Take-up of benefits is markedly lower than the national average, reflecting some failure of the welfare state, partly at least because of difficulty in readily accessing advice and information. In addition, the surveys showed concerns about the likelihood that the continuing loss of young people increasingly inhibit the social reproduction of the community.

All these factors; unseen and under-recognised poverty, failing employment bases, an erosion of the skill base, a decrease in the numbers of young people, increases in the dependency ratios of rural communities and a high level of 'anomie' are precisely those which have been associated with the escalation of problem drug use in cities in the last 25 years. Given the sophisticated nature of drug distribution networks, the near saturation of urban drug markets and the increased potential for drug cultivation and manufacture in remote communities, it is perhaps unreasonable not to expect a similar escalation of drug problems in those rural communities with similar levels of deprivation.

Assumption four

Fourth, the assumption is made that the characteristics of the service required are the same as those required in an urban service and that the models of care employed can therefore mirror already existing urban-based services. This assumes first that the characteristics of drug usage are the same and second that the circumstances in which the drug service is set are similar.

In the absence of any adequate needs assessment for rural areas, anecdote would suggest that the first of these conditions is not necessarily the case. A study in East Anglia (Haarhoff, 1995) showed significantly more use of intravenous amphetamines as the drug of choice in rural areas. It suggested that this may reflect the fact that, unlike heroin, it can be manufactured locally, and that the product loyalty of the clientele may have arisen in much the same way as area markets create a loyal consumer base.

Services from around the country say that their feeling is that preferences are for amphetamines, cannabis and hallucinogenic mushrooms (i.e. those drugs which can be readily made or harvested) as opposed to cocaine or heroin (which rely on more sophisticated distribution networks). There is also a continual awareness of the use of veterinary drugs although whether this is a real problem or simply stands out for its novelty, is a moot point. Locally, one of the rurally-based needle exchange workers was recently asked how dangerous it was to have shared injecting equipment with a sheep! Thus the characteristics of the drug-using population would appear to be different from their town dwelling cousins and, given that most research and most national policy is based on providing a service for injecting opiate users, this clearly merits some attention.

The circumstances in which the services are set are much more observably different, and much of this revolves around problems of confidentiality and problems of access. The first of these reflects the fact that there is less anonymity in the country, partly because of the lower population concentration, and partly because of the frequent blurring of professional and social roles in such communities (Howland, 1995). It is thus more difficult to use drugs unobserved and more difficult to seek confidential help for fear of being stigmatised.

The more conservative nature of rural society tends to make this stigmatisation more intense and more obvious than in its urban counterpart, to the point where families are often as stigmatised as drug users. In England and Wales there are fifty per cent more exclusions in rural schools for drug use than in city schools (Rickford, 1995), while in Scotland sentences for drug use are significantly harsher in the country than in the city. Thus there are difficulties in accessing specialist help because of its scarcity, and in accessing generic help for fear of being discovered.

In addition, it can be difficult to access generic help (both primary health and social services) because of local monopolies of care which can potentially extend over a wide geographic area. For instance, if a GP in a city is disinclined to provide 'shared care', it is often not too difficult to find another GP who will, reasonably close at hand. This is clearly not the case in the country, where the drug user may have to travel prohibitively long distances to find an alternative, with the possible outcome that help is not sought and the problem escalates. There is thus potential tension between, on the one hand, primary care as being the 'ideal purveyor' of care (as suggested in recent health policy statements with regard to drug services) and, on the other, their effective monopoly of local health care and their willingness, or not, to become involved in drug problems.

This difficulty extends into other service areas as well. For instance, if the only pharmacist for a 40-mile radius is your aunt, and you don't want your parents to know that you are receiving a methadone prescription, you have a dilemma, the end resolution of which may be the decision not to accept care and the possibility of worsening whatever problems may already exist.

It would therefore appear that, despite national assumptions to the contrary, the ground for the existence and, indeed, the continuing escalation of rural drug problems, is fertile indeed. The levels of poverty and deprivation that are commonly held to be instrumental in the development of the more damaging forms of drug use in inner cities, exist at roughly the same levels in the country, although they may express themselves differently (their measurement by standard indices may in fact be slightly skewed towards an underestimate of rural deprivation). Although the logistics of accurate needs evaluation in geographically widespread areas have so far precluded the development of satisfactory techniques for so doing, both the rapidly increasing uptake of services in those rural areas that provide them and the countrywide anecdotal evidence of rural drug workers support this.

There are certain peculiarities of an urban environment to do with access, confidentiality and attitude which demand that the delivery of services be rethought in a way that does not simply mimic urban services and which may need to be unique not just in each area but in subsections of each area.

Rural policy and resources provision

There is little – if any – in the way of local, national, or European policy directed specifically towards the phenomenon of rural drug use. Indeed those task force statements recently published in Scotland and in England and Wales show little awareness of the problem or its peculiarities of presentation, let alone give any idea as to how they might best be approached. If, however, drug problems are seen as being part of a broader canvas of a community's socio-economic difficulties, then there do exist some national strategy statements as to the more general ways in which these might be addressed.

Government policies, both centrally and locally, emphasise the need for the diversification of rural economies away from agriculture. They support the need to foster rural enterprise and to tackle the difficulties of rural exclusion and the decline of rural services while simultaneously cherishing heritage.

The House of Lords' report: 'Future of a rural society' (1994) emphasises a close integration of economic and social development with a prerequirement of 'effective institutional arrangements'. It suggests the need for an absolute involvement of local communities, a multi-agency approach and a flexibility of partnerships and contracts to allow adaptation to diverse local circumstance. The Arkleton Trust (1994) pointed out that three problems underlay strategy: a lack of available skills, the fact that disadvantaged sectors tend not to participate in organised forums and the continuing need to involve new people in local strategies.

Strathclyde Regional Council (1991) identified problem areas as being transportation and isolation, economic decline, problems of access to information and advice, problems of service delivery, the disproportionate impact of service rationalisations (such as school closures) and low-earned incomes combined with relatively high shopping and transport costs. They proposed that these problems be dealt with directly by ensuring a fair share of resources relative to needs (including cost and time factors), by providing transport and by improving the efficiency of inter-agency referrals. They also published a series of good practice guidelines which included greater flexibility of services, better service integration to maximise resources, the promotion of cross-sectoral partnerships with a view to maximising the role of the voluntary sector, and the targeting of those in greatest need. They also pointed out the need for a fund equivalent to the Urban Programme, while avoiding its huge administration and opportunity costs.

Despite their general agreement as to the generalities of need, these various statements lack any indication as to the specific requirements for their translation into practice. Nor do they attempt to approach the difficulties encountered in previous attempts to deal with rural problems, mainly in the 1950s and 1960s in Third World countries. For instance, previous projects often found attempts at change were dominated by local notables to the exclusion of adequate participation by local people (Curtin and Varley, 1991). There was also often a lack of appreciation for the need to be clear about those structures which were to be responsible for the devolution of power (Wright, 1990). Perhaps most importantly, though, was that, despite the prime objectives of development initiatives having emerged from the localities, most projects were, in practice, externally formulated by groups put together by state agencies (Wright, 1990). Similar dangers are obviously inherent in the above calls for local rural partnerships intended to bring together agencies of central and local state with some community representatives and funded by a national rural fund.

The challenges, therefore, would seem to include the adequate involvement of all sections of the community, how to build partnerships in reality, how to resolve and manage conflicts within the community, and what and how clear the role of the state is in fostering and supporting initiatives. Proper local empowerment and adequate resource provision are essential in addressing these as is a good training for community leaders.

In England the Rural Development Commission has been set up for some years, although its 27 designated Rural Development Programmes to date cover only one third of England geographically and five per cent of the population (Confederation of Scottish Local Authorities, 1992). These are constituted by representatives from local authorities, private, voluntary and other rural interest schemes for targeted areas. Criteria for inclusion include unemployment levels, the range of employment, the rate of population decline, the rate of extramigration, local age structure and the level of access to service and facilities. Earnings levels, housing and levels of sickness do not contribute, however, and so, for the reasons outlined above, may tend to skew the interpretation of criteria. There does not seem to be information available as to how effective or not these approaches have been in addressing rural problems.

Supranationally the European Regional Development Fund finances projects which encourage socio-economic regeneration through job creation and infrastructure development projects (Rickford, 1995). In particular, Objective 5b facilitates the development of rural areas. To qualify, the area requires a low level of socio-economic development (such as over-reliance on agriculture as a main employer), low levels of average income and low population or significant outward migration. Its priorities are training, diversified community business development, environmental projects, community development and the promotion of heritage and tourism. It encourages measures to promote locally active agriculture and forestry projects, the development of sound rural infrastructures and the encouraging of new business. There are two other possible sources of funding, both of which require a GDP per head of less than 75 per cent of the European Union average. Objective 1 seeks to strengthen rural economies and to address problems of peripherality by encouraging the development of business, tourism and environmental industries. Objective 2 has similar intentions in those areas hit hardest by industrial decline.

The recent absorption of previously Eastern Europe countries, with their relatively higher levels of poverty, is likely to reduce the future amount of such funding available in the United Kingdom.

Drug service characteristics

It seems to be widely agreed that drug users require a range of those services which are known to be effective both in terms of individual well-being and from a public health perspective. In addition to basic education and health and social care, these would include:

- Access to information and education
- Good quality counselling and support services
- Drop-in facilities
- Crisis care
- Detoxification
- Substitute prescribing services
- Needle exchange facilities
- 'Time fill' activities
- Residential rehabilitation
- Good quality aftercare.

In addition, the special needs of women as a particularly stigmatised group, and as a group who can have especial difficulty in accessing services, requires special attention.

Organisation

With these problems and these requirements in mind it is important that there is good and effective coordination in order to make the best use of scarce resources in such widespread and diverse settings. Too often in the past service delivery has been dependent upon the idiosyncratic and judgmental beliefs of policy makers about what good care entails. The key to effective rural drug services is partnership involving true multi-agency, cross-sectoral working, good liaison practices, and a blurring of the distinction between generic and specialist services. The establishment of these requires the development of appropriate organisational and network structures, an agreement of common purpose, integration of approach, equality of partners, flexibility of practice to allow for renegotiation when adapting to local circumstance and adequate resources.

This has been facilitated to some extent by the advent of Drug Action Teams throughout the UK. Although some questions remain about their effectiveness in communicating local issues to central government agencies, the DATs are the most appropriate promulgators and owners of strong, consensual policy and strategy. For this to be effective the DATs need to ensure that their membership includes decision making representation from all relevant agencies and that communication with the more locally responsive drug fora is maximised.

Drug fora, in their turn, need to feel that they have some say in, and hence ownership of, any strategy that might be conceived, and need to ensure that their representation is as geographically and professionally diverse as possible. The constituency of these groups should not be limited to specialist representatives but should also include representation from any generic agency that can have some impact. This may include, for instance, health promotion, community education, police, church organisations, youth workers, relatives groups, users groups, and so on. The Criminal Justice System is another important participant, given the need to provide a wider range of sentencing options.

Needs assessment

Prior to setting up a service, however, it is useful to have some idea of the depth and the type of need. The difficulties of establishing this have already been alluded to but its importance remains. There is, for instance, little point in setting up a service which caters predominantly for injecting opiate users if the popular drug of choice locally is amphetamine. In urban areas the most successful recent needs assessments have tended to be based on 'snowballing' techniques, in which contact with one group of drug users leads to contact with another group, and so on.

Intuitively this would seem to be the method most likely to succeed in rural areas, but attempts to adapt methods proven in urban settings, such as 'capture–recapture' techniques, have so far been found wanting. In one area the final estimate of drug users turned out to be half the number of individuals using the needle exchanges and one quarter of the number receiving methadone prescriptions. This is perhaps reflective of the fact that rural drug use is less of a cohesive entity than its urban counterpart, tending to be composed of more discrete groups which often have little in the way of cross-group communication and who tend, for reasons outlined above, to be well hidden. More research is needed to allow this technique to become more accurate, although it is probably the most promising.

In the meantime it is worth reflecting that the main impetus behind the growing recognition that rural areas experience drug problems has been the observations, statistics and anecdotes of services set up in such areas. Often there was little initial idea as to what those problems might be and agencies have often had to change and adapt their service as a response to perceived need. In some ways this could be considered to be a form of 'field testing' in which previously untested but commonly held assumptions are explored naturalistically.

In point of fact there are usually some indicators as to what is required to be gleaned from generic sources such as youth workers and health-care workers. It may be, however, that, in the absence of any reasonably accurate techniques of need assessment, the most appropriate way forward is to assume that a drug problem exists and to set up an embryonic service that is flexible enough to adapt to whatever local circumstance may be uncovered.

Community attitudes

The difficulties of disproportionately low levels of confidentiality and high levels of stigma require that substantial efforts be made to convince communities that there is a real problem. The more obvious ways of addressing this involve the use of public meetings and media campaigns as a way of educating and desensitising the community to the point of accepting the fact that there is indeed a problem and therefore to accept and support services. This in turn can make the use of services more readily acceptable to drug users and hence encourage earlier intervention in their problems. This could very usefully be a function of the local drug fora.

Perhaps the most immediately effective method, however, is the encouragement of the relatives of service users to form strongly supported and highly visible family support groups with a view to their greater empowerment and the subsequent lessening of community stigma. By the same token the setting up of user groups and self-help groups can help to highlight the problem to the broader community, form the basis of further service development, and provide a more accurate assessment of local need (Pugh et al., 1996).

Generic services

Generic workers will inevitably play a vital part in underpinning whatever services are set up, first in an attempt to integrate and 'normalise' drug problems into generic care and second to support and maximise the effect of inevitably thinly spread specialist resource. The issue of 'care monopolies' mentioned previously means that concepts such as 'shared care' cannot be entirely relied upon to provide maintenance of care in, for instance, substitute prescribing and reliable, readily accessible specialist services need to be available to fill the resultant gaps. To be effective, as in urban services, education and support of generic services needs to be a strong component with a view to increasing their skills and confidence and decreasing their reliance on specialist services. This has the advantage of freeing the latter to deal with the more difficult end of the spectrum problem. A spin-off to this is, again, the lessening of community stigma, thus allowing drug users to approach generic services with less fear, earlier in the development of their problem.

Indeed the whole issue of who is a provider perhaps needs to be re-examined in rural areas. Frequently recognition of problems and subsequent entry into priority care services occur from already existing rural organisations such as churches, or more informal neighbourhood networks of support and care. These will vary in impact from area to area but are well worth identifying and supporting. For instance, in the USA, the 'Alliance of Black Churches Health Project' (Schorling, 1993) exploited their position as naturally occurring, convenient gathering places to provide entry points to mental health care. Their experience, however, suggests that some care needs to be taken to avoid losing sight of their original purpose, with the subsequent disenfranchisement of their original users (Sarason, 1972).

Specialist services

Specialist services themselves should attempt to be as flexible as possible. They should try to maximise accessibility while remaining aware of the understandable disinclination of drug users to become too visible in their own communities.

Outreach work, much of which has been developed in rural areas, is an essential basis of any service, providing both funnelling and filtering functions for specialist services in areas where drug users do not wish to make contact with generic workers. The common understanding of outreach as an occupation that is practised on street corners, however, is inappropriate, given that the bulk of rural drug use is hidden. Outreach, therefore, ideally becomes domiciliary and as such requires subtler and more sensitive approaches.

Outreach workers can also be used to good effect to provide community-based needle exchanges from health centres, community centres, or other local sites. These can function as satellites to the central static sites which will inevitably be difficult for rural users to access, especially given Stimson's original finding that city-based users were unlikely to travel more than a mile to access needle exchanges (Stimson et al., 1988).

Community pharmacists can, also, usefully provide more localised needle exchange, as can the partial devolution of such facilities to drug agencies. More recently there has been an increase in interest in the idea of 'backpacking' needles, i.e., allowing outreach workers to carry needles with them on their travels. A number of such schemes are currently being piloted. Further, perhaps more radical, thinking suggests that drug users themselves can be used as a network to enable needle distribution. At its most extreme, attempts have been made to involve dealer networks in the distribution of injecting equipment, and in providing entry points to services. There are areas of the country where this has been tried in a (very!) unofficial way and anecdotal report suggests that this can be an effective way of minimising the sharing of equipment and of helping disseminate information.

The use of drug users already in contact with the service as a form of outreach may be a useful way of providing a service in those areas with idiosyncratic drug-using characteristics, and the development of self-help groups can be a very effective way of providing support. At the very least this approach can help to obtain a better idea of the services required and, at best, it can provide the basis for the subsequent development of a substantive service.

Counselling and support services (including the provision of drop-in facilities) are best provided by local drug agencies who should attempt to make their services as geographically accessible as possible. This may involve the use of satellite facilities such as community centres, church halls, health centres or whatever else is to hand. Integration into the community will increase the likelihood of services becoming acceptable and therefore of being contacted for assistance by relatives or users. It is also worth allocating time to be spent with those generic workers (e.g., teachers, social workers) who bear the brunt of the community's psychological difficulties, with a view to gleaning information and providing support (Yellowlees, 1992). This has the added advantage of raising the profile of drug services and, in the process, helping to make both services and drug problems more readily acceptable to the community at large. Similarly, and for the same reasons, substitute prescribing services should be devolved as far as possible. This may, for instance, mean a series of satellite clinics run out of local drug agencies by GP sessional workers under the supervision of a consultant psychiatrist.

This approach has the advantage of encouraging true multi-agency working and networking. It encourages both cross-sectoral cooperation and a high level of mutual reliance between specialist and generic workers, which maximises the efficient use of scarce resource. An alternative is the shared care approach, although the problems that arise if one practice which covers a large geographical area is unwilling to provide such a service, and to which there is no alternative, have already been alluded to.

In-patient detoxification and residential rehabilitation will inevitably (and appropriately) remain centre-based. In Ayrshire the home detoxification of opiate and amphetamine users has been very successfully combined with the already well-proven home detoxification of alcohol users, to the point where this aspect comprises 35 per cent of the team's activities. The service consists of short-term, high-intensity support from community psychiatric nurses with appropriate prescribing from the GP. Its success appears to be dependent on a high level of communication between themselves, the in-patient detoxification service and the various drug agencies as to what and when is the most appropriate form of after care and support. For example, an opiate user might approach either a drug agency or a GP with a request for detoxification. The request will then be passed to the home detoxification team who will visit the client and determine the likelihood of detoxification at home being successful. If this is thought to be the case, then the appropriate prescription will be sought from the GP and the appropriate level of support (at least daily visits) negotiated with the local drug agency. If it is thought that success at home is unlikely (either because of lack of community support or because of a history of serious complications of withdrawal) then arrangements will be made for admission to a detoxification bed. Successful (or indeed unsuccessful) admission will be followed by a minimum of five weeks of intensive support (again in conjunction with the local drug agency), while negotiating the most appropriate form (if any) of continuing intervention. This may take the form of retrying detoxification, maintenance prescribing, admission to the local rehabilitation facility, continuing counselling through drug agencies or the outreach services or, indeed, no further action. The key here is the high level of continuing cooperation and communication between the various parts of the drug services network.

Resources

Finally, there is no escaping the fact that providing an adequate and effective service for drug users in rural areas is more expensive than providing a comparably adequate service in urban areas (Chalifoux, 1996). Precisely the same individual and public health arguments apply, however.

Fewer people can be seen for the same amount of money. Travelling times and expenses are greater. The need for and amount of liaison time is greater when dealing with a less concentrated group of generic workers. There does, however, need to be a commitment to ensuring that rural drug users do not continue to be disadvantaged in the services they receive.

Some of this commitment needs to be directed towards addressing more general rural issues in order to minimise the levels of deprivation and poverty which can only further nurture an already significant drug problem. The rest needs to be directed towards ensuring ready and reasonable access to drug services designed specifically for the area concerned, rather than being an ineffectual mirror of urban services.

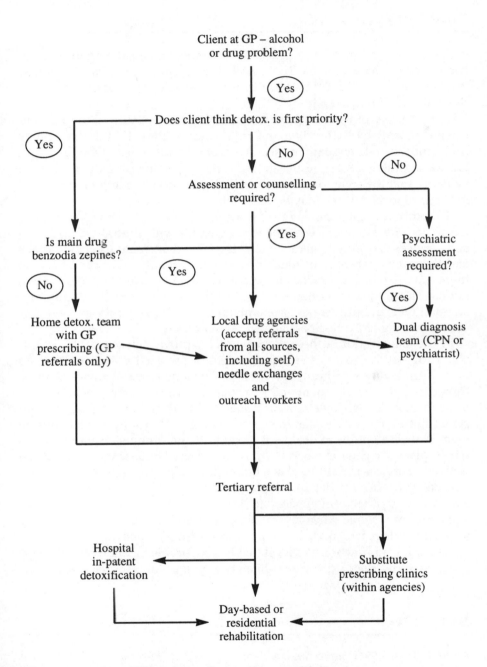

Figure 8.1   A possible scheme for service provision

Summary

In summary then, there is evidence of substantial and escalating drug problems in rural environments. Their roots often seem to lie in largely similar levels of poverty and deprivation to those seen in urban areas (albeit expressed in different ways).

For a variety of reasons there are difficulties in attracting recognition of these problems by both urban and rural communities. This in itself poses problems when developing services. Further difficulties arise when attempting to accurately assess need, although there is some (mainly anecdotal) evidence that the styles of drug usage, both in terms of drug preference and in terms of local culture, may be different.

To complicate matters, there are some peculiarities of rural communities which require attention. First, poor compliance with centrally-based, distant services is common, because of long and inconvenient travelling times and the relative scarcity of reliable, reasonable quality child care. Second, there can often be a reluctance to accept services in nearby and often 'rival' towns. Third, there are often very real concerns about confidentiality and stigma given the difficulties in maintaining rural anonymity and the frequent blurring of professional and social boundaries.

To adequately address these problems and to provide an accessible, acceptable drug service requires strong, coherent, consensual policy making. As well as involving significant specialist and generic service providers, there should be a real involvement of the various local communities, including the users themselves, when determining policies. Efforts need to be made to help communities understand that there is a problem and to support and educate them in their attempts to deal with it. Support and training also needs to be put in place for generic workers, who will inevitably bear the brunt of the problem. Services should be characterised by multi-agency cooperation and efficient and effective networking, both between the various specialist organisations and between generic and specialist workers. Flexibility and imagination are required when determining the nuts and bolts of service delivery in order to adequately address the problems referred to above.

Last, if it is to function at a level that is comparable to and equitable with urban services, then a disproportionately high level of resource is required.

References

Arkleton Trust (1994), *Supporting and Animating Community-based Rural Development in Europe.*

Blank, M.B., Fox, J.C., Hargrove, D.S., Turner, J.T. (1995), 'Critical Issues in Reform-ing Mental Health Strategy', *Community Mental Health Journal*, 31, (6), 511–23.
Chalifoux, Z., Neece, J.B., Backwater, K.C., Litwak, E., Abraham, I.L. (1996), 'Mental Health Services for Rural Elderly', *Community Mental Health Journal*, 32, (5), 463–80.
Commins, P. and Keane, M. (1994), *The Developing Rural Economy, Problems and Prospects in the National Economic and Social Council: New Approaches to Rural Development*, Report No. 97, Dublin: NESC.
Confederation of Scottish Local Authorities (1992), *Local Strategies to Tackle Rural Disadvantage*, NA9OSLD. Doc, CSLA.
Coward, R.T. and Jackson, R.W. (1983), 'Environmental Stress in the Rural Family', in McCubbin and Figley (eds), *Stress and the Family*, New York: Brunner/Muzel.
Curtin, C. and Varley, T. (1991), 'Populism and Petit Capitalism in Ireland – An Appraisal', in S. Whatmore, T. Marsden and P. Lowe (eds), *Rural Enterprise – Shifting Perspective on Small-scale Production*, London: David Fulton.
Edmonds, H., Williams, N., Shucksmith, M. and Gemmell, A. (1996), *Scottish Rural Life Update*, Scottish Office: Edinburgh.
Fox, J., Blank, M.B., Kane, C.F. and Hargrove, D.S. (1994), 'Balance Theory as a Model for Co-ordinating Delivery of Mental Health Services', *Applied and Preventive Psychology*, 3, (2), 121–29.
Haarhoff, G. and London, M. (1995) 'A Comparative Study of Injecting Opiate and Amphetamine Users in a Rural Area', *Addiction Research*, 3, (1), 33–8.
Hill, C. (1988), *Community Health Systems in the Rural American South*, Boulder, Colorado: Westview Press.
House of Lords (1994), *The Future of Rural Society*, London: HMSO.
Howland, R.H. (1995), 'Treatment of Persons with Dual Diagnoses in a Rural Com-munity', *Psychiatric Quarterly*, 66, (1), 33–49.
Pugh, R., and Richards, M. (1996) 'Speaking Out, a Practical Approach to Empow-erment', *Practice*, 8, (2), 35–44.
Reading, R., Raybold, S., Jarvis, S. (1993), 'Deprivation, Low Birth Weight and Childrens' Height, a Comparison Between Rural and Urban Areas', *British Medi-cal Journal*, 307, 1458–62.
Rickford, F. (1995), 'Needles in the haystacks', *Community Care*, 2–8 November.
Sarason, S. (1972), *The Creation of Settings*, San Francisco: Jossey-Bass.
Schorling, J. (1993), 'The Alliance of Black Churches Project', in *Partnerships in Health Care*, New York: Rochester.
Scottish Council of Voluntary Organisations – European Regional Development Fund, *Focus on Fact*, Issue 29, April 1997.
Shelter (1997), *Scotland's Rural Housing: At the Heart of Communities*, Edinburgh: Shelter.
Shucksmith, M. (1991), 'Scottish House Condition Survey, Survey Report', Scottish Homes.
Shucksmith, M. (1994), 'Disadvantage in rural Scotland', Summary Report, Perth: Rural Forum.
Stimson, G., Alldritt, L., Dolan, K. and Donaghoe, M. (1988), 'Preventing the Spread of HIV in Injecting Drug Users – the Experience of Syringe-exchange Schemes in England and Scotland', NIDA Research Monograph, 90, 302–10.
Strathclyde Regional Council (1991), 'Seminar on Rural Deprivation – Summary and Options for Action', Report by the Chief Executive of Strathclyde Regional Council, Glasgow.

Wright, S. (1990), 'Development Theory and Community Development Practice', in H. Butler and S. Wright (eds), *Rural Development: Problems and Practice*, Aldershot: Avebury.

Yellowlees, P.M. and Hemming, M. (1992), 'Rural Mental Health', *The Medical Journal of Australia*, **157**, 152–4.

9 Working with women who use drugs

Mary Hepburn

Introduction

Illicit drug use has been steadily increasing for almost 20 years. However, there has been a disproportionately large rise in the number of women and particularly young women of childbearing age who use drugs (Ministerial Group on the Misuse of Drugs, 1988). While this increase has occurred throughout society, problem drug use is closely associated with socio-economic deprivation (Scottish Home and Health Department, 1994). While young women who use drugs share many of the problems experienced by men, there are also a number of gender specific issues. These include the direct effects of drug use on women's roles – both biological and social – as mothers, and their wider roles as carers within families. Additional problems arise because of society's perceptions of women's appropriate social role, its views of appropriate behaviour for women and, consequently, its views of these effects and of drug use by women in general. Drug-using women will frequently experience deprivation and poverty, if not because of the uneven social distribution, then as a consequence of problem drug use *per se*. They therefore experience the medical and social problems due to deprivation, which are added to and exacerbated by the problems directly due to their drug use. Women who use drugs therefore require specific services designed to meet their needs.

131

General health problems

Many of the general health problems associated with drug use are common to women and men. Poor diet and undernutrition are common, and become worse when drug use becomes more chaotic. Weight is therefore a good objective indicator of stability of drug use and is particularly helpful when monitoring pregnant drug-using women. Poor diet and hygiene cause dental decay, which provides a focus of infection as well as causing toothache which may be precipitated by and foil attempts to reduce or stop use of painkilling drugs, such as opiates.

Injecting drug use causes vascular damage, the consequences of which will depend on the site affected. These can include serious effects such as stroke or loss of limbs, but can more commonly be less dramatic. Even minor vascular problems such as loss of accessible veins, with the associated difficulties of venous access, can make pregnancy more difficult to monitor and labour more hazardous. Use of the lower limbs as injection sites, often results in swelling due to reduced venous drainage which will again be exacerbated by pregnancy. Injecting drug use can also cause infection both locally and systemically. Locally abscesses and phlebitis can exacerbate vascular damage caused by the actual act of injecting. Systemic infections due to injecting can cause such conditions as endocarditis with its associated damage to the cardiac valves. This will necessitate the use of antibiotic cover during any medical procedures or events – including childbirth – which may increase the risk of presence of bacteria in the bloodstream. The risk of transmission of blood-borne viruses, including HIV, Hepatitis B and C has additional implications for women because of the risk of vertical transmission from mother to baby.

Women may finance their drug use by prostitution, bringing not only the risks of violence but also of sexually transmitted diseases (again including hepatitis B and HIV) of importance to any future or current pregnancy. There is also the risk of unplanned or unwanted pregnancy.

Reproductive health

Menstrual disorders

Women who have a significant drug problem are often amenorrhoeic either because of a direct effect of opiate drugs such as heroin or methadone, or simply because of poor nutrition and low body weight. While both can also inhibit ovulation, amenorrhoea can occur with or without ovulation and neither amenorrhoea nor any disturbance of the menstrual cycle can be assumed to indicate infertility. An unplanned pregnancy, even if not unwelcome, can be disastrous for a woman with a significant drug problem; a chaotic lifestyle may jeopardise custody of the unborn baby while an additional baby may destabilise precariously maintained custody of existing children. Regardless of the presence or absence of menstruation or the regularity of their cycle, drug-using women should be advised about and provided with appropriate effective contraception.

Methods of contraception

Methods such as the oral contraceptive pill which require rigorous user compliance and an organised predictable lifestyle are rarely suitable for drug-using women. Methods which are long-lasting and as far as possible independent of lifestyle – such as progestogens by injection or implant or intrauterine contraceptive devices (IUCD) – are most likely to be effective. While length of action is the advantage of depot hormonal methods, this can also be a relative disadvantage; infrequent follow-up can be more difficult and failure of follow-up potentially more catastrophic since the duration of action of such drugs, however long, is still finite. The IUCD has a long duration of action and will probably retain some effectiveness for even longer. It has often been regarded as unsuitable for drug-using women because of the perceived increased risk of pelvic infections. However, this risk only applies to the time of insertion and removal, while new progestogen-releasing intrauterine devices are actually claimed to protect against infection (Toivonen et al., 1991). Both methods are therefore potentially suitable for drug-using women, while for those who are certain that their families are complete, sterilisation may be the most appropriate method. Sterilisation may also be indicated at a younger age or at times, such as the immediate post-partum period, which would not be considered appropriate for the general population. Adequate and accurate counselling is obviously essential in such circumstances.

Fertility

While anovulatory amenorrhoea can reduce fertility, this effect is usually reversed by control and reduction of drug use. Unfortunately the same does not apply to infertility resulting from blockage of the fallopian tubes due to pelvic infection resulting from sexually transmitted diseases. In addition to effective contraception women should therefore be advised to use barrier protection against infection, not just to protect themselves from life-threatening infections such as HIV, but also to protect their future fertility. While non-penetrative sexual intercourse and use of male condoms will provide the most effective protection, not all drug-using women will be able to use these methods. Other approaches, such as the use of pessaries, foams or sponges (the latter much criticised and withdrawn from the market), may certainly be less effective. They are, however, better than nothing and the use of any method, no matter how ineffective, if it is the best that can be achieved, should be encouraged. It is important to ensure that drug-using women are helped both to protect their fertility and to control it until the time is appropriate and they choose to have a pregnancy.

Pregnancy

Drug-using women are often regarded as unsuitable to have children first because of the effects of maternal drug use on pregnancy and the unborn child and second because they are considered by virtue of their drug use to be incapable of caring for their children. However, drug-using women do not differ from non-drug-using women in their motivation to have children and to be effective parents. Illicit drug use can and does affect foetal well-being but this is also true of legal drugs such as tobacco and alcohol, and their use is certainly not incompatible with good childcare. The problems due to maternal drug use should therefore be kept in perspective.

Effects of maternal drug use on pregnancy

Drug use by pregnant women can affect the baby in two ways. It can affect foetal growth and well-being *in utero* and it can lead to withdrawal symptoms in the neonate. Both of these effects will depend on the drugs used, their dosage and pattern of use. Teratogenicity (developmental abnormalities caused by drugs) is not a particular problem for this group, apart from the well-documented cranio-facial abnormalities which can be associated with problem alcohol use, and the suggestion that benzodiazepine use may be associated with an increased rate of cleft palate.

Many illicit drugs, including opioids (e.g., opiate drugs, such as heroin and morphine, and non-opiate-derived drugs with a similar action, such as methadone and dihydrocodeine), benzodiazepines and cocaine, increase the risk of low birth weight and preterm delivery and, consequently, the associated risks of stillbirth or neonatal death. There is also an increased risk of cot death. These effects have been well-documented by many centres (Hepburn, 1992). Such outcomes, however, are the result of many factors and are caused not only by the use of illegal drugs but also by the legal drugs – tobacco and alcohol – as well as factors associated with socio-economic deprivation. It is therefore difficult, if not impossible, to attribute outcomes to specific drugs or to quantify the contribution from drug use. The possible exception is cocaine, which is a powerful constrictor of blood vessels and whose use has been reported to cause an increased risk of placental separation as well as damage to developing organs such as the brain, bowels or limbs. There is no good evidence that use of amphetamines or ecstasy is associated with significant obstetric problems, while a significant factor in the risk to the foetus from the use of cannabis may result from the fact that it is commonly smoked in combination with tobacco.

Maternal drug use in pregnancy can also result in withdrawal symptoms in the baby. If the mother's use of drugs is erratic, or the drugs she uses are short-acting, these effects can occur before birth. Smooth muscle spasm due to opiate withdrawals can result in the foetus releasing bowel contents or meconium, which, if then inhaled, results in severe respiratory problems. Postnatal withdrawal symptoms in the baby are commonly seen with maternal use of opiates or benzodiazepines but rarely with other types of drug. Many of the symptoms are not dissimilar to those experienced by adults. Babies may be irritable and jittery, have vomiting or diarrhoea and, despite being hungry, they do not feed effectively. Consequently they may exhibit excessive weight loss. A spectrum of severity of symptoms is seen ranging from mild irritability to severe cerebral irritation with convulsions. Convulsions are, however, rare and typically babies are irritable and hungry but ineffective feeders and poor sleepers. They may pose a major childcare challenge to mothers already struggling to learn new skills. While overall there is a general correlation between the level of maternal drug use and the severity of neonatal withdrawal symptoms, this correlation does not necessarily apply to individual cases, and the baby's condition at birth cannot be predicted from the mother's pattern of use nor can the severity of her habit be deduced from the baby's condition. The presence or absence of neonatal withdrawal symptoms or their severity should not therefore be the basis for decisions about child custody, and in that context merits consideration only because a mother with a sick child will require additional sympathy and support.

Management of drug use in pregnancy

Substitution therapy

Management will depend on the type of drug used. In the case of opiate addiction the prescribing of substitute medication is frequently recommended since antenatal detoxification is still widely regarded as unacceptably hazardous to the foetus. This has not been the experience in Glasgow, however (Hepburn, 1997), where detoxification and maintenance or any combination of the two have always been available as treatment options to all opiate-using women.

There is no evidence that maintenance benzodiazepine prescribing is of significant benefit during pregnancy and, since benzodiazepine use causes significant problems including withdrawal symptoms in the baby, it is not justified. While detoxification is indicated in the foetal interests it should be covered by a reducing regime using a longer-acting benzodiazepine such as diazepam to prevent maternal convulsions.

There is debate over the role of substitute prescribing for amphetamine use. Amphetamine use causes no major foetal complications and any concerns arise from the possible effects of intravenous use and from a chaotic lifestyle. None of the other commonly used drugs justify management by substitute prescribing during pregnancy.

Which agency prescribes substitute medications will depend on local circumstances. However, most maternity services will see too few pregnant drug-using women to acquire the necessary skills and prescribing will often be more appropriately undertaken by the local addiction services. Many women will already be receiving prescribed medication when they become pregnant, while others who are using illicit drugs will require assessment to decide if or what they should be prescribed. In all cases, however, the various options should be discussed with the woman and a plan of management agreed. Regardless of prescribing arrangements it is essential that there should be close collaboration between maternity services and those who may be prescribing during pregnancy and who will undertake prescribing after delivery.

Antenatal detoxification

While experience in Glasgow has not shown detoxification at any gestation or at any speed to be unduly hazardous to the foetus, rapid reductions in levels of opiates or benzodiazepines should arguably be carried out on an in-patient basis under obstetric supervision. Outpatient detoxification is also an option but, even with much slower reduction in drug levels, this is often less successful.

Rehabilitation

While the maternity ward is the ideal setting for initial stabilisation, rapid reduction or detoxification of pregnant drug-using women, it cannot provide the setting for subsequent comprehensive rehabilitation for those women who require it. Although scarce, some residential facilities do exist for pregnant women, or for women or couples with children, but finding one which deals with the required combination is difficult and places are often unavailable. Pregnancy provides strong motivation for behavioural change and can provide the stimulus for an attempt to achieve long term abstinence. However, for many women such a goal will be either unachievable or inappropriate at that time, and achieving sustained stability of drug use and lifestyle while remaining in the community will often be a more realistic objective.

Objectives of drug management

Management objectives may be slightly different during pregnancy. The short-term goal of a good pregnancy outcome may allow women to achieve greater stability or reduction in levels of drug use than at other times, but the need to increase levels again after delivery should not be regarded as failure. Methadone use has many benefits particularly in stabilising lifestyle and reducing dangers from intravenous use of drugs. However, it should be remembered that methadone, like other opioid drugs, causes problems for the foetus, and the severity of these is similarly dose-related. As the dose of methadone increases there will therefore come a point when the disadvantages outweigh the advantages. Since the main objective is reduction in the total dose of drug consumed, a pragmatic approach should be adopted when deciding appropriate doses of methadone, recognising that very occasional safe use of illicit drugs on top of a relatively small dose of methadone may cause less problems for the baby than total abstinence from illicit drugs in the presence of a much higher dose of methadone.

Management of paediatric problems

The decision to treat neonatal withdrawal symptoms is often based on a scoring chart but, while arguably helpful in concentrating attention on relevant symptoms and providing guidance for inexperienced staff, these scores should not provide the sole criterion for therapy. The mother's ability to cope should also be taken into consideration.

Routine admission to the special care baby unit (SCBU) at birth is illogical since withdrawal symptoms can take several days to develop and, in the absence of medical complications, the babies of drug-using women should routinely go to the post-natal ward with their mothers, with admission to the SCBU only when medically indicated.

Neonatal withdrawal symptoms can be managed either by substitution therapy or by symptomatic therapy. Substitution therapy with gradual reduction can take a long time and consequently often requires admission to the SCBU with resulting separation of mother from baby. Since polydrug use is common, exact substitution is often impossible. Symptomatic therapy, usually to prevent convulsions or improve feeding, rarely involves such lengthy separation and the precise combination of drugs is less important.

Breast-feeding is often regarded as contraindicated for drug-using women since this will result in the baby receiving continued drugs after birth. However this is precisely what happens when babies are given substitution therapy and breast milk, by providing a combination of drugs exactly matching that taken by the mother, will provide extremely effective substitution therapy. Weaning should always be gradual, and HIV infection in the mother would, of course, be a contraindication to breast-feeding.

Social management

Social support

Many of the social problems experienced by women, either as cause or consequence of their drug use, may be of equal importance in influencing the pregnancy outcome as well as the welfare and custody of their children. During pregnancy, drug-using women, like all women, need help and advice regarding housing, financial and legal difficulties as well as with any other social problems they may be experiencing. Involvement of social services is often viewed as punitive and unnecessary unless serious deficiencies in childcare develop. It is precisely this late involvement of social services – often simply with the task of removing the child from the mother's custody – which results in this hostile perception. Earlier involvement of the social worker in a preventative and supportive role not only promotes a more positive relationship with the drug-using woman but also reduces the social work department's workload.

Parenting skills

It is widely assumed that the demonstration of poor parenting skills by drug-using women is entirely attributable to their drug use – but this is not necessarily the case. They may have had no opportunity to learn them because of an absence of appropriate role models, and the necessary skills will not miraculously appear if they stop using drugs! Appropriate tuition in parenting skills on a one to one or small group basis should be provided during pregnancy, and a slightly extended post-natal stay in hospital will enable skills to be assessed and acquired under supervision.

Multidisciplinary care

In the management of pregnant drug-using women, it is vital that a multidisciplinary approach is adopted with close collaboration between not only health-care professionals in hospital and in the community, but also between healthcare services, addiction and social services (SCODA and LGDF, 1997). In addition to regular contact, planning meetings around 32 weeks' gestation are invaluable in identifying problems, setting goals and planning support networks. A further meeting held postnatally allows review of progress, reports on childcare and a transfer of management back to the community with planning for ongoing support. While the numbers of people involved in these meetings and the formality of the proceedings can be varied according to the individual woman's needs, their occurrence should be routine. To omit them because the woman's drug use is under control is to fail to recognise the natural history of problem drug use and the risk of subsequent relapse. It is also poor practice in multidisciplinary management.

Pregnancy provides an ideal opportunity for developing relationships between the women and the workers who will provide ongoing care and support after delivery. While all services will not contribute equally at all stages, continuity of care is important and will be promoted by good communication between services, women and their families.

Service provision

Whether they have children, are pregnant or are contemplating pregnancy, women's role as mothers should always be considered by those who provide services for drug-using women. Regardless of their function, services should be accessible by any route including self-referral, while provision of help with both medical and social problems on one site will facilitate and encourage attendance and will allow opportunistic management of problems. For example, provision of well woman and contraceptive care within addiction services, or provision of help with problem drug use in maternity services, will help women to become pregnant when they choose to and maximise their chances of having a healthy baby. All services should be non-judgemental and should consider the drug use in the context of the rest of the woman's circumstances rather than in isolation. Health-care services should recognise that non-attendance, especially for screening or preventive care, is a feature of socio-economic deprivation, and not necessarily attributable solely to drug use, while addiction services should recognise the need for appropriately trained and experienced staff and appropriate content of service provision.

Conclusions

The rising incidence of problem drug use among women emphasises the need to provide them with appropriate help. The same range of therapeutic options is available to both men and women who use drugs. However, in discussing management plans with women, the possibility of a present or future pregnancy should be borne in mind, as should the effect on their options of any existing children. Women's particular requirements should be recognised and their views taken into account when planning services. Experience confirms that appropriate services will be enthusiastically used by women (Hepburn and Elliott, 1997).

References

Hepburn, M. (1992), 'Socially Related Disorders: Drug Addiction, Maternal Smoking and Alcohol Consumption', in A.A. Calder and W. Dunlop (eds), *High Risk Pregnancy*, London: Butterworths.

Hepburn, M. (1997), 'Drugs of Addiction', in F. Cockburn (ed.), *Advances in Perinatal Medicine: Proceedings of the XVth European Congress of Perinatal Medicine, 10–13 September 1996, Glasgow, Scotland*, Carnforth: Parthenon Publishing.

Hepburn, M. and Elliot, A. (1997), 'A Community Obstetric Service for Women with Special Needs', *British Journal of Midwifery*, 5, (8), 458–88.

Ministerial Group on the Misuse of Drugs (1988), *Tackling Drug Misuse: A Summary of the Government's Strategy. 3rd Edition*, London: HMSO.

Scottish Office Home and Health Department (1994), *Drugs in Scotland: Meeting the Challenge*, Report of the Ministerial Drugs Task Force, Edinburgh: HMSO.

Standing Conference on Drug Abuse (SCODA) and Local Government Drugs Forum (LGDF) (1997), *Drug Using Parents. Guidelines for Interagency Working*, London: Local Government Authority (LGA).

Toivonen, J., Luukkainen, T., Allonen, H. (1991), 'Protective Effect of Intrauterine Release of Levonorgestrel on Pelvic Infection: Three Years' Comparative Experience of Levonorgestrel and Copper-Releasing Intrauterine Devices', *Obstetrics and Gynaecology*, 77, 261–4.

10 The treatment of drug users in prison

J. Kennedy Roberts and Brian A. Kidd

Imprisonment for most people is a subjective concept. Their perception of imprisonment may be based on many sources of information: perhaps childhood memories, when the vague menace of imprisonment was held over their heads as a consequence of continued unacceptable behaviour. Documentaries, soap operas or the media may also have contributed to their perception. Few people, we imagine, could have passed a Victorian prison with its gaunt and forbidding exterior without a shiver. It is not the intention of this chapter to portray prisons as Dante's 'Inferno', with the legend above the door 'abandon hope all ye who enter here'.

Imprisonment is, however, an extremely stressful experience. It has been well said that the loss of liberty due to imprisonment is the punishment, and the conditions in the prison itself should not be part of that punishment. Despite the best efforts of highly trained and caring prison staff, imprisonment is an experience which even the most stoical, mentally and physically robust inmates find difficult to cope with. It is not just the loss of freedom and liberty and having to live a regimented life with all decisions virtually being removed from oneself. The prison has rules, some of which may seem trivial, punitive or even incomprehensible to the inmates. A frightened prisoner admitted to jail for the first time may be dreading being locked up in a cell with only a chamber pot and several other frightened and possibly equally bewildered strangers for company. Much can be and is done to allay inmates' fears and to mitigate against the worst excesses of imprisonment by what on the whole is a caring prison service. Despite the best efforts of staff, however, bullying, violence and injury including fatalities and suicides are often a feature of prison life. Untried prisoners on remand may have an especially difficult time because their futures are so uncertain. They have the anxiety of an impending trial which may be postponed, and this uncertainty adds a further frightening dimension to what is already an awesome experience. Prisoners on remand also frequently have fewer regimes available to occupy them. Enforced separation from family and loved ones may be more than some can bear. They may be housed in an institution which is difficult for their family and friends to visit. Some drug users become detoxified for the first time and emerge from a drug-clouded existence into this dark and sometimes unacceptable reality. The coping mechanisms and support systems people may have used in the community are no longer available to them.

The Prison Doctor's Perspective

The prison medical officer has an important influence on treatment options. Many of the readers' of this textbook will have contact with prisons. This chapter aims to describe the prison doctor's perspective, and how it interacts with that of the person using the prison medical service.

As well as the obvious issues of authority and control, which affect how prison medicine is perceived, there are characteristics of the prison environment which affect how drug users can be supported while in prison. The most striking feature is that the prison medical officer dealing with drug users has a captive audience. The service users can be observed to a much greater extent than would occur in a community setting. Medication can be easily supervised. The person's whereabouts are known at all times. These in turn influence the treatment options chosen in prison.

The chapter also discusses the links between the length of time spent in prison, and the treatment options. The importance of arrangements to ease the transition from community to prison, and vice versa, are also reviewed. The overall aim must be to produce a consistent response to drug use, with good communication between the relevant helping agencies.

The extent of the problem – the national picture

Drug users pose an extensive problem for the prison service in the UK. Recent work estimated that as many as 6 500 dependent drug users entered prisons in England and Wales in 1989 (Maden et al., 1991). The total number of inmates is increasing, with figures for England and Wales showing a population of 45 900 in 1993 to 1994, increasing to 51 286 by 1995. The prison service anticipates that the population will be 55 700 by 2000 to 2001 (ACMD, 1996). In Scotland the average number of prisoners in custody is 6 000 males and 200 females. These figures represent approximately 1 in 1 000 of the overall UK population.

Estimates of drug misuse prior to incarceration have shown up to 43 per cent misusing drugs in the six months prior to arrest (Maden et al., 1992). In this survey 11 per cent were injecting and 11 per cent were drug-dependent, with 9 per cent using opiates. Cannabis was the main drug used – 34 per cent of cases. Figures about drug use inside the prison are less robust – relying heavily on self-report. However, studies do show drug use continuing in prison, with many users continuing to inject or even beginning to inject while in prison (Bridgwood and Malbon, 1995). Outside the prison setting, estimates of the number of drug users also vary widely. The Scottish police force estimates that between 50 and 70 per cent of the total crime they deal with is drug-related. The Scottish Crime Survey reveals that 23 per cent of all respondents have used illegal drugs. The figures for 16–19 year olds show an even higher prevalence of 39 per cent. It has been estimated that acquisitive crime by drug users costs from £58 to £864 million per year, representing up to one fifth of all acquisitive crime in the UK. These figures obviously link the healthcare issues of problem drug use with criminality.

The 1996 Task Force Review of drug services in England included services in prisons and made recommendations based on its findings. Though aimed at an English audience, it has relevance throughout the UK. In Scotland the 1995 report of the Ministerial Drug Task Force (HMSO, 1994) remains the strategic framework for tackling drug misuse. These two reports form the basis for a comprehensive drug strategy throughout the UK. Within the Prison Service many medical officers welcomed the HM Prison Service Drug Strategy (1995) which may be summarised in three statements. The strategy:

1 Advocates the development of a range of interventions for drug misusers, including use of methadone within prison which more closely reflects its use in the community.

2   States that for those assessed as opiate-dependent on admission and who are serving short sentences, this (methadone) might be provided on a maintenance basis but will normally be administered with a view to reducing the dose, leading to abstinence over time.
3   Introduces a random mandatory drug-testing programme for all inmates on reception, suspicion of drug use or who are identified as persistent drug offenders.

The aim is that each prison should develop a local strategy to reduce drug misuse with the strategy focussing on three areas:

1   Reduction of supply/availability of drugs in prison.
2   Reducing the demand for drugs in the prison and rehabilitating drug misusers.
3   Measures to reduce the potential for damage to the health of prisoners, staff and the community as a result of drug misuse.

Prison medical officers are therefore responsible for developing more comprehensive services for the drug users in their prison. We will now look at some of the practical aspects of assessing and treating a drug user in prison.

The consultation

The consultation is the foundation and cornerstone of most doctors' medical practice. It is the subject of many studies, and its essential elements are well documented. When considering a consultation by a drug user in prison it is essential to look at some vital elements. In reality, before, during and after the consultation, doctors have many expectations, and indeed requirements, of their patients. First, a legitimate medical reason for attending; then to accurately report their symptoms, their severity, their duration and the extent to which their lives are affected by them. Second, doctors require their patient to submit to an examination and possibly further investigations. During the examination cooperation is expected. The patient is expected to respond appropriately, not to fake symptoms or signs in order to lead one to a false conclusion. Third, doctors expect patients to accept their diagnosis and treatment plan. Fourth, they expect patients to take the treatment as conscientiously as possible and to return at a pre-arranged time. At that time they are expected to report honestly and accurately success, failure or whatever outcome has resulted.

With drug addicts in general, and within the prison service in particular, most of these expectations and requirements are quite simply not met. The prison consultation with drug users is centred around the prisoner/patient requiring drugs to alleviate their physical or mental misery. Obviously value judgements, morality and philosophy occur in medicine, but where possible they are best kept separate from medical practice. Doctors, however, will have a view as to what constitutes their patient's needs as opposed to their wants. Patients likewise have expectations that their needs are met and may or may not be prepared to differentiate needs from wants. These perspectives are represented in Figure 10.1.

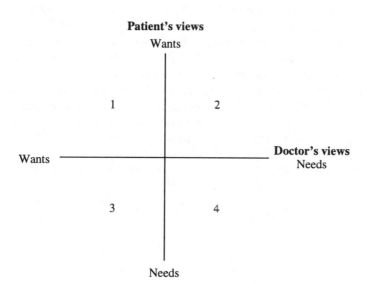

Figure 10.1

We can plot visually where the consultation is taking place with regard to these interfaces. The patient might well be satisfied with the doctor who had a treatment plan that was in quadrant one, but would they be satisfied with a treatment plan in quadrant four? Whether the patients' needs were being met, or if this was an appropriate practice of medicine, is a different proposition. It may be possible to practice in quadrant one for a short time, but wants would soon outstrip resources or safe prescribing levels and the word 'no' might have to appear for the first time. The question of setting limits and saying 'no' are particularly important in the prison setting, when consistency and fairness hold even more relevance than in the community or hospital practice. The balance between consistency and treating people as individuals may be as difficult as 'walking a tightrope' but feels more like 'walking the plank'.

Assessment and intervention

Assessment is performed not just through the consultation with the patient but in conjunction with many other agencies. It is vital to glean as much information from their GP, statutory and voluntary agencies, family and all those concerned in the patient's welfare. The assessment will lead to the formulation of the treatment plan to intervene when possible and will focus appropriate resources accordingly. The prison service must never ignore the treatment plan that has been in place in the community and, where possible, should continue that plan, especially when the sentence is short and reoffending is common. There will be transfer of patients between the prison and the community and indeed between different prisons. It is important, therefore, that there is consistency and continuity of practice within the prison service in line with the prevailing view of best practice in the community (ACMD, 1996). Within the community patients can choose doctors who will treat drug misuse. Within prisons such a choice does not exist. The prison doctor therefore must reflect best practice at all times. For the purpose of selecting appropriate treatments for drug users it is helpful to divide the inmates of the prison population into four broad groups:

1   Those in treatment programmes in the community who conform well with their treatment plan.
2   Those in treatment programmes in the community who continue to use illicit drugs.
3   Those who in the community are chaotic drug users and are not on a programme.
4   Those who misuse drugs for the first time while in prison.

The intervention would depend upon the following variables:

- The nature of the drug problem (severity, quantity of drugs, risk, etc.)
- The duration of drug misuse
- The length of time the prisoner will be in custody.

Where possible, the treatments are in line with those available in the community. Psychological support, counselling and regular review and monitoring are just as important as revision of a prescription. Resources, however,
are limited and it must be recognised that prisons are not hospitals, nor are
they drug treatment centres. At times, prisons who cope particularly with
remand prisoners may appear to be a cross between a casualty clearing
station and an acute psychiatric ward. The numbers of inmates passing
through some prisons, along with the rate of turnover, may preclude such
matching of prison programmes to those outside. However, essential considerations such as confidentiality should never be compromised. What is
practical may resemble what is represented in Table 10.1.

Table 10.1   Assessment and intervention: drug users in prison

Type of prisoner	Community programme	Chaotic illicit drug use
Remand prisoner	Continue maintenance if treatment to be continued on release	Detoxification programme
Convicted: less than 3 months sentence	Continue maintenance if treatment to be continued on release	Detoxification programme
Convicted: more than 3 months sentence	Detoxification programme	Detoxification programme
Convicted: presents during course of sentence	1 Detoxification 2 Symptomatic treatment 3 Stabilisation and reduction over less than 3 months	
Pregnant drug user	Consider maintenance if treatment to be continued on release	

This approach is in line with ACMD recommendations (ACMD, 1996). The
aims must be realistic. To expect all prisoners to remain drug-free in prison
and after release is frankly naive. Reduction programmes should reduce the

harmful effects of sudden drug withdrawal and help prisoners adopt the drug-free option. If prescribing is indicated it is important that the initial dosage is appropriate to avoid withdrawal symptoms, always bearing in mind that opiate withdrawal is subjectively severe but objectively mild (Gossop, Bradley and Philips, 1987). Drug misusers will display other behaviours which may require treatment. Many inmates will have underlying mental health problems which may be exacerbated by detoxification and may only become apparent when the patient is drug-free.

In the prison setting, long-term maintenance will not be appropriate except in exceptional circumstances. Support and harm reduction packages as well as counselling – both individual and group – is vital. It may be possible to utilise existing therapeutic programmes within the prison, but it must be acknowledged that comprehensive approaches using specialist personnel would be ideal.

Many inmates will have no access to a GP or primary health care services when they are discharged. Through-care is essential. In a drug treatment approach which promotes abstinence, it is unfortunate that the associated decreased tolerance significantly increases the risk of possibly fatal overdose post discharge. Involvement of outside agencies, therefore, is not just desirable but is vital in order to avoid potential unnecessary deaths. It is a controversial issue, but should the prison service be reintroducing opiate substitution to prisoners who have been detoxified prior to release? Such an approach is unlikely to gain support, but the alarming number of deaths shortly after discharge from prisons highlights the need to address the issue of transition back into the community. The 1996 ACMD report acknowledged that through-care was given little importance and stated that, until prisoners' needs on release were being addressed, no strategy for dealing with drug use in prison was likely to be successful (ACMD, 1996).

Whatever treatment programmes or personal care plans are devised for a patient in prison, consistency is paramount. Should prescribing be considered, it may not be possible to provide different levels of prescribing for inmates who are located together. The prison may not have the facilities to provide different units and drug-free areas to accommodate those at different stages in their treatment. The reality is that, if one individual obtains more prescribed drugs than others, it can lead to severe disruption and violence such as bullying and other intimidation. Individuals may be offered counselling and support to individual needs, but to prescribe an individual a different prescription from the others may lead to resentment, poor compliance and programme failures. It is probably not possible to prevent the influx of illicit drugs into prison, so regular and random urine analysis is required to improve compliance in treatment programmes.

The gender factor – male/female differences

It is facile to say that men are different from women. There are so many differences that in reality a separate book would be required, never mind a paragraph in a chapter. There are, however, important differences which can result in management problems (Loucks, 1998):

- *Separation from their family*   Women undoubtedly take this worse than men. They feel guilty that their children are suffering for their crime. They may run the risk of having their family being taken into care temporarily or permanently
- *Underlying mental health problems*   Over 30 per cent of women admitted to a Scottish Prison have previous admissions to a Psychiatric Hospital and a similar percentage has a history of self-harm
- *Sexual abuse*   Eighty per cent have been sexually abused by a male member of their own family
- *Experience of violence*   Over 50 per cent have witnessed violence as a child of such a nature that their mother received injuries – normally at the hands of their father or step-father – that required hospitalisation.

Women are much more likely to consult, and have been prescribed, psychotropic drugs by their GP, and are much more willing to talk about their difficulties. Working with female prisoners presents very different problems and requires a very different approach from those in male establishments. Treatment programmes for women in Canada and Australia are based much more on a therapeutic model, and are many years ahead of what is currently available in most prisons in the UK (Lightfoot and Lambert, 1992; Hurley and Dunne, 1991).

Conclusion

Opiate users do change over time. Treatment can lead to change. Psychological interventions and support, as well as medical treatments, including replacement prescribing, are of great importance. The treatment of drug misusers is emotive and liable to throw up discussion around the questions, 'Is it a medical problem?' or 'Does anything work for a self-induced condition?' Although the ultimate aim of most doctors is to achieve abstinence in their patients, because of the risk to the individual and possibly the public, harm reduction must be part of any treatment package. Intervention with the use of prescriptions for various agents, particularly methadone, have been the subject of many research articles. While not wishing to comment on the efficacy of any particular pharmaceutical intervention, it is best remembered that many of the side effects of drug withdrawal are psychological. Explanation, education and psychological support make a major difference in the success rates of treatment programmes.

There is evidence that those in treatment programmes are less likely to reoffend. It has been estimated that the risk of imprisonment is reduced by a factor of 5 if an individual is in a treatment programme as opposed to being a chaotic drug injector (Gruer, 1996 – personal communication). Research suggests that individuals on programmes engage in less criminal activity than drug users outside such programmes (Yancovitz et al., 1991). Studies done at HM Prison, Edinburgh, found that prisoners who had gone through a treatment programme were less likely to inject in prison than those who had not done so (Shewan, 1994). At present there is great variation between different prisons and the service offered to drug users within them (ACMD, 1996). The difficulties in providing a unified service that is in continuity with the community is made difficult by the fact that there is not widespread agreement on the treatment of problem drug use.

Prescribing of replacement drugs in prison is fraught with risks if not carried out in a safe and professional manner. Through-care agencies must pass accurate information to prison medical staff, allowing them to make appropriate objective decisions about care. Poor information at this stage will inevitably result in methadone being prescribed unsafely. A methadone death in prison would surely set back replacement prescribing in prisons for years. Indeed, recent reports of three such deaths occurring in Brixton prison in 1994 are now raising questions about the appropriateness of methadone prescribing in prison and highlight the need for tight systems to avoid abuses.

What must be fully appreciated is that any treatment is unlikely to shorten the process that naturally might take up to 20 years. However, the high mortality rate among those still injecting is alarming. While abstinence must be the ultimate goal, we must still consider harm reduction as the mainstay of treatment for drug users – in prison as well as the wider community. Indeed, prison may offer a first point of contact with stability which must not be squandered.

References

Advisory Council on the Misuse of Drugs (1996), *Drug Misusers and the Criminal Justice System. Part III: Drug Misusers and the Prison System – an Integrated Approach. Report by the Advisory Council on the Misuse of Drugs*, London: HMSO.

Bridgwood, A. and Malbon, G. (1995), *Survey of the Physical Health of Prisoners 1994*, Office of Population Census and Surveys, London: HMSO.

Gossop, M.R., Bradley, B., Phillips, G. (1987), 'An Investigation of Withdrawal Symptoms Shown by Opiate Addicts During and Subsequent to a 21 Day In-patient Methadone Detoxification Procedure', *Addictive Behaviours*, 12, 1–6.

HMSO (1995), *Tackling Drugs Together. A Strategy for England 1995–1998*, London: HMSO.

HM Prison Service (1995), *Prison Drug Strategy*, London: HMSO.

Hurley, W., Dunne, M.P. (1991), 'Psychological Distress and Psychiatric Morbidity in Women Prisoners', *Australian and New Zealand Journal of Psychiatry*, 25, 461–70.

Lightfoot, L. and Lambert, L. (1992), 'Substance Abuse Treatment Needs of Federally Sentenced Women. Report No. 2 (Draft)', Correctional Services, Canada.

Loucks, N. (1998), 'HMPI Cornton Vale'.

Maden, A., Swinton, M. and Gunn, J. (1991), 'Drug Dependence in Prisoners', *British Medical Journal*, 302, 880–1.

Maden, A., Swinton, M. and Gunn, J. (1992), 'A Survey of Pre-arrest Drug Use in Sentenced Prisoners', *British Journal of Addiction*, 87, 27–33.

Shewan, D., Gemmell, M. and Davis, J.B. (1994), 'Drug Use and Scottish Prisons', *Scottish Prison Occasional Paper No. 5*.

The Task Force to Review Services for Drug Misusers. Report of an Independent Review of Drug Treatment Services in England (1996), London: Department of Health.

Scottish Office Home and Health Department (1994), *Drugs in Scotland: Meeting the Challenge. Report of Ministerial Drugs Task Force*, Edinburgh: Scottish Office.

Yancovitz, S.R., Des Jarlais, D.C., Peyser, N.P., Drew, E., Friedmann, P., Trigg, H.L. and Robinson, J.W. (1991), 'A Randomised Trial of an Interim Methadone Maintenance Clinic', *American Journal of Public Health*, 81, 1185–91.

11 Recreational drug use and the club scene

Natalie Morel

Introduction

Drug use is common in UK dance culture. This chapter describes the development of dance culture and outlines aproaches to drug use, including the development of safer dancing guidelines. The example of a safer dancing project in the Highlands of Scotland is used to illustrate the value of local involvement, including the role of clubbers themselves.

A history

The dance music club scene of today is not a new phenomenon. Whatever the media might print or what politicians might banter about 'new evils' and 'wars', drug use and youth culture have been intertwined for decades. The present links between dance and drugs can be traced back as far as 'all-nighters' in Southport at the height of Northern Soul, a movement resulting from the rather obscure partnership between the white working-class youth of 1970s Northern England and African-American soul recordings from the previous decade. Amphetamine helped people to feel they could 'make the most' out of a dance night. A boost of energy was required after often having travelled for several hours or worked all day before reaching an event and then having to queue, before being engulfed by the sounds of soul and surrounded by people. When trying to place that initial incident, the first time music, movement and psychoactive substances came together, we could travel even further back in time. Consider the Shamanic rituals of Latin America, carried out for generations before being discovered by the rest of the world, or journey across to the African Continent, to tribal initiations and celebrations. On a recent visit to the theatre to see Les Ballets Africains, a professional dance company from Guinea, it was surprising to see so many moves that are replicated on dance floors across Britain.

Within these belief systems that have been passed on for hundreds of years, there exists a rational purpose and reasoned cost-benefit analysis for the behaviour of combining drug use and dance. Whether for the health and well-being of a community, to worship, or explain the unexplainable, the occurrence and purpose of drug use has been ingrained into the social and cultural organisations of communities, folded into the complexities of dealing with everyday life.

Freeze-frame. Now step back and watch the course of history speed past. Poets whose works form the part of many school childrens' education, supping laudanum from pewter goblets, their psychoactive experiences become the fodder of innumerable standard grade English Literature exams. The turn of the century; young dancers, singers, theatre goers; different layers of a class system mixing together in night clubs and 'gentlemen's establishments'; the ladies toilets littered with small cardboard pill boxes; the first reporting of social cocaine use on our shores. Forward a couple of decades, contributors to the fields of Art, Psychology, Literature and Science openly reporting their drug use as an influence upon their work. The late 1960s, early 1970s Britain sees substance use issues high on the generational agenda for the first time. The concept of recreational use is first described (Collin, 1997; Thornton, 1995). The movement of Northern Soul brings young people together in their hundreds. By the mid 1970s, people are not only talking about drug use, they are singing about it.

Throughout our history we can see that the attitudes and experience of substance use are interconnected with the desire to express new-found freedom in other life style areas (in a historical and/or personal sense). An escape, or alternative to the formal and often socially restrictive, due to the character of human existence or the nature of that particular social structure. Whether it is about the availability of sexual relationships, the recognition of being part of a different generation or the drive towards a sense of 'togetherness', a style of drug use can be symbolic of a generation's attitudes and values.

Towards today

The 1980s saw economic change, conservatism, individual attainment and competitive drive. Drug use moves away from hallucination towards stimulation. A push to get ahead or a rush to escape the fast moving environment. The late eighties sees again a youth push – the Acid House movement.

Young people in a fast-moving and constantly changing, constantly competing society. This is reflected in the style and speed of Acid House music and dance (Collin, 1997). The yellow smiley face, adopted as the movement's symbol, embellished on any and every item of clothing. Sweating heat, lights flashing at frightening speed to keep up with the beat, glowsticks, waving hands and whistles. There appeared to be a sense of belonging, a shared experience in the music. In hindsight it has been said that this sense of belonging was not only a reflection of attitudes, values and perceptions but also needs of the time being expressed.

From the late eighties to the present day. The links between the music and drug use of today have grown from the most diverse and heterogeneous melting pot since our expeditious history began. Some clubbers will tell you it started out in the gay disco diva scene of the USA. Others believe that underground clubs in Berlin played a part. There are even those convinced that the House Music of the 1990s stemmed from the free parties at the back of Sainsbury's in Ladbroke Grove, London. The generation of Italian and Piano tunes, balearic beats, taking clothes off to dress up and dance, was born (Champion, 1997). Wherever you plant the roots of today's club scene, two fundamental factors remain the same. First, the recreational drug use of the 1990s has its place in a wider historical context (Champion, 1997; Furlong and Cartmel, 1997). It is not a virus affecting a weaker society without warning, it is a formula of behaviours that can be closely linked to the attitudes, values and beliefs of parts of our communities. Second, this form of drug use and the clubbing scene that goes with it are unique in some ways from previous blasts of media, political and social interest in drug issues (Thornton, 1995). We shall go on to discuss this point further.

It's not just about a larger than usual number of people trying to get to London's Elephant and Castle on a Friday night, or people queuing around the block from Liverpool's Bold Street to Wolstenhome Square every Saturday. The influence of the clubbing scene upon our British culture goes much further. 'The Face' magazine is seen by many as a reflection of how the 'hippest' people in their late teens – twenties are living their lives. In the March 1997 issue, in a corner of page 215, appears an article called 'Modern Life is Rave-ish' (Grundy and Garret, 1997). It is a piece of writing that could be filed among any social anthropologist's research ! Albeit tongue in cheek, the article gives an illustration of some of the less obvious influences the so called E-Generation has had on all our lives: 'A sizeable percentage of the UK's prison population ... Drinking Lucozade even when you are not ill ... Blokes hugging each other and "nuffink" funny going on ... Pubs employing resident DJs ... La Luz (the night club in the television series "Brookside") ... The "rave episode" of Inspector Morse ... Buying anything apart from petrol at all-night garages ... The Daily Star's music page being called "Rave".' In a one-column article is crammed a wealth of information about how recreational drug use and its associated music have influenced our legal system, our attitudes to personal space, one might even say, sexuality, our attitudes towards alcohol and finally the television and newspaper media. Certainly not a small feat for something passed off as just another youthful fad. What we are really looking at is an entire industry. Major companies are buying into its style, the music, its imagery, the attitudes, to sell products. From ice lollies to cars, the force of today's youth culture reflected in the clubbing scene has stamped its mark in all our lives.

Drugs and clubbers

Studies worldwide have attempted to define clubbers in an effort to describe and quantify them as a target group. To quantify by age, gender, socio-economic status, even attitudinally, is to deny the first rule of being part of this group – i.e., anything goes (Barnard et al., 1996; Forsyth, 1995; Galt, 1997; Solowij and Hall, 1992). Anyone from doctor to student, right-wing nationalist to SWP member can be found on the dance floor. Attitudes on many subjects are left with the stewards at the doors. Talking to clubbers during the course of outreach work, one can see that attitudes to drug use are often similar (even between users and non-users) when views on wider issues can be from opposing camps of thought (the danger here is that 'street myths' about substance use spread and can become ingrained very quickly). However comparable worldwide patterns have emerged.

The majority of recreational users in clubs are aged 17–26 years, and more males than females admit to drug use. Crew 2000, a peer-led project working particularly with this form of drug use in their recent work at the 'Rezerection' event in Ingliston in Scotland, found that although 26–30 year-olds only made up seven per cent of the study group, all of this age group reported being current drug users (Mullen et al., 1997).

The illicit substances used by this group vary over time in terms of levels of use, but anecdotal evidence would indicate that the range of substances has stayed fairly constant over the last ten years (Galt, 1997). Ecstasy, amphetamine, cannabis and LSD are the preferred (illicit) substances (Mullen et al., 1997). Quantity and level of use may be influenced by regional differences in availability. The use of stimulant drugs reflects the energy associated with the music and social aspect of this way of life. Use often necessitates combining, enhancing and counteracting the different effects with a number of substances. Multiple drug use is viewed as normal and acceptable behaviour. Clubbers will often monitor their own and friends' behaviour in order to assess whether there is a need to use any more of the same or different substances throughout the night. Relaxants and depressants such as cannabis, alcohol or temazepam, can then be used to combat 'the come-down', the effects of excess energy output and fluid loss. Worth noting is the fact that alcohol is seen as the most commonly used drug amongst this group and is used in both the energetic and chill out setting.

Clubs and clubbers

For many of us the inside of a dance club in 1997 is what was portrayed in the media with thousands of pale-faced, bug-eyed sixteen-year-olds, palms raised in the air framed by waves of lasers in the typical snapshot style of the docu-drama. Scenes like this can be found in the real world, but it is certainly not the be all and end all image of today's clubbing chic. A group of people so stereotyped as a whole by many sources, are actually made up of several different groups. These groups can be differentiated by their style of dress, or the particular style of music they prefer; what was once House music went on to become house and techno, which further divided into hard-core, happy, hardfloor and intelligent techno, and so on.

For so long we (adults and professionals) have cast aside this particular lifestyle as being all of the same mould. In the meantime an entire culture has grown and developed. In this culture peer groups' issues can be discussed and individuals empowered. This empowerment comes from their knowledge of this movement and their ability to make decisions within and about it, whether that be drug taking or the choice of shoes they wear (Kellner, 1992).

So, away from the docu-drama image, what constitutes a club? The Scottish Drugs Forum have produced a set of guidelines (commissioned by the Ministerial Drugs Task Force) for running safer dancing events and providing better venues (Scottish Drugs Forum, 1995). Guidelines in England and Wales stemmed from Dr Russell Newcombe's work (Newcombe, 1992), but this is now being replaced with the London Drug Policy Forum's 'Dance 'til Dawn Safely' document (Baker, 1997; London Drug Policy Forum, 1996), modelled on the Scottish paper and sponsored by the Home Office. The Scottish guidelines include advice concerning security, health and safety, environmental issues, information provision and support. These are issues as relevant to those in attendance at an event as the music itself. They are as much a part of defining a club as the physical premises. If chill out facilities for people to cool down and relax are not available the atmosphere of an event can change, people can become confused or uncomfortable in a crowded environment. This can be just as important to non-drug-using clubbers.

Events can occur anywhere. Some years ago parties in the Scottish Highlands were held on top of hydroelectric dams. From a neighbour's house to
a purpose-built multiplex, a variety of physical environments could be
called a 'club'. This poses problems for any drug information provider –
where to provide the information! Whether in the rural community or a
small village in a far-flung corner, an inner city, or a market town one can
find a club, or a party where the bass of the music causes brick dust to fall.
The dance music scene and associated drug use can be found in some form
all over Britain.

Other views of clubbers

In light of legislative changes we can see how the concerns from different
agencies and many areas of society can influence this particular movement
and its ensuing behaviours. For example, the Criminal Justice and Public
Order Act (1994), and its references to people congregating to listen to 'repeti-
tive beats' can have an impact. Rt. Hon. Barry Legg, MP's Private Members
Bill on Public Entertainment Licensing, published in February 1997, gives a
new emergency licence revocation power, allowing for (immediate) closure
of a club on the basis of a report received from the Chief Police Officer that
drugs are being used on the premises. The existence of 'chill out' areas in
clubs, in Scotland as well as England, has been given as evidence for drug
use on the premises and lead to requests to close clubs providing such facilities. Many club patrons, DJs, owners and drug users complain that neither
they nor their representatives were afforded involvement during its development, resulting in what they see as uninformed practice. One clubber at the
Highland event 'Clear' (to be discussed further) said, 'Some people don't
seem to think that you can put drugs and a brain into the same body'.

It is a moral assumption that determines that drug use has to be equated
with dependency which, in turn, has to be equated with an inability to
control one's own behaviour. However unrealistic that may seem to drug
users and workers, it is a theme that is often only subtly conveyed in
discussions, but actions certainly speak louder than words. There is a distinct lack of useable communication channels for this group of young people to convey their messages and ideas to statutory bodies (Cripps, 1997;
Furlong and Cartmel, 1997). We are not even able to gain an insight into
their needs, because as a group they are rarely picked up by physical or
mental health services. Yet a wealth of youth media speaks the words,
paints the pictures (and sells the linked products) on drug issues. Unlike
alcohol and tobacco companies, who can provide revenue for publications,
illicit drugs are not usually given advertising space.This might give a freer
editorial attitude to discuss issues.

Visit a local newsagent, pick up a copy of *MixMag, The Face, Muzik Magazine, I-D* or even *Cosmopolitan*. Take a close look at the covers. If you haven't been thrown out for loitering yet, thumb through the contents. You will find glossiness, style, intelligence, and colour. You will find music items, clothes items, celebrity items, how to wear your hair this season, the famous barometer, what's in and what's out. Among it all you will find drugs information. 'Who was caught on camera with the X brand mix of alcohol and guarana' this week, will appear beside a mention that human ecstasy studies are underway in Britain. 'A phone call with Liam Gallagher ... Do you drink fruit teas or just get a kick out of caffeine?' The top ten places to be seen in London/Glasgow/Manchester will also be found hidden among cool club wear and the latest DJ/'celeb' sex scandal. This tells us five things:

1   Drug issues are prevalent in youth culture.
2   Whether people are users or non-users, they have access to some forms of drug information (rarely monitored or supported by statutory input).
3   Drug use does not stand alone, it is linked to other youth attitudes and behaviours.
4   Young people are open to discussing such issues.
5   A forum for raising awareness about drug issues already exists in the form of this type of media.

Raising awareness amongst clubbers

This is probably a good stage at which to define a clubber, within the context of 'safer dancing'. But first to define the term 'safer dancing' itself. The term really stems from work undertaken in Manchester, viewed by many as the capital of clubland at the end of the 1980s.

A series of events led to the then (and still now for many) controversial decision to develop harm-reduction strategies as ways of improving the safety of young people attending events. The Lifeline drugs project was brought in to provide realistic information, while Manchester City Council and Police Force worked to ensure that clubs were run more responsibly. Stewards were given training and wore clear, visible identification. It was at this time that Dr Newcombe produced the first 'Safer Dancing Guidelines' (Newcombe, 1992). Peanut Pete, a now infamous character among clubbers, was seen by the public for the first time in information leaflets on a variety of drug issues. It would not give the reader a complete picture of drug use and work in the club scene to refer so briefly to Lifeline and Peanut Pete, a source of inspiration as well as resources. In the preface to the book *If it Weren't For the Alligators*, Rowdy Yates refers to

Lifeline's meandering history: 'Often, I think, we were groping around in the dark. Alone. Speaking in Slogans. Dream Dancing. Embarrassed or frightened of awakening our fellow slumberers. Stubbing our toes in the pitch black. Gripping our barked shins and hissing under our breath'. He describes a process that many drug issue-based projects go through, fighting taboos, questioning actions and rationalising to unseen funding sources. Along with other 'founders', over its 21-year history Lifeline has had its hand in working across the drug use 'spectrum' and now epitomises the move towards involving the target group in understanding and promoting clear drugs information.

Here was the framework for an approach to what is now commonly known as recreational drug use. With this in mind, and in conjunction with the development of a strong youth following, we can see again that clubbers are informed about drug issues from varied sources, and often have liberal attitudes towards drug issues. These attitudes are not illogical, in that they are the culmination of considerable experience, information gathering and sharing. Indeed, in the introduction to the SDF's guidelines for good practice at dance events (Scottish Drugs Forum, 1995), Lord James Douglas Hamilton states, 'We do not want to deprive young people of a source of entertainment, but we want them to enjoy themselves safely. This is their right and I am sure that young people will increasingly demand high standards in the venues they use.'

We are certainly dealing with a shrewd consumer, how do we serve their complex needs? Our response can be broken down into three areas: Drug, Set and Setting.

- *Drug*   We can provide informed data about substances, their positive and negative consequences (Scottish Drugs Forum and Enhance RDP, 1996).
- *Set*   We can research the needs of this specific group, or set. By using the following guiding principles (Stead et al., 1996), we can inform, evaluate and improve practice:
  a) positioning – the positioning of drug use in young people's lives is characterised by stylish imagery versus its illicit nature. This tension and contradiction enhance its attractiveness; it is both alternative and accessible;
  b) breadth – our responses need to be as broad as the factors influencing drug use;
  c) targeting – clubbers are a separate group of drug users (they do not often consider their use to be either chaotic or dependant) with different needs.

● *Setting* Raising the awareness of club-goers, although a complex process in itself, only solves one part of the equation. When discussing the Drug–Set–Setting model in the instance of an individual's use, the setting makes reference to many different factors; when we refer to it in terms of the clubbing scene or type of drug use as a whole, the defining factors can be stretched even further. 'Setting' outlines the environment in which behaviours occur. This might be the physical surroundings of the club itself, but it refers to more than just a building. Going back to the SDF 'Safer Dancing Guidelines' we can see how multi-faceted that definition can be, including supplies of drinking water, air temperature and overcrowding. All are part of the surroundings, part of the setting which can influence behaviour. From first aid facilities to information provision, all these factors have to be considered by club owners and promoters. The cost in terms of time and people resources, as well as financially for training and supporting staff in these areas, can make this seem an impossible option. But, as patrons become more aware, it is in the interest of owners and promoters to be as well informed. In what is becoming a more and more consumer-driven market, it is possible for us to promote such training as an investment.

In this sense it is possible to give a tangible example of harm reduction as a balance of care, control and education. Statutory organisations, paramedical staff, police and health/drug workers all have knowledge to share, either in the form of training club staff or a presence at events. Responses to these issues need to be multi-agency, to ensure that existing knowledge and information is continually exchanged and resources are shared, and to ensure that owners and promoters can see what can be gained from implementing such guidelines.

Case example – the CLEAR project

Needs assessment work in the Highlands of Scotland provided information about dependant drug use and related service provision, but also identified a level of 'recreational use' comparable to levels of use in urban areas, a conclusion also drawn in a study by Gardner and Peck (1996) of drug use in the Scottish Highlands. This group of users rarely feel they experience the type of drug-related problems with which they believe existing services can offer assistance, resulting in only sparsely available information.

In order to investigate this form of drug use in a Highland context, funding from the National Services Division of the Scottish Office was used to support further work. From existing information, and from work in other geographical areas (Galt, 1997), it was felt likely that the target group would be relatively young (15–26 years) and that many users would be linked to the dance music scene. With these two initial parameters set, the next task was to find out where these people socialised in Highland and what they did while there. Health promotion staff donned their trainers to attend local events. Initial contacts were made through conversations, buying drinks, helping to load and unload sound systems! We got to know local DJs, clubbers and promoters, and within weeks Health Promotion had set up an information stall at a weekly event 'Jungle Palace'. By placing ourselves next to the cigarette machine, patrons were able to glance over at the information available without committing themselves. At our first event, much of the real discussion took place in the ladies' toilets, where we were able to offer plastic bottles and cups to replenish water supplies. At subsequent stalls, once we had become a regular feature, people would come up and openly ask questions, tell us what was currently available, and eat all the sweets and mints we had on offer (our first attempt at a marketing approach, to 'make the stall appealing').

It was 'put around' by word of mouth that Health Promotion wanted to find out more about the Highland Club Scene, and a group of interested parties was brought together, including local clubbers, DJs and promoters, to form the CLEAR group. The name was chosen by the group to represent their willingness to give honest, clear information and to outline their need for clear, honest, factual information in return. After many long discussions in a variety of settings, the group decided that the best way to get existing information over to clubbers and get the story on their views of drug use was to hold a dance event. It was felt that a flagship dance event could also involve raising the awareness of professionals in the field as well as those working with young people in other settings. The group wanted to involve existing agencies in Highland, but also groups throughout Scotland who worked in clubs and at events.

With an overall aim of 'developing an understanding of young people within the context of recreational drug use and the dance music scene', the three main tasks of the initiative were:

- To organise a multi-agency forum for free discussion around recreational drug issues and the club scene
- To run a flagship safer dancing event as an opportunity to provide young people with health information, relevant professionals with information regarding safer dancing guidelines and the health board with unbiased information about young people's recreational drug use and attitudes
- To produce an information resource based on the needs of young people in Highland.

We were able to secure the boardroom at Highland Health Board's headquarters for the multi-agency forum. Already feeling empowered by the support for the proposal, the CLEAR group felt quite comfortable about meeting on such formal territory. As well as curiosity, the kudos of the setting was an enticement for other agencies to attend. Representatives from Northern Constabulary, NHS Trusts, local support groups for alcohol users and ex-young offenders, as well as staff and promoters from local clubs, were present. The full CLEAR group, as well as friends and interested clubbers, were also in attendance. Presentations looked at issues around health and drug use, consumer trends in alcohol and drug use and safer dancing guidelines. Ensuing discussions were frank and open. For some organisations, it was the first time they had sat around the same table with young people (some of whom openly stated that they were drug users) on equal terms. Taking people out of their normal setting and placing them in a unique context proved to be a positive move for all concerned. It was an opportunity to dispel myths and seek clarity and new information as well as support for the dance event. Cripps (1997) argues that 'The obstacles to working with young people around drug issues can be summed up in one word: Adults. Professionals, parents and adult institutions all face one major problem in trying to access young people – we haven't a clue what they are doing'.

After this meeting the CLEAR group felt that they had gone part of the way to bridging this gap. In order to build on what had happened so far and to ensure we maintained our growing credibility, the organisations Crew 2000 and Enhance, currently working in Edinburgh and Glasgow respectively, were asked to add their experience to the project. Both groups include peer-led support and harm reduction in their philosophies. With a wealth of knowledge in outreach work and the club scene, their support was inestimable in terms of experience, information and networking among young people and other organisations. Northern Constabulary were involved from the early days of the project, offering assistance in developing user-friendly and effective security policies and ensuring safety. Highland Health Board provided administrative support to the group. Throughout, the CLEAR group provided organisations with clear messages and were surprised at their effectiveness. It was not to be promoted as a drug-free 'rave'; this it was felt would discourage a large percentage of our target group – users and non-users – because of the connotations that they link with such an event (the emphasis being on control at the expense of care and education). Instead, clubbers would be informed by way of posters and leaflets that the security policy involved searching everyone that entered the premises and offered the opportunity to 'opt out' and return their ticket.

Local DJ talent gave us ample choice for the whole affair. But a bigger name would also be required to reflect the event's size and credibility. With this in mind we contacted agents and explained the nature and purpose of the dance event. Many were willing to offer their client's services, and eventually we settled upon a national name – David Holmes. His particular style was not dissimilar to the type of techno preferred elsewhere in Highland, but the slightly slower pace was favoured in order to introduce clubbers to a less intense pace of music. With Health and Safety inspections completed we also procured a venue.

Advertising the event presented Health Promotion with a whole new set of problems. The CLEAR group made it quite apparent that a mention in the Health Promotion Department's monthly newsletter was not going to secure any ticket sales. Posters were placed all over the region in record shops, youth clubs, cafés and corner shops. There were slots on local radio, faxes and phone calls to national radio dance music shows, music magazines, local papers – and there was flyering of other clubs. All these were new approaches to marketing a health promotion concept. Because we wanted the event to represent an ideal situation, we did not feel the need to overtly promote the Health Board's links to the project until people arrived at the event. Some groups (and some of the post-event media coverage) felt this was a covert approach. The CLEAR group felt that funding was the only influence the involvement of statutory agencies had on the style of the event and (as with the previously mentioned concept of a 'drug-free rave') it could incorrectly bias the target group. Talking to people in the following months who had not attended the event, supported the group's concerns. One individual had 'heard' that everyone who attended would be arrested because the Health Board wanted to 'get rid' of drug users, illustrating the difficulties of communication with such groups.

A clubber and graphic designer involved in the group produced flyers for the event. This showed a bottle of water with a CLEAR label on it, the other side gave details of the event. The image was used to illustrate that all clubbers have to replace lost fluids when dancing. The end product was stylish enough for people to stick on their bedroom walls and yet still have associations with health messages.

Free buses from every Highland locality brought over 700 young people to the biggest regional event for years. Security staff greeted clubbers who had viewed the security policy while queuing. Members of Crew 2000 and the CLEAR group gave away free T-shirts with the message 'Eat Fruit – Drink Juice – Live to Dance' emblazoned across the back, while others handed out questionnaires to clubbers. The questionnaires were designed to take advantage of the opportunity to gain information about attitudes and drug use. Despite concerns before the event, a one on two sample was achieved with no spoiled papers. This provided invaluable information which added to the value of the event.

As expected, drug use was common. Ninety-two per cent used alcohol, and 75 per cent cannabis. Amphetamine (66 per cent) and ecstasy (63 per cent) were also commonly used. Results indicated that 84 per cent of clubbers felt that drug users should have access to drugs information which they wanted for safety reasons (69 per cent), or to help them to make informed choices (23 per cent). When asked the same question about non-drug users, again 84 per cent felt that they, too, needed access to drug information. Similar reasons were given again of safety (34 per cent), education (43 per cent) and also to prevent prejudice against drug users (16 per cent). Friends (63 per cent) were given as the main source for drugs information, with television the second most important information source (38 per cent) Over half of the respondents had come across 'good' drugs information leaflets. Good leaflets were 'stylish', 'balanced', 'had cartoons in them', 'came as postcards'.

The event had an even split of males and females, and there were no significant differences between the reported levels of drug use. Three quarters of those completing questionnaires were aged between 15 and 25 years old but, although only making up less than a quarter of the numbers, those aged between 25 and 36 years plus reported a significantly higher level of regular use across all substances mentioned, age being the only area to show any statistically significant differences.

The results have shown that there are many different sources from where clubbers get their drug information. The issue is not simply about telling them that drugs can be bad for them, as there are a variety of other issues that need to be addressed – in health and social areas. It is about time that we took notice of what type of information this group want and made ourselves (adults and professionals) more of a useful resource to this target group.

It was not only the clubbers who had closed doors opened to them through this event. Agencies from all over Highland that include working with young people in their remit were invited to attend a pre-event presentation. For many it was the first time they had been to a dance event – a daunting experience – but many had questions for the young volunteers working at the Crew 2000 and Enhance stalls, as well as being rather surprised at the sight of people pushing around a pram full of (free) condoms! It was a chance to see the inside of one part of an illusive youth culture.

Local and national press covered the event. Some journalists later spoke of having attended in order to be the first to get the 'worst scenario' story. They were surprised by the candour of these young people, their existing knowledge and eloquence about issues, their appreciation and acceptance of services on offer, and press coverage was positive.

When the CLEAR group met after the event, the main theme was one of empowerment – not only of the group, but also of the people they had worked with and people who had attended the event. Group members felt that they would be more able to approach services (club owners or health services) with issues and ideas in the future. The CLEAR project showed young people and adults alike that the community of young people in Highland have an active role to play in defining and providing services for their needs. CLEAR group members are already acting as safer dancing consultants to events throughout the area, others are involved in progressing user involvement in other projects and development of a drug issues book is ongoing. One group member who had always been ready to expect the worst when dealing with, in his words, 'big companies and important people' summed up why the project had worked for him, 'It's about giving us space to decide what we want. Being honest about what we can have. Opening channels for us to fight for what we need and ... Giving us the things we need to do what we can do'.

Conclusions

It is easy for professionals to regard dance culture as one phenomenon, but it is not homogeneous. Approaches have to be based on work with local clubbers. This work must itself respect the clubbers. Contacts based on the assumption that professionals have all the knowledge and clubbers need only to listen will not work. Material and initiatives must be tailored to the local club scene, and revised frequently to take account of changing patterns and trends.

References

Baker, O. (1997), 'Dawn Raid', *DrugLink*, **12**, (1).

Barnard, M., Forsyth, A. and McKeganey, N. (1996), 'Levels of Drug Use Among a Sample of Scottish Youth', *Drugs; education, prevention and policy*, **3**, (1), 81–9.

Champion, S. (ed) (1997), *Disco Biscuits*, London: Sceptre.

Collin, M. (1997), *Altered State*, London, New York: Serpents Tail.

Cripps, C. (1997), 'Workers with Attitude', *DrugLink*, May–June, 15–17.

Forsyth, A. (1995), 'Ecstasy and Illegal Drug Design: A New Concept in Drug Use', *The International Journal of Drug Policy*, **6**, (3), 193–209.

Furlong, A. Cartmel, C. (1997), *Young People and Social Change. Individualisation and Risk in Late Modernity*, Buckingham: Open University Press.

Galt, M. (1997), 'Illicit Drug Availability in Rural Areas and Attitudes Towards Their Use – Young People Talking', *Health Education Journal*, **56**, 17–34.

Gardner, B.W. and Peck, D.F. (1996), 'Drug Use in the Scottish Highlands', *Drugs; Education, Prevention and Policy*, **3**, 3, 285–94.

Grundy, G. and Garret, S. (1997), 'Modern Life is Rave-ish', *The Face*, March.

London Drug Policy Forum (1996), *Dance till Dawn Safely*, London: LDPF.

Kellner, D. (1992), 'Popular Culture and the Construction of Post Modern Identity', in S. Las and J. Freidman (eds), *Modernity and Identity*, Oxford: Blackwell.

Mullen, R., Sherval, J. and Skelton, L. (1997), 'Young People's Drug Use at Rave/Dance Events', Edinburgh: Crew 2000.

Newcombe, R. (1992), *Safer Dancing Guidelines for Good Practice*, Manchester: Lifeline.

Scottish Drugs Forum (1995), *Safer Dancing: Guidelines for Good Practice*, Glasgow: Scottish Drugs Forum.

Scottish Drugs Forum and Enhance Recreational Drugs Project (1996), *The Survivor's Guide to Drugs and Clubbing*, information leaflet, Glasgow: Scottish Drugs Forum.

Solowij, N. and Hall, W. (1992), 'Recreational MDMA Use in Sydney: A Profile of Ecstasy Users and Their Experiences with the Drug', *British Journal of Addiction*, 87, 1161–72.

Stead, M., Hastings, G. and Tudor Smith, C. (1996), 'Preventing Adolescent Smoking: A Review of Options', *Health Education Journal*, 55, 31–54.

Thornton, S. (1995), *Club Cultures, Music, Media and Sub-cultural Capital*, Cambridge: Polity Press.

12 Sex workers
Moira C. Paton

Introduction

Sex work is known as the 'oldest profession', perhaps one of the most famous historical figures being Mary Magdalene. In *Whores in History: Prostitution in Western Society*, Roberts (1992) charts the social history of sex work back to the second millennium BC. In more recent times recognition of prostitution as a social problem emerged in the middle of the nineteenth century (Darrow, 1984). 'Respectable' society feared that prostitutes would spread syphilis (then incurable) to their customers, and so into the wider population. Thus, although 'mortality rates from syphilis were relatively small when compared with diseases of poverty such as TB' (Roberts, 1992), the first Contagious Diseases Act in 1864 provided for the compulsory examination of women working as prostitutes in naval ports and garrison towns.

The advent of HIV has once again put sex workers centre stage. It is sometimes difficult to believe that we have learned a great deal about the transmission of infection and about successful and unsuccessful interventions, since the Contagious Diseases Act failed to prevent the enormous spread of STDs before and during the First World War. It seems as though many have not recognised that (i) by definition, sex work involves a client as well as a sex worker, and (ii) that risk is not associated with belonging to a certain group or category, but with specific behaviours. The media regularly portray prostitution *per se* as a transmission route for HIV. That the real issue is unsafe sex, and that this is practised by a large proportion of the population, is less frequently recognised.

As Morgan Thomas (1992) has pointed out, 'people focus on the prostitute as though prostitution were something that prostitutes do on their own

169

and amongst themselves' (p. 71). In fact, as Plant (1990) notes, clients vastly outnumber sex workers in all settings. Commercial sex is a worldwide phenomenon, and there is a high level of demand for paid sexual services.

In relation to HIV transmission in Africa and the eastern United States, Conant (1988) comments that 'it is evident that continued use of the prostitute label not only distorts the complexity of the social factors of HIV transmission but also, because of the pejorative nature of the label, directs attention to women's immorality as a source of HIV transmission rather than men's sexual adventuring.' For these reasons, the terms sex work or sex industry, and sex worker will be used, except when quoting others. Appropriate terminology for everyday use in a service setting should be determined locally and in conjunction with sex workers themselves.

This chapter is primarily concerned with sex workers and not clients for the simple reason that little work on clients has been carried out. That which has (e.g., Barnard et al., 1993), has tended to focus on describing the characteristics of clients and estimating numbers. There is little to distinguish between descriptions of clients and those of a general cross-section of the sexually active male population.

Most of the available evidence relates to female sex workers. There may be a number of reasons for this, not least the fact that women comprise the majority of the visible sex work scene. For this reason, the chapter focuses on issues relating to female sex workers. Issues pertaining to male sex workers are discussed where relevant and where data is available.

Sex is sometimes traded for drugs and other goods outside what we would recognise as the commercial sex scene. While this chapter is focussed primarily on those involved in commercial sex work, many of the issues raised will be pertinent for other drug users.

The chapter is aimed at those who wish to undertake needs assessment work, develop or improve services for IV drug-using sex workers in their area, or commission research activity in this field. It examines the range of issues involved, considers what is currently known and provides some pointers for those wishing to design and implement local services. While the risks of HIV and other infections imply a need to provide targeted harm-reduction strategies and services, people who use drugs, are involved in the sex industry, or are associated with both activities, have as much right to mainstream social and health care services as any other member of the public. The emphasis nowadays is on 'needs-led', 'people-centred' services, which address issues of accessibility in the widest sense of the term. That this chapter focuses on the needs of intravenous drug-using sex workers in no way implies that it is only this sub-group of sex workers who may need specially tailored services, or who may find mainstream services stigmatising or inaccessible. All services used by the population at large must ensure that they are 'user-friendly' and accessible. This is discussed further below.

Current understanding

Working environment

In general terms, sex workers, whether male or female, can be grouped into three categories according to their working environment:

1 Those who work from the streets, bars and discos, and who seek out their clients.
2 Those who work primarily in and from a specific building, e.g. saunas, massage parlours, private flats and brothels.
3 Those who work through escort agencies, visiting massage services, and through media advertising or the placement of cards in telephone boxes (Morgan Thomas, 1990; Waldorf and Murphy, 1990).

The most frequently requested services are vaginal sex, oral sex and masturbation. (Matthews, 1990; Blakey and Frankland, 1994)

Much of the available evidence shows that, on the whole, the stereotypical image of the streetworker and her pimp is not reflected in the reality across much of the UK. While anecdotal evidence suggests no difference in this respect between drug-using and non-drug-using women, data is thin on the ground. Some sex worker women will work to provide money for a partner's drugs. For some of these women, it may make little difference that her partner does not fit the common image of the pimp.

Blakey and Frankland (1994), in a study based in Glamorgan, note that some women moved from street work to agencies and parlours and back. The drug-using status of these women was not reported. It has been suggested that heavy drug users may be more likely to work from streets and bars than from saunas or massage parlours for two reasons. First, that sauna or parlour managers may not be keen to engage someone with a known or obvious drug habit. Second, it may be that heavy users will not find it convenient to work regular, set hours, and may find that they can earn more when they negotiate their own fee and no cut of their takings has to be passed over to an agent (Harcourt and Philpot, 1990).

There is some evidence that IV drug use is more common among those who work from streets or bars than among other sex workers (e.g., Morgan Thomas, 1990). This would certainly seem to be confirmed anecdotally, but little data is available on sex work within saunas and massage parlours, or on those whose initial contact with a client is by telephone. Such groups are particularly 'hidden' and thus difficult to research. A recent exception is the work in Glamorgan referred to above (Blakey and Frankland, 1994). That study was in contact with 200 women who worked primarily from massage parlours or escort agencies. These women represented 49 per cent of all sex workers contacted.

Population size

It is very difficult to assess the full extent of the overlap between IV drug use and the sex industry because both are largely hidden activities. Engaging in sex work is in itself not illegal, unlike soliciting or procuring sex and living from the 'immoral' earnings of the sex industry. Figures recorded by the criminal justice system reflect local policing and charging policies rather than provide accurate counts. For example, of the 1 046 offences relating to prostitution recorded by police in Scotland in 1995, 78 per cent were recorded in Glasgow, as were 86 per cent of both the 761 court appearances made and the 743 cases proved (Home Department, The Scottish Office). Evidence from survey-based work suggests that these figures mask the true extent and geographical spread of the sex industry (see later in this chapter). The statistics do not differentiate between those charged with procuring or soliciting for sex, but it is known that sex workers are far more likely than clients to be cautioned or brought before the Courts. As will be seen later, regional variations in policy can impact on the extent to which local service interventions can address issues of harm reduction.

The available evidence suggests a great deal of local variation in the size and situation of the sex-working population, and in the overlap with the drug-using population. For example:

- In 1990, 59 per cent of female sex workers using a drop-in service in Glasgow city centre were injecting drug users (McIver, 1992)
- McKeganey et al. (1992) estimated that around 1 150 women worked on the streets of Glasgow over a 12-month period. Seventy-one per cent of the 206 women interviewed were injecting drug users. By 1996, the figure was 75 per cent. (McKegany et al., 1996)
- A study in London in 1991 found 33 per cent of women contacted through street-based outreach work were injecting drugs (Rhodes et al., 1991)
- An Edinburgh-based study in 1989 found 25 per cent of their sample to be drug users (Morgan Thomas et al., 1989)
- 18 per cent of a Glamorgan sample (Blakey and Frankland, 1994)

reported having injected drugs in the previous year. It should be noted, however, that only 51 per cent of that sample were working on the streets, and thus direct comparisons cannot be drawn with studies of street-based workers.

The little evidence available (e.g., Morgan Thomas et al., 1989) suggests that injecting drug use may be more common among women sex workers than among their male counterparts. Many sex workers who inject drugs did so before becoming involved in sex work, and the main reason for engaging and continuing in sex work is in support of their (or a partner's) habit (e.g., McIver, 1992). Poly-drug use may be a factor among sex workers, some drugs being taken to ensure 'fitness' for work at a given time (e.g., amphetamines taken to counteract the sluggishness induced by barbiturates).

HIV and other infections

Injecting drug use and unprotected sexual activity are the most important routes for the transmission of HIV in Europe. Are sex workers at increased risk of HIV or other sexually-transmitted diseases? What is the impact of the overlap between drug use and sex work?

Sex work plays a significant role in the transmission of HIV in certain African countries (see McKeganey et al., 1992). This is probably not the case in Britain (Plant, 1990). Differential rates of transmission reflect the different social, cultural and political contexts within which the sex industry operates. However, although 'there are few studies which have systematically investigated the epidemiology of HIV prevalence among injecting drug using and non drug using sex workers, or among drug injectors involved in sex work' (Rhodes, 1994, p. 28), there is some evidence to suggest that HIV is more prevalent among drug-injecting sex workers than among non-drug-injecting sex workers. McKeganey et al., (1992) tested saliva from 159 street-working women in Glasgow. Four were HIV positive, all positive samples coming from those reporting involvement in drug-injecting. Those testing positive represented 3.5 per cent of their total drug injecting sample. The researchers estimate that around 29 HIV positive drug-using women may work on the streets of Glasgow over a 12-month period.

An Edinburgh study (Morgan Thomas, 1990), based on self-reporting, found five male sex workers from a sample of 102 reporting an HIV positive status. All had injected drugs and reported having shared needles with someone known to be HIV positive. Twelve women from a total female sample of 103 reported being HIV positive. Nine of these reported injecting drugs and having shared with someone known to be HIV positive. Three women attributed their infection to sexual transmission, all having had sexual partners known to be HIV positive. Few studies have looked at the prevalence of other sexually-transmitted diseases among drug-injecting sex workers. A study in London (Ward et al., 1993) found that STD infection (including HIV) was not associated with duration of sex work, numbers of clients or reports of condom failures, but was associated with youth and with increasing numbers of non-paying sexual partners.

The risks of unsafe drug use in terms of the transmission of both Hepatitis B and C are well recognised, and increased risk, particularly of Hepatitis B, has been linked to unprotected sexual activity (BMA, 1996; British Liver Trust Information leaflet). There has been little work on the extent to which these infections are prevalent amongst drug-using sex workers.

Risk behaviour

We have already noted that it is engaging in specific activities which increase sex- and drug-related health risks, not the fact that one belongs to a particular group or sub-group. There is a fair body of evidence to suggest that sex-working women are generally diligent about condom use during the course of their work. The work by Taylor et al. (1993) in Glasgow found that almost 100 per cent reported condom use with clients. A study of female drug users involved in sex work in London notes 70 per cent reports of always using condoms with clients (Rhodes et al., 1994). Blakey and Frankland (1994) note that the 100 per cent self-reporting use of condoms in all commercial encounters found in Glamorgan may reflect a 'reluctance on the part of the women interviewed to give an "unacceptable" answer'. However, these findings are consistent with those from a number of other studies from around the country (e.g., McKeganey et al., 1992; Ward et al., 1993).

Of more concern is the consistent finding that male clients continue to press for unprotected sex. In Glamorgan, for example, 92 per cent of women reported that they had been asked for unprotected sex, and 86 per cent that clients offered more money for sex without a condom (Blakey and Frankland, 1994). In Edinburgh, two-thirds of male sex workers and three-quarters of female sex workers reported requests for unprotected sex (Morgan Thomas, 1990). Possibly sensitive to the perceived unacceptability of such behaviour, few sex-working women report acceding to clients' demands for unprotected sex. It may be that drug-using sex workers are more likely to agree to such activity due to the additional and perhaps more immediate need for money for drugs. Most evidence for this is anecdotal but compelling. Matthews (1990) records one woman: 'I'll do anything to make my money when I'm turkeying ... you have to take that risk when you need the money.'

One fifth of the women in the Glamorgan study reported having experienced condom failure in the course of the previous month's work, the same proportion found in Edinburgh (Blakey and Frankland, 1994; Morgan Thomas, 1990). Again, there is insufficient evidence to judge whether sex workers are more at risk of condom failure than are other sexually active women. The higher rate of sexual activity involved will in itself increase this risk.

Many writers have commented upon the extent of unprotected sexual activity within the general population. Rhodes (1994) notes that 'levels of condom use among drug injectors and their sexual partners are similar to those reported in the heterosexual population as a whole'. He further reports that, similar to the population at large, injecting drug users are more likely to use condoms with casual partners than with primary partners.

Although there is little published evidence, it may be that sex-working drug injectors are more likely to engage in unprotected sex with partners than are drug injectors not involved in sex work. A need to differentiate between work and personal life could be a factor. Day and Ward (1990) quote a female sex worker 'How could I? [use a condom with her partner] He would be like a client. It's different for people who don't work' [i.e. sex work]. Few studies have compared injecting behaviour between sex workers and non-sex workers. We know that while the sharing of needles has generally declined over recent years, the impact of situational factors on unsafe injecting behaviour is significant. Perception of risk has more to do with interpersonal and social factors than individual ones (Rhodes, 1994). Little is known of sex workers' perceptions of their sex-related risks, and whether or how these might impact on perceptions of injecting behaviour risks. Further work should focus attention on exploring the social and situational factors which impact on such perceptions and behaviour. It is certainly important, and urgent, that we address the cultural, societal and interpersonal factors which affect sexual behaviour. We have, thus far, been more successful in reducing risk-related injecting behaviour than in tackling unsafe sex (Rhodes, 1994). As already noted, this may involve additional complexities in the case of sex workers in terms of their relationships with non-commercial partners.

Violence

Research by Blume (1990) suggests that women who use drugs may be at more risk of violence or rape than non-drug-using women. The old double standard was much in evidence in her research, with an intoxicated male being held less responsible for rape than one who was not intoxicated. A woman who was intoxicated was, on the other hand, thought to be more to blame for her rape than was a non-intoxicated woman in the same circumstances. Involvement in the sex industry may mean being at even greater risk of physical and sexual violence. Many writers and researchers have commented on the levels of violence experienced by sex workers (e.g., McIver, 1992). Since 1991, seven women sex workers were murdered in the course of their work in Glasgow alone.

Use of health and other services

Many injecting drug users, and women drug users in particular, are reluctant to seek health care. The greater stigma experienced by women drug users, as reflected in the criminal justice system, and by their fears of losing care of their children, may influence the extent to which female drug users seek help (Pilley et al., 1997). Although there is little published evidence, it is reasonable to guess that drug-injecting women who are also involved in sex work face even more stigma than their non-sex-working sisters. It may be doubly difficult to seek help in such circumstances.

Summary

The main risks for female injecting sex workers are therefore in their personal lives, rather than in their working lives. There are five areas where those drug users who are also sex workers may face additional risk:

1   An even further increased risk of rape and sexual assault.
2   A potential increased likelihood of acceding to client demands for unsafe sex.
3   An increased incidence of condom failure.
4   An increased risk, in some areas and depending on local policing policies, of being brought to the attention of the police as a drug user, and all that entails.
5   Double stigma and, consequently, a potentially increased reluctance to seek health care.

Providing a service

Before going on to consider the question of appropriate and accessible service provision, a brief look at social policy issues is helpful.

Social policy issues

We have already noted that the sex industry has been of concern to policy makers since the mid-nineteenth century, although attempts to proscribe sex work activity have been made since the times of earliest recorded history (Roberts, 1992). Morgan Thomas (1992) summarises the 'solutions' to the perceived threat to public health which have been attempted over the last hundred years or so as: (i) regimentation, (ii) abolition, (iii) prohibition and (iv) toleration. Like many other writers she notes that such attempts have not enhanced public health: 'All these strategies have attempted in some way to regulate or eradicate the sex industry. In addition, they have failed to improve the situation of the sex worker with regard to preventing the transmission of STDs within commercial sexual contacts, and in many cases have made it worse. The primary aim should be to control STDs, including HIV infection, and not to control the sex worker.'

The impact of local policing and charging policies has already been mentioned. Anecdote suggests that it is not so long ago that women walking in the streets of many towns and cities were regularly stopped and searched for condoms. If found, these were taken to imply that the woman was a sex worker and were confiscated, the woman often being cautioned or charged. Not a helpful way of protecting health! It is thought that this happens less frequently nowadays, but some police forces, as evidenced by the statistics cited earlier, still devote substantial resources to cautioning and charging sex workers. Such activity can force sex workers into more covert and dangerous situations. Furthermore, being charged and fined means sex workers have to work for longer periods of time to meet the additional financial burden, not to mention the added strains on already hard-pressed local courts. This may also encourage compliance with clients' demands for unprotected sex, for which higher prices can be charged. Such policies may merely force sex workers to travel further afield to other towns and cities where they perceive the possibility of an easier working life (Freeman, 1997).

Recent comment has noted that local prescribing policies may impact on the extent to which some drug-using sex workers need to work in this field at all, and on the extent to which safer sex practices can be insisted upon in the commercial situation. There is some evidence, for example, that there has been an increase in sex work activity in Liverpool since an earlier policy of prescribing both equipment and drugs for injecting was reversed (Williamson, 1997). It can be seen, then, that the social policy context within which the sex industry operates can affect markedly the risks involved in the work.

Targeted or generic service provision?

In terms of service provision, whether the most appropriate response is the development of specialist services, carefully designed service specifications for more mainstream services or a mixture of both, will depend on the size and 'reach-ability' of the local injecting drug-using sex-working population. In many areas outside the larger towns and cities, it can be difficult to identify the existence of any sex work at all, let alone determine its size and shape. In these circumstances, it may be more appropriate to focus attention on ensuring generic services are accessible and acceptable. For example, a recent study in Lanarkshire found that the total number of female sex workers in the area was not large enough, nor concentrated in one place, to justify the development of specialist services (McKenna and Parkin, 1996). It recommended making existing health provision more accessible, particularly in respect of the location and opening hours, and urged more interagency liaison and networking. The need to ensure wide availability of a variety of types of condoms was emphasised. Where there is an identifiable population of drug-injecting sex workers, consideration should be given to the provision of specially designed and targeted services. Such services can be very helpful in addressing both those needs which sex-working drug users share with other drug users, and those which are more directly associated with sex work. It should not be assumed, however, that all drug-injecting sex workers will use targeted services even if they are available. Many will wish to use more generic services for some or all of their needs. The most common models are outreach and drop-in services operating within a harm-reduction framework. Examples of each of these models are briefly described below.

Outreach services

Outreach services can be 'stand-alone', linked to specialist centre-based provision or linked to the provision of regular satellite sessions. Rhodes (1994) notes that outreach work with drug users in general is limited in two respects. First, in terms of the numbers it can reach, and second, 'because most interventions focus on individuals and target changes in individual knowledge, opinion and behaviour, they have a limited capacity for changing peer group and social norms about drug use and risk behaviour'.

Outreach work can be the model of choice when sex work is not concentrated in a particular patch, when the size of the sex-working population does not warrant a centre-based facility, or when other constraints prevent such provision. The likelihood that most drug-injecting sex workers will be street-based, and therefore more easily accessible to outreach workers, may make Rhodes' first concern less of an issue. A link to a centre-based project or the provision of satellite sessions may prove a useful means of addressing the second.

The literature provides a number of examples of outreach work with sex workers, although they vary in the extent to which injecting drug use is an issue for the target group (e.g., Matthews, 1990; Blakey and Frankland, 1996). The outreach project operated in Aberdeen by Drugs Action was in contact with over 280 women working around the harbour area during 1996, and provides condoms and lubrication, needle exchange, advice, information and referral to other agencies. It has distributed panic alarms and is planning the provision of self-defence sessions. In recognition of the fact that many drug users experience violence or abuse from men, the service is provided by female workers. Sex workers contacted are invited to attend regular women's sessions held in Drugs Action premises, and topics for discussion have included drug use, sexual health, being a mother and a drugs user, assertiveness, violence and relationships.

Drop-in services

Drop-in centres which are based near red-light areas and operate during 'working' hours, are well placed to provide a range of services. For example, the Glasgow-based service which is run by the Social Work Department and has been operational since 1987, provides access to on-site medical and nursing care, shower facilities, food and hot drinks, and information and support on a range of issues from legal problems to welfare rights. Such facilities may provide a useful base from which to facilitate the development of peer initiatives or otherwise address issues of social or cultural norms and risk behaviour.

There can be some tension between the drug-using and non-drug-using sex workers who use such services (McIver, 1992). Clear guidelines about what behaviour is acceptable are helpful, and it is important to involve the users of the service in drawing up and enforcing them. Within an overall philosophy of 'the fewer rules the better', McIver (1992) notes that the Glasgow drop-in facility prohibits the taking of drugs on the premises, and forbids verbal or physical violence towards other users or staff. She notes that denial of a service 'to punish someone' is counterproductive in terms of safeguarding health, but comments that 'the lack of rules forces the staff to consider other ways of controlling behaviour which can be extremely taxing'.

A framework for service development

A great deal of attention has been paid in the literature to factors associated with 'help-seeking' behaviour, with more recent models focusing on the social factors involved (Hartnoll, 1992). These models emphasise the importance of peer opinions, social norms and lay referral systems, and are potentially more fruitful than the individualistic models which have been at the forefront in the past (Rhodes, 1994).

Since the advent of HIV there has been a shift in emphasis away from an examination of the determinants of help-seeking behaviour towards studies of the extent to which services can reach out to hidden populations (Hartnoll, 1992). This approach is endorsed by Rhodes (1994) who contends that 'while it is vital to understand the determinants of help-seeking behaviour among drug users to help provide more appropriate intervention responses, in the interests and immediacy of public health there is a greater urgency to reach out to drug users who do not and will not seek help'. These are not competing imperatives. It is not feasible to take all services out to people and, in any event, taking services to people is in itself not a guarantee that these services will be used or that they will be effective. It is known that the factors which influence help-seeking behaviour include awareness of services, their perceived accessibility and appropriateness, perceptions of service and treatment effectiveness, and perceptions of health and welfare (Rhodes, 1994). This information is of direct practical value because these are issues which can be addressed, to a greater or lesser extent, by service providers themselves. More attention needs to be paid to identifying the specific factors which make some services more accessible (in the widest sense) and more effective than others.

There has been no systematic exploration of perceptions of the availability, accessibility or effectiveness of either generic or targeted services from the point of view of drug-injecting sex workers. However, that which we do know about the preferences of female drug users, the problems and failures of existing services, and the needs of drug-injecting sex workers can be put together to provide a preliminary framework or checklist for the development of more accessible and effective services. As local needs and priorities are identified, the basic framework can be modified and extended.

The specific needs of female sex workers who inject drugs, and those needs shared with non-sex-working drug injectors have already been described. Recent work (Pilley et al., 1997) has shown that, in terms of preferences, women drug users favour services which emphasise self-help, peer education and participation, and address their health and social problems in a holistic manner. A number of problems of existing services have been identified in the literature. These include:

- The majority of drug users are not in contact with services at all (Rhodes, 1994)
- Reports of drugs services failing to make themselves attractive to women, many not even advertising the fact that they provide services specifically for women (Pilley et al., 1997)
- The unwillingness of many GPs to accept drug-using patients to their list (Rhodes, 1994)
- A report that many drug users feel that staff attitudes can be unwelcoming and off-putting (Pilley et al., 1997)
- Women drug users being unwilling to use services for fear of having their children taken from them (Pilley et al., 1997)
- A lack of attention to issues around sexuality, sexual behaviour and safer sex, particularly in terms of women's sexual health (Rhodes, 1994)
- The culture within specialist drugs agencies and the generally lower priority given to developing services for women (Pilley et al., 1997)
- A lack of strategic planning and inter-agency working (Pilley et al., 1997)
- A need for better terms of employment, and more training and support for staff (Pilley et al., 1997).

On the basis of the above, a preliminary framework or checklist would comprise factors relating both to identified service needs, and to service 'attributes'. These elements are further elaborated below.

Identified service needs

These include services which address the wider needs of women, for example, housing, finance, benefits and legal issues, childcare, domestic violence and general health care, as well as those more specifically targeted at sexual health and safer drug use. The provision of clean injecting equipment and advice on its use is important. Issues of prescribing have already been touched upon above, and are discussed more fully elsewhere (e.g., Williamson, 1997). A range of condoms should be readily and freely available, and women should be encouraged to identify those which might be most appropriate and acceptable for different purposes.

In relation to sexual health, the need to help women develop strategies for insisting on safer sex with partners is important (Rhodes, 1994). Elements of such strategies – the eroticising of condoms for example (Morgan Thomas, 1990) – could be of particular value to sex-working women. Safer sexual behaviour is an issue for society in general. Issues around sexual health are more difficult to tackle than those around injecting behaviour.

We have already noted that there has been more positive change in the latter, in part reflecting the greater attention it has received. Changing norms and perceptions of risk in terms of injecting drugs may be hugely difficult, but is perhaps less difficult than changing the sexual norms accepted by the vast majority of the population. Many of the more successful strategies for reducing drugs-related harm, particularly those which address interpersonal and cultural norms, may also prove helpful in changing sexual behaviour norms.

Services require to examine how they might assist sex-working women reduce their vulnerability to violence and sexual assault during the course of their work. This might include providing panic alarms or self-defence lessons, and facilitating the exchange of information on particular clients who have exhibited violent behaviour, for example. Other strategies, for example, working in pairs or taking note of car number plates, can be shared and encouraged.

Service attributes

Although some issues will be of more relevance to certain models of service provision than others, a range of factors for consideration by all service providers, specialist and generic, can be identified.

Where specialist service provision is being considered in an area with a visible sex-working population, the value of planning and developing the service in conjunction with potential users themselves cannot be overstressed. A number of descriptions of how this has been done in various areas can be found in the literature (e.g., McIver, 1992; Matthews, 1990; Blakey and Frankland, 1994). COYOTE, (Call Off Your Old Tired Ethics) is an international network of sex workers and service providers which lobbies on legal and social issues, facilitates peer initiatives, and has produced a number of papers aimed at sharing information on good practice. It has to be noted that it may be particularly difficult to engage drug-injecting sex workers in service planning and development, and it may be appropriate to consider some form of payment for women willing to give time to such activities. In any event, potential providers should be prepared to withstand a considerable degree of suspicion in the initial stages of consultation (McIver, 1992; Matthews, 1990).

Blakey and Frankland (1994) comment that 'experience from the Cardiff project highlights the importance of winning support from the wider community. In the absence of local understanding and acceptance, long-term support for projects may be hard to maintain in times of scarce resources'. In particular, a good working relationship with the police and other elements of the criminal justice system will be invaluable (McIver, 1992).

Of prime importance, perhaps, are issues which relate to staff: attitudes and qualities, training, support, and conditions of employment. All staff involved in providing services for female drug users need to be aware of the various forms stigma and discrimination can take, and the impact this can have on women's lives and their perceptions of service accessibility. The additional stigma faced by drug-using sex workers has already been noted. McIver (1992) comments on the difficulties posed for staff by the realities of the lives of many sex-working drug-injecting women, and on the need for toleration and a non-judgemental approach. She suggests that appropriate support to staff might include stress management, and individual and team supervision. She further notes some of the practical issues to be considered by specialist projects, for example, staff safety in terms of the location and working hours.

Pilley et al. (1997) note the need for both general and specific skills development through training, and in particular comment on the need for further training in respect of working with drug users who have dependent children. McIver (1992) stresses the importance of clear policies in terms of childcare and other issues where there may be a dilemma about the extent to which services have a monitoring role. In respect of the Glasgow project, she comments that 'if the service were to become a monitoring point for other workers then women would cease to trust it and use it'.

Although there are particular issues for specialist projects in terms of the choice of staff, generic providers should also give some attention to attitudinal issues when selecting and training staff. In relation to the choice of staff for specialist projects, Blakey and Frankland (1994) note that the Glamorgan project identified a list of five required skills and five desirable qualities, and further asked that the project worker be 'tough-minded, non-judgemental, stable, mature and creative'. A number of writers have commented on the potential impact of staff gender on perceptions of service accessibility (e.g., Pilley et al., 1997). It may be that services specifically targeted at female sex workers should consider the advantages of a female-only staff. This is an issue which should be discussed with potential service users as services are being designed.

There is little in the literature on peer education in terms of drug-injecting sex workers. Rhodes (1994) notes that peer initiatives 'lay the foundations for intervention responses which encourage consumer advocacy, involvement and organisation', and are founded on social rather than individualistic models of health and help-seeking. On a different note, McIver (1992) comments on a policy of being open to employing staff who have previously been sex workers. Further work in the area of peer initiatives for drug-injecting sex workers should be encouraged.

Pilley et al. (1997) comment on the poor conditions of employment of many workers in drugs projects, primarily related to the short-term nature of funding and a lack of strategic planning. This needs to be addressed both in terms of good employment practice and in the interests of providing high quality services staffed by a motivated workforce.

Practical issues, including location, opening hours and advertising, are important in terms of service accessibility. Providers need to ensure that service planning takes these issues into consideration from the point of view of potential service users, and be prepared to modify them as necessary. We have already noted the value women place on services which take a holistic view of their needs and which recognise that they may prioritise things differently from providers (Pilley et al., 1997). In terms of specialist provision, as wide a range of services as possible should be provided from the one location, or taken out to women. However, no one service can expect to meet all needs, and services will frequently find themselves requiring to be a conduit to other providers. Accurate information on other services is essential, and referral protocols may be a helpful tool in terms of striving towards 'seamless' provision. The need for joint working and planning has already been noted.

Research and evaluation

Given the importance of social and situational factors on perceptions of accessibility and effectiveness, it may be appropriate that, in addition to research which seeks to identify the universal factors involved, more attention is focused on exploring these issues at a local level. This would imply an 'action research' type approach, with services designed to be sensitive to particular local needs and circumstances, and capable of being modified as these change. In addition to facilitating the development of better services for users, and assisting providers to more successfully reach out to non-users, such an approach can benefit both commissioners and providers in times of scarce resources and competing priorities by making available some evidence of effectiveness and efficiency.

Pilley et al. (1997), in their survey of services for women problem-drug users in Scotland, note that 'The development of women's services was often blocked in agencies by a history of failed initiatives which littered the way, prejudicing attitude to future development but not necessarily causing agencies to evaluate where they had failed. Blame for failure was thus often ascribed to women users and their characteristics' (p. viii). Not exactly 'client-centred'! This is not to suggest that all services should have a formal research element built in. Rather that providers make a conscious effort to explore local perceptions of availability, accessibility and effectiveness and modify their services accordingly. This is perhaps less difficult for specially targeted services as their provision implies the existence of an identified population of sex-working drug users whose views can be sought. The importance of inter-agency liaison has already been noted, and for providers of generic services, inter-agency networking and collaboration may be an important means of accessing the views of a group whose voices might otherwise remain unheard.

Conclusions

It has been seen that while sex work is a potential route of transmission of HIV and other STDs, in Britain the main risks are where this overlaps with injecting drug use. Most risks faced by drug-using sex workers are in their personal lives and are shared with other drug users. The additional risks posed by sex work may be addressed by ensuring the accessibility and acceptability of general services, by specialist projects, or by a combination of the two. More attention requires to be given to safer sexual behaviour in both generic and drugs services, and this also needs to be tackled at a general population level. The double stigma attached to drug-using sex workers can be a barrier to approaching helping agencies.

References

Aberdeen Drugs Action, *Annual Report* 1996–7.
Barnard, M., McKeganey, N. and Leyland, A. (1993), 'Risk Behaviours Among Male Clients of Female Prostitutes', *British Medical Journal*, **307**, 361–2.
Blakey, V. and Frankland, J. (1994), 'HIV Prevention for Women Prostitutes and Their Clients', Cardiff: Health Promotion Wales.
Blume, S.B. (1990), 'Chemical Dependency in Women: Important Issues', *The American Journal of Drug and Alcohol Abuse*, **16**, 297–307.
British Medical Association (1996), *A Guide to Hepatitis C*, London: Board of Science and Education.
Bury, J., Morrison.V. and McLachlan, S. (eds) (1992), *Working with Women and Aids*, London: Routledge.
Conant, F.P. (1988), 'Social Consequences of AIDS: Implications for East Africa and the Eastern United States', in R. Kulstad (ed.), *AIDS 1988*, Washington, DC: American Institute for the Advancement of Science.
Darrow, W. (1984), 'Prostitution and Sexually Transmitted Diseases', in K.K. Holmes, P.A. Mardh, P.F. Sparling and P.J. Weisner (eds), *Sexually Transmitted Diseases*, Maidenhead: McGraw-Hill.
Day, S. and Ward, H. (1990), 'The Praed Street Project: A Cohort of Prostitute

Women in London', in M.A. Plant (ed.) (1990), *Aids, Drugs and Prostitution*, London: Routledge.

Freeman, J. (1997), report in *The Herald* newspaper, November 22.

Harcourt, C. and Philpot, R. (1990), 'Female Prostitutes, AIDS, Drugs and Alcohol in New South Wales', in M.A. Plant (ed.), *Aids, Drugs and Prostitution*, London: Routledge.

Hartnoll, R.L. (1992), 'Research and the Help-Seeking Process', *British Journal of Addiction*, **87**.

Home Department, The Scottish Office, Statistics supplied by the Civil and Criminal Justice Statistics Department, 429–37.

McIver, N. (1992), 'Developing a Service for Prostitutes in Glasgow', in J. Bury, et al. (eds), *Working with Women and Aids*, London: Routledge.

McKeganey, N. and Barnard, M. (1996), cited in McKenna, C. and Parkin, S.G. 'The Sex Industry in Lanarkshire and Related Needs of Female Sex Workers', unpublished report commissioned by Lanarkshire Health Board.

McKeganey, N., Barnard, M., Leyland, A., Coote, I. and Follet, E. (1992), 'Female Streetworking Prostitution and HIV Infection in Glasgow', *British Medical Journal*, **305**, 801–4.

McKenna, C. and Parkin, S.G. (1996), The Sex Industry in Lanarkshire and Related Needs of Female Sex Workers', unpublished report commissioned by Lanarkshire Health Board.

Matthews, L. (1990), 'Outreach Work with Female Prostitutes in Liverpool', in M.A. Plant (ed.), *Aids, Drugs and Prostitution*, London: Routledge.

Morgan Thomas, R. (1990), 'AIDS risks, alcohol, drugs and the sex industry: a Scottish study', in M.A. Plant (ed.), *Aids, Drugs and Prostitution*, London: Routledge.

Morgan Thomas, R. (1992), 'HIV and the Sex Industry' in Bury et al. *Working with Women and Aids*, London: Routledge.

Morgan Thomas, R., Plant, M.A., Plant, M.L. and Sales, D. (1989), 'AIDS Risks Amongst Sex Industry Workers: Some Initial Results from a Scottish Study', *British Medical Journal*, **299**, 148–9.

Pilley C., Shucksmith, J. and Philip, K. (1997), 'Services to Women Problem Drug Users: A Review of Provision and Practice in Scotland, Report of a Project to the Scottish Home and Health Department.

Plant, M.A. (ed.) (1990), *Aids, Drugs and Prostitution*, London: Routledge.

Rhodes, T. and Hartnoll, R.L. (1991), 'Reaching the Hard to Reach: Models of HIV Outreach Health Education', in P. Aggleton, P. Davies and G. Hart (eds), *AIDS: Responses, Intervention and Care*, Lewes: Falmer Press.

Rhodes, T. (1994), *Risk Intervention and Change*, London: Health Education Authority.

Roberts, N. (1992), *Whores in History: Prostitution in Western Society*, London: Harper Collins.

Taylor, A., Frischer, M. and McKeganey N. (1993), 'HIV Risk Behaviours among Female Prostitutes in Glasgow', *Addiction*, **88**, 1561–4.

Waldorf, D. and Murphy, S. (1990), 'Intravenous Drug Use and Syringe-Sharing Practices of Call-men and Hustlers', in M.A. Plant (ed.), *Aids, Drugs and Prostitution*, London: Routledge.

Ward, Day, Mezzone, Dunlop, Donegan, Farrar, Whitaker, Harris and Miller (1993), 'Female Prostitutes in London – Prostitution and Risk of HIV', *British Medical Journal*, **307**, 356–8.

Williamson, K. (1997), *Drugs and the Part Line*, London: Canongate.

13 Co-morbidity
Malcolm Bruce

Introduction

> These patients are often on the margins of psychiatric services, alienated by their
> poor compliance, social instability, and behavioural problems, and by the inflexi-
> bility of service structures to accommodate them.
>
> (Cantwell and Harrison, 1996)

The above quotation refers to patients with a substance misuse problem
and a severe mental illness (i.e., co-morbidity or dual diagnosis). For the
purposes of this chapter, the term co-morbidity will be used throughout
and one diagnosis will be drug misuse. Some research does not distinguish
clearly between alcohol and other drugs of misuse or between misuse and
dependence, so extrapolation to individual groups needs to be done with
care. The second diagnosis will not be confined to severe mental illness but
will include other psychiatric disorders including personality disorder.
Co-morbidity has implications on aetiology, diagnosis, management and
prognosis.

In terms of an individual patient's history, one condition occurs first. In
the case of an initial substance misuse problem, intoxication, withdrawal,
or chronic effects with or without continued drug use, can lead to psychiatric complications and long term 'co-morbidity' issues. However, drug-
induced psychiatric states are not co-morbidity and should be seen as
secondary phenomena. In the case of an initial psychiatric condition, this
may be precipitated in a vulnerable individual by drug misuse, but in
addition there is increased drug use within this group for a variety of
reasons such as common risk factors between psychiatric illness and substance misuse. Some suggest a preferential use of particular drugs for 'symp-

tomatic relief', others that a sense of control is exerted by the use of drugs in some people who have psychotic phenomena. In the long term, exacerbation of psychiatric illness, involvement in the criminal justice system and poor compliance may all be complicated by drug misuse in someone who has an initial psychiatric condition.

Drug misuse has become endemic in our society. The proportion of young people who have known someone taking drugs has increased from 15 per cent in 1969 to 65 per cent in the present day (White and Poole, 1995). There seems to be no reason why people with psychiatric illness should be excluded from this rise in drug misuse, and there is a suggestion that they have an increased risk of substance misuse. What in 1969 was a very small number of patients, has now become a much larger group. This change is underlined by three editorials in the *British Journal of Psychiatry* in 1997 dedicated to: co-morbidity of mental disorders and substance misuse (Hall and Farrell, 1997); service provision for this group of patients (Johnstone, 1997); and suicide and substance misuse (Neeleman and Farrell, 1997).

This chapter will review some of the evidence regarding the size of the problem and then deal with separate diagnostic groups. There will also be reference to planning strategies and service implications of these findings.

Prevalence

The British Psychiatric Morbidity Survey gives the most recent prevalence data for the UK (Meltzer et al., 1996). Approximately one third of the general population sample had some form of psychiatric morbidity. Of those with psychiatric morbidity, one third had a substance misuse disorder. This translates to a general population sample of 5 per cent having heavy drinking problems and 5 per cent having a substance misuse disorder. Of those that had a substance misuse disorder, the majority by far use cannabis, followed by benzodiazepines and then other drugs. In young men, substance misuse disorder is much more common than any other psychiatric disorder. Of the 5 per cent of the general population that had a substance misuse disorder, one third also had an additional psychiatric illness. The number that form this group are those with a co-morbidity. This means that, excluding alcohol, approximately 1.5 per cent of the population have a co-morbid condition, with the typical drug being cannabis. When looking further into this study, Gill and colleagues (1996) showed that in institutions – most typically psychiatric hospitals – there may be less heavy drinking in the population but drug misuse increased up to 10 per cent of the sample. Again, there was typically cannabis but frequently benzodiazepine abuse. Almost all of this sample had an additional psychiatric diagnosis. A further group assessed was the homeless population, and this showed near 30 per cent prevalence of drug misuse, again typically cannabis, but also opiates along with benzodiazepines. Co-morbidity in this sample was about 15 per cent.

In the United States, the epidemiological catchment area study (Regier et al., 1990) showed similar prevalence patterns. In addition, schizophrenia was found to have a multiple of 4.6 times the risk of substance misuse compared to the general population, and affective disorder has a multiple of 2.6 times the risk of a substance misuse disorder. The US National Co-morbidity Survey also looked at prevalence and correlates of drug use and dependence in the United States (Warner et al., 1995). The estimate of a lifetime dependence was approximately 5 per cent similar to the British Psychiatric Morbidity Survey. Others have examined the same data and give figures of co-morbidity, but they are not confined to substance misuse disorder (Kessler et al., 1994). When compared with mental health patients who are severely mentally ill, patients with co-morbidity were found to be younger, have increased feelings of anger, more involvement with the criminal justice system and more suicidal threats (Barry et al., 1996).

In the heterogeneous group of co-morbidity, Lehman and colleagues (1994) have tried to define sub-groups for service planning. Four of these groups warrant further definition. The first group is 'definite co-morbidity but not current'. These patients have either a current mental disorder or substance misuse disorder, but not both. They also have a past history of the inactive condition. The second group is 'substance-induced organic mental disorder, current'. These patients have no history of an independent mental disorder. Group three, 'possible dual diagnosis, current'. Here the relationship of substance misuse disorder to the mental disorder is unclear. Finally the fourth group, 'definite dual diagnosis, current'. These patients have both a current mental health disorder and a substance misuse disorder, and they are independent. The patients for their study were recruited from state- and university-operated psychiatric hospitals in the United States, and the percentage of patients falling into each group are Group 1 – 17 per cent, Group 2 – 16 per cent, Group 3 – 15 per cent and Group 4 – 24 per cent. In Group 1, these were typically mental health disorder patients in view of the setting of recruitment for this group. It is argued that these patients should be considered for service needs as Group 4. The past history of substance misuse in the context of a relapsing mental health disorder, will require relapse prevention input to ensure that the substance misuse disorder does not recur. The Group 2 patients with a substance misuse organic mental state do not technically have co-morbidity. However, they are often found in psychiatric settings because of the psychiatric treatment they require. It was felt that services should be provided concentrating on treating their substance misuse. It was also always possible that once the acute psychiatric syndrome had resolved, this would then result in the finding of a premorbid co-morbid independent mental health disorder. They felt that although psychiatric hospitals were well equipped to deal with acute behavioural problems, the patients themselves did not integrate well into a psychiatric setting and their on-going needs were not addressed. Once discharged from hospital they frequently dropped out of follow-up care. Strictly speaking, this group is outside the scope of this chapter and, although presenting problems for service planning of psychiatric services, they frequently also appear in general medical settings, the criminal justice system and accommodation for the homeless. This group is not discussed further in this chapter. Despite rigorous research methodology, some patients could not be placed into Group 2 or 4, yet had symptoms of both a mental health disorder and substance abuse disorder. In this study it was found that, over time, the diagnosis became more clear and patients were either rediagnosed as group 2, and then referred on to a substance abuse treatment programme, or group 4. Group 4 is in essence what the rest of this chapter is about. That is, patients with current definite independent co-morbidity. Within the psychiatric setting, the incidence varied in that schizophrenia and major depression were most common, followed by anxiety states and bipolar affective disorder. Typically the drugs abused were alcohol rather than illicit substances, and cannabis rather than other drugs. However, the full range of illicit drugs was found within this group.

As with alcohol, chronic substance misuse can lead to residual states where psychiatric symptoms persist despite stopping the substance of misuse. It again becomes difficult to decide whether there is true co-morbidity in a particular case, or whether there is a secondary psychiatric phenomena related to the primary drug misuse. Such an example is 'cannabis psychosis'. The phenomenon of cannabis intoxication is well documented, as is the association of cannabis with schizophrenia. The validity of any separate diagnosis of cannabis psychosis is questioned and some say should be dropped (Thomas, 1993). However, there are residual phenomena which are unique as secondary phenomena to primary drug misuse such as 'flashbacks'. But these again are not true co-morbidity states and are not discussed further.

It has been suggested by others that initial drug misuse, particularly cannabis, at an early age may be developmentally important and lead to subsequent psychosocial adjustment difficulties and an apparent increase in co-morbidity (Fergusson and Horwood, 1997). The evidence suggests an increased incidence of mental health disorder following early substance misuse. However, when factors such as maternal age, gender, changes in parents, childhood sexual abuse, IQ, self-esteem, novelty-seeking behaviour and parental attachment are controlled, then the association between cannabis use and a subsequent mental health problem is lost. It is suggested that those who elect to use cannabis at an early age are a high-risk population and would independently be at high risk of developing subsequent mental health difficulties also. However, in areas outside mental health, early cannabis use was associated with increased juvenile offending, leaving school without qualifications or getting work, but this is again outside this chapter.

Prior to discussing the individual psychiatric disorders and particular management issues related to co-morbidity, special attention should be given to the problems of criminal behaviour and violence associated with co-morbidity. A key finding from the McArthur Violence Risk Assessment Study was that co-morbidity could increase the risk of violence four-fold. Co-morbidity and violence was associated with greater risk of refusal to continue treatment, inability to function effectively in daily life, several changes of residence, poor anger control, impulsive personality with poor behavioural controls, violent fantasies, pervasive delusions, and having had a head injury with loss of consciousness (Dyer, 1996). The new phenomenon of arresting patients during hospitalisation has been explored in a New York study, which found that more than 90 per cent of those arrested during their hospitalisation had a diagnosis of substance misuse or personality disorder in addition to their psychiatric diagnosis. The study did not explore whether the substances themselves contributed to the violent incident, but the association between substance misuse and severe violent incidents during hospitalisation remains (Volavka et al., 1995). In a British study looking at a newly-opened Psychiatric Intensive Care Unit, a previous history of drug abuse was associated with violent incidents (Walker and Seifert, 1994). In a Swiss study, the single most powerful variable to discriminate between patients with and without a criminal record was found to be a diagnosis of alcohol or drug misuse (Modestin and Ammann, 1995). Whether the increase in violent incidents found in patients with co-morbidity is additive or synergistic for substance misuse and mental health, remains to be seen. Smith and Hucker (1994) have reviewed extensively the literature on schizophrenia and substance abuse and its association with violence. Their conclusion was that, while there is circumstantial evidence to support an increased risk among this group, the mediating mechanisms remain unclear. From a service perspective, the issue remains, and security and staff safety should reflect the increased risk.

Schizophrenia

In Smith and Hucker's (1994) review of schizophrenia and substance misuse, they list complications leading from the co-morbidity including increased rates of violence, suicide, non-compliance with treatment, earlier psychotic breakdown, exacerbation of psychotic symptoms, relative neuroleptic refractoriness, increased rates of hospitalisation, tardive dyskinesia, homelessness, and overall poor prognosis. However, they also point out that should the substance misuse problem be dealt with, then the overall prognosis is better than for poor prognosis schizophrenia. Substance abuse is the most prevalent co-morbid condition associated with schizophrenia (Regier et al., 1990) and a review of the literature by Cuffell (1992) suggests that the prevalence of substance misuse among patients with schizophrenia is increasing.

In the chronology of co-morbidity, in at least 80–90 per cent of cases, substance misuse tends to occur first (Strakowski et al., 1995; Kovasznay et al., 1993). When the first psychotic episode occurs, there is a suggestion that it may have an earlier onset and be more abrupt and with less negative symptoms of schizophrenia than those who do not misuse substances. Typical drugs of abuse are cannabis and amphetamines, but many of the American studies report extremely high rates for cocaine which are much less readily available and more expensive in Europe. In an Australian study looking at self-report of substance misuse in patients with schizophrenia, 40 per cent of patients used cannabis and 8 per cent used amphetamines with 20 per cent using more than one substance. Other substances were benzodiazepines, cocaine and rarely opiates. Patients associated their substance misuse with the initiation or exacerbation of their schizophrenic illness. Despite this, their substance misuse continued. Initial reasons for starting drugs were either peer pressure or in 30 per cent of cases to relieve dysphoria and anxiety, less frequently just for experimentation. Continued use in 80 per cent of cases was because the drugs were perceived as relieving dysphoria or anxiety, or to enhance social interaction within their cultural sub-group. It seemed more socially acceptable to have a substance misuse disorder than to have a mental illness in the form of schizophrenia, and substance misuse gave the patients a sense of identity. This may also contribute to the reasons for the increased association between substance misuse patients who deny having a diagnosis of schizophrenia, and are resistant to follow-up attempts. Patients preferred activating drugs in the form of amphetamine, cannabis, hallucinogens or cocaine, as they were felt to relieve the depression or dysphoria and the negative symptoms of schizophrenia, even at the price of exacerbating some positive symptoms (Baigent et al., 1995). Another study looked at expectations and motives for using substances in different groups of patients with schizophrenia. Three groups were compared: non-using patients, patients with a past history, or a current history of substance misuse. Expectations of reducing craving and physical withdrawal effects was the only distinguishing feature between current substance misuse and the other two groups. In the past substance misuse group compared to the non-using group, statistically significant differences were found for: social and sexual facilitation, perception of cognitive enhancement, global positive and negative effects, and increases in arousal and anxiety. As to motives, coping and pleasure enhancement were the aims for the current and past substance misusers, but not seen as an issue with people with no substance misuse history (Mueser et al., 1995).

The environmental catchment area study database in the United States identified 231 people with schizophrenia, with approximately 31 per cent having co-morbidity. These patients with co-morbidity were found to be young males with depressive symptoms or possibly negative symptoms of schizophrenia (the screening tool used was not able to differentiate clearly between these diagnostic categories). It was felt the mood disturbance or negative symptoms of schizophrenia may be an identifiable trigger for substance misuse in this condition, and could be amenable to treatment, therefore clinical effort should be made towards this end (Cuffel et al., 1993).

Relapse in schizophrenia is associated with substance misuse. In one study looking at compulsory admissions for 'dangerousness' in a mixed diagnostic group, patients with a positive urine for drugs recovered more quickly over a five-day period than those with no drugs in their urine. The exception was when patients had a history of personality disorder in addition to their severe mental illness (Sanguineti and Samuel, 1993). Others have reported higher readmission rates for abuse rather than for dependence syndrome. The 'natural history' of co-morbidity in schizophrenia shows that over a seven-year follow-up period in 29 subjects, of those that abused substances 46 per cent still continued to abuse substances at follow-up. In those that had a dependence syndrome 69 per cent continued to abuse substances at follow-up. This suggests a chronic relapsing condition (Bartels et al., 1995).

Poor compliance is associated with relapse and in one study 50 per cent of patients were non-compliant with treatment prior to admission. Current substance misuse was then associated with non-compliance and decreased out-patient contact at follow-up at six months was also associated with worse symptom severity (Owen et al., 1996). In an American study of primarily cocaine users rather than cannabis users, co-morbid patients were found to be younger, less independent and had more hospitalisations and did not attend out-patient follow-up, were less compliant, and had four times as many relapses as those that did not abuse substances. Seven out of the nine patients who relapsed during the study period of one year were found to be substance misusers (Swofford et al., 1996). Others have found five times increased risk of relapses over a one-year period in a similar group (Gupta et al., 1996).

The effects of substance misuse on treatment response in chronic schizophrenic patients have shown that young substance misusers had higher rates of visual and olfactory hallucinations and decreased treatment responsiveness of auditory and tactile hallucinations as a result of their continued substance misuse (Sokolski et al., 1994).

In summary, many patients with schizophrenia and co-morbid substance misuse end up in a 'revolving door' and prevention of substance misuse and non-compliance may help to prevent this phenomena (Haywood et al., 1995).

The problem of service delivery to patients with co-morbidity has been reviewed extensively by Drake and colleagues (1993). In their paper they reviewed 13 projects in addition to their review of the literature, and came out with nine key principles of treatment for this group. The nine principles are: assertiveness, close monitoring, integration, comprehensiveness, stable living environment, flexibility in specialisation, stages of treatment, longitudinal prospective, and optimism.

Assertiveness is seen as outreach with practical issues being addressed particularly with regard to basic needs, the focus being on engagement and stabilisation. Close monitoring may involve the use of the Mental Health Act, or probation, or close monitoring with the consent of the patient utilising frequent urine testing and, in some cases, aversive drugs such as antabuse or antagonists such as naltrexone. Integration of services would involve the removal of exclusion criteria within treatment facilities and expanding the options of treatment for patients. Comprehensiveness would involve not just looking at the psychiatric illness itself, but improving the skills, social networks and activities of the patient and providing them with structure. A stable living environment would involve provision of safe housing which would be substance misuse-free, and involve on-site support. Flexibility and specialisation would involve an eclectic approach with the emphasis on gradual recovery, low arousal and attention to psychotic symptoms. Stages of treatment would involve the initial engagement, followed by motivational interviewing, treatment and then relapse prevention. A longitudinal perspective would have to be taken in view of the relapsing nature of the condition. And, finally, optimism in the face of this chronic illness would be required for patients, relatives, and care-givers including clinicians, all of whom should receive support in the form of self-help groups and peer supervision.

Johnston (1997), in her review of the case for specialist services, outlines the need for integration. Psychiatric staff often lack training, expertise and confidence in the treatment of substance misuse disorder, and only experience these patients in crisis, i.e., when intoxicated or in withdrawal states. This often results in patients being confronted with a punitive response. This is perpetuated by specific exclusions of substance misuse disorder from these units, so that staff fail to gain experience in the overall management of substance misusers who are not in crisis. Substance misuse staff also have the converse problem in that their experience of general psychiatric conditions is not as up-to-date as their colleagues in a psychiatric unit. Many may also work in a high confrontational, high arousal environment with a low tolerance of relapse which would be likely to exacerbate schizophrenia. Parallel treatments can lead to mis-communications, contradictory recommendations and non-compliance and are not seen as in the best interests of the patient. In the United States, dedicated teams for co-morbidity providing 24-hour care with caseloads of 12 patients per keyworker, have been shown to decrease hospitalisation, increase functioning and show 50 per cent abstention from substance misuse at three-year follow-up (Drake et al., 1996). However, Johnston argues that with the difference in training of staff in substance misuse in the UK, such units may not be necessary and indeed have not been shown to be cost effective at this stage. Options put forward are for increased training of respective staff within the separate units. A second option is joint clinics, and a third option co-morbid teams. At present, the move is towards services available locally in the community. However, as patients need to be given a stable living environment away from their previous substance misusers network, they may be better served away from their previous environment and therefore local services are not necessarily a priority.

Mood disorders

The American Epidemiological Catchment Area (ECA) Study Dataset has been used to look at the association between mood disorder and substance misuse, particularly in adolescents (Burke et al., 1994). This analysis showed a four-times increased risk of subsequent substance misuse if a mood disorder had developed before the age of 20, compared to those who developed mood disorder after the age of 20. Although an association, the researchers argue that this provides clinically important information suggesting early treatment of mood disorder in adolescents may subsequently reduce substance misuse disorder. They also suggest that the targeting of this group prior to the development of substance misuse would allow prevention strategies to be implemented. Retrospective studies have investigated associations between depressive episodes with co-morbid substance misuse compared to those with depressive episodes with no co-morbidity. These have shown that substance misuse co-morbidity is associated with younger males of lower social class (Fabrega et al., 1993). In substance misuse populations, opiate drug dependance syndrome patients in a methadone maintenance programme have been screened using the general health questionnaire, and 60 per cent were found to be 'cases'. The major component of this is likely to be symptoms of depression. However, no formal diagnoses were made (Darke et al., 1994). Likewise the mechanism in intravenous user suicide, with a 30-times increased risk, is unclear but may be attributable to depression (Neeleman and Farrell, 1997).

Prospective studies have been done in bipolar affective disorder but only in the United States and the substance misuse pattern of cocaine as the most commonly reported drug limits extrapolation to UK populations. In the ECA Dataset, bipolar affective disorder with co-morbidity had rates of approximately 40 per cent. Other mood disorders have much lower prevalence rates, and overall mood disorders were associated with a prevalence of 19 per cent with substance misuse. Bipolar affective disorder and co-morbid substance misuse is associated with twice the risk of hospitalisation, younger age of onset of the affective disorder, and four times the risk of other co-morbid conditions, most commonly post-traumatic stress disorder, but included other conditions such as phobic anxiety and other anxiety disorders. The hypothesis put forward in this study by Sonne and colleagues (1994) was that substance misuse would either exacerbate bipolar affective disorder or the substance misuse would attenuate the bipolar affective disorder as patients would be using it as a form of self-medication. Their study suggests that patient perception is an agreement with the second hypothesis, but the data supports an exacerbation of the bipolar affective disorders. Numbers of pure drug misusers within this study were small and much of the results apply to a mix of alcohol and drug misuse. A further study looking at 188 cases with a co-morbidity rate of 35 per cent in bipolar affective disorder analysed the data comparing three groups (Feinman and Dunner, 1996). The first group was bipolar affective disorder only. The second group, bipolar affective disorder with late onset substance misuse. And the third group, initial substance misuse disorder with later onset of bipolar affective disorder. The most common drugs abused by this group, in more than 50 per cent of cases, were stimulants, typically cocaine or amphetamine. Across the groups findings were:

- An increased family history of substance misuse in those with a diagnosis of substance misuse
- A female preponderance in those with an exclusive affective disorder.
- A male preponderance in early onset substance misuse with subsequent affective disorder
- Fewer suicide attempts and panic attacks within the exclusively affective disorder patients.

Rapid cycling of the affective disorder was more common in those with an initial diagnosis of bipolar affective disorder. Those who demonstrated mood changes rapidly over a period of days or hours were patients with an initial diagnosis of substance misuse.

Neurotic and stress-related disorders

The literature shows a clear increase in the prevalence of alcohol disorder in relation to anxiety states, but there is much less data on substance misuse. The American ECA Study found that, of those who had an anxiety disorder, 24 per cent also had a substance misuse disorder (odds ratio 1.7) (Regier et al., 1990). Two studies in tertiary clinics for anxiety-related disorders have shown prevalence rates of approximately 10 per cent in New Zealand (Page and Andrews, 1996) and 31 per cent in the United States (Goldenberg et al., 1995). The New Zealand study tried to examine the hypothesis that secondary anxiety states were associated with an increase in prescribed or self-medication in a substance specific manner and that there was an association with continued drug misuse related to the perpetuation of the anxiety-related disorder. They found with relation to sedative hypnotics an eight times greater than expected risk of substance misuse when compared to a general population sample. They were unable to show differences across different sub-categories of anxiety disorder, but if the study had been comparing anxiety disorders against other diagnostic groups, they may have found substance specific effects. Benzodiazepine use in this group is important clinically as it has been found to block the response to some behavioural treatments, and may require management prior to the initiation of treatment for the anxiety disorder. The American study (Goldenberg et al., 1995), compared initial onset anxiety disorder against initial onset substance misuse disorder and looked for substance-specific and diagnosis-specific interactions. They found little support for the self-medication hypothesis, but did find an increased risk of opiate misuse in those with an initial diagnosis of post-traumatic stress disorder. However, their strongest finding was for an avoidance of stimulant drugs in those with a primary diagnosis of anxiety disorder. This was not found in those with a primary diagnosis of substance misuse disorder.

Obsessive compulsive disorder

The prevalence of obsessive compulsive disorder (OCD) is generally felt to be under-reported. This also applies to patients with substance misuse disorder who may have co-morbidity. In a study selecting its patients from a substance misuse setting, co-morbidity of OCD was found to be at 11 per cent, at least four times the incidence of that found in the general population (Fals-Stewart and Angarano, 1994). Accurate diagnosis of OCD within substance misuse patients has been shown to be important as regards outcome (Fals-Stewart and Schafer, 1992). An outcome study at 12-month follow-up, showed that patients with co-morbidity who received treatment for their OCD and substance misuse stayed in treatment longer, showed greater reduction in OCD symptom severity and higher overall abstinence.

Post-traumatic stress disorder

Much of the research in this field is on combat-related trauma and there is limited literature on non-combat-related trauma. That which exists is often primarily concerned with co-morbid alcohol misuse and substance misuse is not defined specifically. In those with post-traumatic stress disorder (PTSD), the prevalence of substance misuse varies widely depending on the population screen. Typical figures are in the region of 35–45 per cent (Brown and Wolfe, 1994). Prevalence in non-combat-related PTSD, for example, that found in civil violence in Northern Ireland, has show substance misuse rates of about 8 per cent in those with or without PTSD. The comparison here between combat-related and non-combat-related PTSD suggests no increase in prevalence of substance misuse in this group. However, further follow-up may reveal increasing prevalence of substance misuse (Deering et al., 1996). The course of symptoms in PTSD has been shown to begin with hyper-arousal, progress on to avoidance behaviour and peak with intrusive re-experiencing of the trauma. The time course for this can be a period of years and, when substance misuse has been observed in this group, it has been found to parallel the development of the PTSD. This supports the hypothesis that substance misuse in PTSD is a form of self-medication. In addition, there seems to be a selective use of sedatives, primarily alcohol, cannabis, heroin and benzodiazepines, which would depress hyper-arousal and induce 'numbing' on exposure to stimuli specific for the PTSD and also suppress or 'forget' re-experiences. It has also been found that these patients avoid stimulants such as cocaine and amphetamines (Bremner et al., 1996). Theoretically, the outcome for co-morbid PTSD patients may be worse if their sedative substance misuse is not addressed. Sedatives withdrawal induces hyper-arousal, which is associated with symptoms of PTSD and become a stressor leading to established coping mechanisms, primarily drug misuse.

Eating disorders

An extensive review of the current literature has been carried out by Holderness and colleagues (1994). In this they present the three main theories of the association between substance misuse and eating disorders: eating disorders are a form of addiction; substance misuse is a form of self-medication; or the two disorders have a common aetiology, such as dysfunctional families. In all studies, bulimia is found to be more strongly associated with substance misuse than anorexia. Typical prevalence of substance misuse in bulimic patients is 20 per cent. In anorexic patients substance misuse tends to occur in 15 per cent or less and some studies suggest that the main drug of misuse is amphetamines. Community samples of bulimic patients have confirmed the expected prevalence of 20 per cent (Welch and Fairburn, 1996). The drugs misused were, in descending order, cannabis, amphetamine, benzodiazepines and then other drugs. In clinical samples, sub-groups of bulimics have been postulated with a 'multi-impulsive' disorder, the substance misuse being associated with increased suicide attempts, stealing and sexual intercourse. No studies have been done looking at treatment for co-morbid conditions or assessing outcome following different treatment models. The clinical implications then of the co-morbidity of eating disorders and substance misuse remains unexplored.

Personality disorder

The research in this area comes exclusively from the United States and deals primarily with the anti-social personality disorder (ASPD) sub-type. The ECA Study found a prevalence of ASPD in five per cent of males and just less than one per cent of females. When there was a diagnosis of substance misuse disorder, 18 per cent were found to be co-morbid with

ASPD. Higher prevalence rates are found in different populations, for example, in intravenous drug users, prevalence is as high as 44 per cent with ASPD. When the diagnostic criteria 'onset prior to the age of 15 with conduct disorder' is removed, this results in a diagnosis similar to antisocial personality disorder used in the ICD 10 and then prevalence rises to near 70 per cent. (Cottler et al., 1995). Co-morbidity of substance misuse and ASPD remains a major public health concern because of the callous unconcern for the feelings of others and the association with injecting drug use and the Human Immunodeficiency Virus. Opiate substance misuse patients with co-morbid ASPD who engage in methadone maintenance programmes in the United States have been shown to do no worse than those without this co-morbid condition (Gill et al., 1992). However, in Australia compliance within a methadone maintenance programme has been found to be poor in intravenous users with ASPD and the use of benzodiazepines have been particularly associated with aniety and depression (Darke et al., 1994). ASPD was predicted by being a younger male, with poor social funtioning and involvement in the criminal justice system. From a preventive point of view, targeting pre-adolescents and adolescents with conduct disorder with co-morbidity of substance misuse would seem to make clinical sense, as there may be a narrow window of opportunity to prevent substance disorders once drug use has begun (Reebye et al., 1995.)

Attention deficit hyperactivity disorder

The research in this area is also exclusively from the United States, and uses a slightly different diagnostic system to the ICD 10, where these patients would be classified as having hyperkinetic disorders. The hypothesis put forward by these researchers is that attention deficit hyperactivity disorder (ADHD) in childhood progresses into adulthood in at least 50 per cent of cases. In adults, ADHD leads to self-medication and co-morbid substance misuse. Drugs used are typically stimulants. Therapeutic trials in adults have been shown to be effective with this group (Schubiner et al., 1995). The detection of the adult form of ADHD needs to be carefully separated from other psychiatric conditions and the symptom profile of inattention, impulsivity and hyperactivity particularly dating back to childhood needs to be established. The inclusion of this category within co-morbidity is not strictly correct as substance misuse in this case is secondary to the adult form of ADHD. If the primary diagnosis is addressed, then the substance misuse would be expected to recede, although this has yet to be confirmed by outcome studies. Initiation of treatment for ADHD, however, should not be done until the substance misuse has at least been stabilised (Wilens et al., 1995). In clinical populations with patients with ADHD, prevalence of substance misuse has been found to be approximately 20 per cent. As with conduct disorder in adolescence, the emphasis should be on prevention of substance misuse and targeting of adolescents with ADHD may reduce subsequent substance misuse disorders in adults. Further details of treatment strategies are outlined by Wilens and colleagues (1994).

Conclusion

In spite of the high levels of co-morbidity, the ability of doctors and particularly psychiatrists to assess substance misuse has been shown to be poor and training responses have been slow. There continues to be a need for doctors to have a low threshold for the detection of substance misuse in the assessment of their patients. Typical figures for in-patient psychiatric units are between 20 per cent prior to drug screening and 35 per cent following drug screening (Appleby et al., 1995; Galletly et al., 1993; Menezes et al., 1996). Depending on the catchment area and the specific type of institution, higher rates of co-morbidity can be found typically among young, male, urban, lower-income groups. Instances can go up to as high as 65 per cent (Cohen and Henkin, 1993). Failure to recognise substance misuse results in incorrect diagnosis, poor management and a worse prognosis. There needs to be an institutional shift to raise the profile of substance misuse problems in psychiatric cases. Substance misuse needs to be seen as 'a problem requiring help' rather than a 'behaviour requiring punishment'. It is not unknown for patients to be discharged from in-patient care if found to be using drugs and, in some instances, the hospital policy may be to call the police should drugs be found. In some cases drug misuse is seen as a reason for exclusion from psychiatric treatment, rather like smoking is seen as a reason for exclusion from coronary artery by-pass surgery. As for treatment there is no conclusive evidence as to whether sequential treatment, initially of the substance misuse and then of the co-morbid psychiatric disorder is indicated, or a simultaneous approach is more effective. However, case studies support a simultaneous approach. In sequential treatment, it is often difficult to retain patients in a substance misuse programme when their co-morbid syptomatology repeatedly induces high-risk relapse cues. It may be that abstinence is not a prerequisite for the treatment of co-morbid conditions but stabilisation is. This chapter has tried to contribute to the debate regarding co-morbidity but, until there is movement on how these patients are perceived, the quote at the beginning of this chapter will apply.

References

Appleby, L., Luchins, D.J. and Dyson, V. (1995), 'Effects of Mandatory Drug Screens on Substance Use Diagnoses in a Mental Hospital Population', *Journal of Nervous and Mental Disease*, **183**, (3), 183–4.

Baigent, M., Holme, G., Hafner, R.J. (1995), 'Self Reports of the Interaction Between Substance Abuse and Schizophrenia', *Australian and New Zealand Journal of Psychiatry*, **29**, (1), 69–74.

Barry, K.L., Fleming, M.F., Greenley, J.R., Kropp, S. and Widlak, P. (1996), 'Characteristics of Persons with Severe Mental Illness and Substance Abuse in Rural Areas', *Psychiatric Services*, **47**, (1), 88–90.

Bartels, S.J., Drake, R.E. and Wallach, M.A. (1995), 'Long-term Course of Substance Use Disorders Among Patients with Severe Mental Illness', *Psychiatric Services*, **46**, (3), 248–51.

Bremner, J.D., Southwick, S.M., Darnell, A. and Charney, D.S. (1996), 'Chronic PTSD in Vietnam Combat Veterans: Course of Illness and Substance Abuse', *American Journal of Psychiatry*, **153**, (3), 369–75.

Brown, P.J. and Wolfe, J. (1994), 'Substance Abuse and Post-traumatic Stress Disorder Comorbidity', *Drug and Alcohol Dependence*, **35**, (1), 51–9.

Burke, J.D. Jr, Burke, K.C. and Rae, D.S. (1994), 'Increased Rates of Drug Abuse and Dependence After Onset of Mood or Anxiety Disorders in Adolescence', *Hospital and Community Psychiatry*, **45**, (5), 451–5.

Cantwell, R. and Harrison, G. (1996), 'Substance Misuse in the Severely Mentally Ill', *Advances in Psychiatric Treatment*, **2**, 117–24.

Cohen, E. and Henkin, I. (1993), 'Prevalence of Substance Abuse by Seriously Mentally Ill Patients in a Partial Hospital Program', *Hospital and Community Psychiatry*, **44**, (2), 178–80.

Cottler, L.B., Price, R.K., Compton, W.M. and Mager, D.E. (1995), 'Subtypes of Adult Antisocial Behavior Among Drug Abusers', *Journal of Nervous and Mental Disease*, **183**, (3), 154–61.

Cuffell, B. (1992), 'Prevalence Estimates of Substance Abuse in Schizophrenia and Their Correlates', *Journal of Nervous and Mental Disease*, **180**, 589–92.

Cuffel, B.J., Heithoff, K.A. and Lawson, W. (1993), 'Correlates of Patterns of Substance Abuse Among Patients with Schizophrenia', *Hospital and Community Psychiatry*, **44**, (3), 247–51.

Darke, S., Swift, W. and Hall, W. (1994), 'Prevalence, Severity and Correlates of Psychological Morbidity Among Methadone Maintenance Clients', *Addiction*, **89**, 211–17.

Deering, C.G., Glover, S.G., Ready, D., Eddleman, H.C. and Alarcon, R.D. (1996), 'Unique Patterns of Comorbidity in Posttraumatic Stress Disorder from Different Sources of Trauma', *Comprehensive Psychiatry*, **37**, (5), 336–46.

Drake, R.E., Bartels, S.J., Teague, G.B., Noordsy, D.L. and Clark, R.E. (1993), 'Treatment of Substance Abuse in Severely Mentally Ill Patients', *Journal of Nervous and Mental Disease*, **181**, (10), 606–11.

Drake, R., Mueser, K. and Clark, R. (1996), 'The Course, Treatment and Outcome of Substance Disorders In Persons With Severe Mental Illness', *American Journal of Orthopsychiatry*, **66**, 42–51.

Dyer, C. (1996), 'Violence May Be Predicted Amongst Psychiatric Patients', *British Medical Journal*, **313**, 318.

Fabrega, H. Jr, Ulrich, R. and Comelius, J. (1993), 'Sociocultural and Clinical Characteristics of Patients with Comorbid Depressions: A Vomparison of Substance Abuse and Non-substance Abuse Diagnoses', *Comprehensive Psychiatry*, **34**, (5), 312–21.

Fals-Stewart, W. and Schafer, J. (1992), 'The Treatment of Substance Abusers Diagnosed with Obsessive-Compulsive Disorder: An Outcome Study', *Journal of Substance Abuse Treatment*, **9**, (4), 365–70.

Fals-Stewart, W. and Angarano, K. (1994), 'Obsessive-compulsive disorder among patients entering substance abuse treatment. Prevalence and accuracy of diagnosis', *Journal of Nervous and Mental Disease*, **82**,(12), 715–9.

Feirnnan, J.A. and Dunner, D.L. (1996), 'The Effect of Alcohol and Substance Abuse on the Course of Bipolar Affective Disorder', *Journal of Affective Disorders*, **12**, (1), 43–9.

Fergusson, D. and Horwood, L. (1997), 'Early Onset Cannabis Use and Psychosocial Adjustment in Young Adults', *Addiction*, **1992**, **32**, 279–96.

Galletly, C.A., Field, C.D. and Prior, M. (1993), 'Urine Drug Screening of Patients Admitted to a State Psychiatric Hospital', *Hospital and Community Psychiatry*, **44**, (6), 587–9.

Gill, K., Nolimal, D. and Crowley, T.J. (1992), 'Antisocial Personality Disorder, HIV Risk Behaviour and Retention in Methadone Maintenance Therapy', *Drug and Alcohol Dependence*, **30**, (3), 247–52.

Gill, B., Meltzer, H., Hindes, K. et al., (1996), 'Psychiatric Morbidity Among Homeless People', OPCS Survey of Psychiatric Morbidity in Great Britain, Report 7, London: HMSO.

Goldenberg, I.M., Mueller, T., Fierman, E., Gordon, A., Pratt, L., Cox, K., Park, T., Laweri, P., Goisman, R. and Keller, M. (1995), 'Specificity of Substance Use in Anxiety-disordered Subjects', *Comprehensive Psychiatry*, **36**, (5), 319–28.

Gupta, S., Hendricks, S., Kenkel, A.M., Bhatia, S.C. and Haffke, E.A. (1996), 'Relapse in Schizophrenia: Is There a Relationship to Substance Abuse?', *Schizophrenia Research*, **20**, (12), 153–6.

Hall, W. and Farrell, M. (1997), 'Co-morbidity of Mental Disorders with Substance Misuse', *British Journal of Psychiatry*, **171**, 425.

Haywood, T.W., Kravitz, H.M., Grossman, L.S., Cavanaugh, J.L. Jr, Davis, J.M. and Lewis, D.A. (1995), 'Predicting the "Revolving Door" Phenomenon Among Patients with Schizophrenic, Schizoaffective, and Affective Disorders', *American Journal of Psychiatry*, **152**, (6), 856–61.

Holderness, C.C., Brooks-Gunn, J. and Warren, M.P. (1994), 'Co-morbidity of Eating Disorders and Substance Abuse Review of the Literature', *International Journal of Eating Disorders*, **16**, (1), 1–34.

Johnstone, S. (1997), 'Dual Diagnosis of Severe Mental Illness and Substance Misuse: A Case for Specialist Services?', *British Journal of Psychiatry*, **171**, 205–8.

Kessler, R.C., McGonagle, K.A., Zhao, S., Nelson, C.B., Hughes, M., Eshleman, S., Wittchen, H.U. and Kendler, K.S. (1994), 'Lifetime and 12–month Prevalence of DSM-III-R Psychiatric Disorders in the United States. Results from the National Comorbidity Survey', *Archives of General Psychiatry*, **51**, (1), 8–19.

Kovasznay, B., Bromet, E., Schwartz, J.E., Ram, R., Lavelle, J. and Brandon, L. (1993), 'Substance Abuse and Onset of Psychotic Illness', *Hospital and Community Psychiatry*, **44**, (6), 567–71.

Lehman, A.F., Myers, C.P., Dixon, L.B. and Johnson, J.L. (1994), 'Defining Sub-groups of Dual Diagnosis Patients for Service Planning', *Hospital and Community Psychiatry*, **45**, (6), 556–61.

Meltzer, H., Gill, B. and Petticrew, M. et al. (1996), 'Economic Activity and Social Functioning of Residents with Psychiatric Disorders', OPCS Survey of Psychiatric Morbidity in Great Britain, Report 6, London: HMSO.

Menezes, P., Johnston, S., Thomicroft, G., Marshall, J., Prosser, D., Bebbington, P. and Kulpers, E. (1996), 'Drug and Alcohol Problems Among Individuals with Severe Mental Illness in South London', *British Journal of Psychiatry*, **168**, 612–19.

Modestin, J. and Ammann, R. (1995), 'Mental Disorders and Criminal Behaviour', *British Journal of Psychiatry*, **166**, (5), 667–75.

Mueser, K.T., Nishith, P., Tracy, J.I., DeGirolamo, J. and Molinaro, M. (1995), 'Expectations and Motives for Substance Use in Schizophrenia', *Schizophrenia Bulletin*, **21**, (3), 367–78.

Neeleman, J. and Farrell, M. (1997), 'Suicide and Substance Misuse', *British Journal of Psychiatry*, **171**, 303–4.

Owen, R.R., Fischer, E.P., Booth, B.M. and Cuffel, B.J. (1996), 'Medication Noncompliance and Substance Abuse Among Patients with Schizophrenia', *Psychiatric Services*, **47**, (8), 853–8.

Page, A.C. and Andrews, G. (1996), 'Do Specific Anxiety Disorders Show Specific Drug Problems?', *Australian and New Zealand Journal of Psychiatry*, **30**, (3), 410–14.

Reebye, P. Moretti, M.M. and Lessard, J.C. (1995), 'Conduct Disorder and Substance Use Disorder: Comorbidity in a Clinical Sample of Preadoleseents and Adolescents', *Canadian Journal of Psychiatry*, **40**, (6), 313–19.

Regier, D.A., Fartner, M.E., Rae, D.S. et al. (1990). 'Co-morbidity of Mental Disorders with Alcohol and Other Drug Abuse: Results from the ECA Study', *Journal of American Medical Association*, **264**, 2511–18.

Sanguineti, V.R. and Samuel, S.E. (1993), 'Comorbid Substance Abuse and Recovery from Acute Psychiatric Relapse', *Hospital and Community Psychiatry*, **44**, (11), 1073–76.

Schubiner, H., Tzelepis, A. and Isaacson, J.H. et al. (1995), 'The Dual Diagnosis of Attention-deficit/Hyperactivity Disorder and Substance Abuse: Case Reports and Literature Review', *Journal of Clinical Psychiatry*, **56**, (4), 146–50.

Smith, J. and Hucker, S. (1994), 'Schizophrenia and Substance Abuse', *British Journal of Psychiatry*, **165**, (1), 13–21.

Sokolski, K.N., Cummings, J.L., Abrams, B.I., DeMet, E.M., Katz, L.S. and Costa, J.F. (1994), 'Effects of Substance Abuse on Hallucination Rates and Treatment Responses in Chronic Psychiatric Patients', *Journal of Clinical Psychiatry*, **55**, (9), 380–7.

Sonne, S.C., Brady, K.T. and Morton, W.A. (1994), 'Substance Abuse and Bipolar Affective Disorder', *Journal of Nervous and Mental Disease*, **182**, (6), 349–52.

Strakowski, S.M., Keck, P.E. Jr, McElroy, S.L., Lonczak, H.S. and West, S.A. (1995), 'Chronology of Comorbid and Principal Syndromes in First-episode Psychosis', *Comprehensive Psychiatry*, **36**, (2), 106–12.

Swofford, C.D., Kasckow, J.W., Scheller-Gilkey, G. and Inderbitzin, L.B. (1996), 'Substance Use: A Powerful Predictor of Relapse in Schizophrenia', *Schizophrenia Research*, **20**, (1–2), 145–151

Thomas, H. (1993), 'Psychiatric Symptoms in Cannabis Users', *British Journal of Psychiatry*, **163**, 141–9.

Volavka, J., Mohammad, Y., Vitrai, J., Connotly, M., Stefanovic, M. and Ford, M.

(1995), 'Characteristics of State Hospital Patients Arrested for Offenses Committed During Hospitalization', *Psychiatric Services*, **46**, (8), 796–800.

Walker, Z. and Seifert, R. (1994), 'Violent Incidents in a Psychiatric Intensive Care Unit', *British Journal of Psychiatry*, **164**, (6), 826–8.

Warner, L.A., Kessler, R.C., Hughes, M., Anthony, J.C. and Nelson, C.B. (1995), 'Prevalence and Correlates of Drug Use and Dependence in the United States. Results from the National Comorbidity Survey', *Archives of General Psychiatry*, **52**, (3), 219–29.

Welch, S. and Fairburn, C. (1996), 'Impulsivity or Co-morbidity in Bulimia Nervosa. A Controlled Study of Deliberate Self Harm and Alcohol and Drug Misuse in a Community Sample', *British Journal of Addiction*, **169**, 451–8.

White, J. and Poole, L. (1995), 'Knowledge and Experience of Young People Regarding Drug Misuse 1969–94', *British Medical Journal*, **310**, 20–24.

Wilens, T.E., Biederman, J., Spencer, T.J. and Frances, R.J. (1994), 'Comorbidity of Attention-deficit Hyperactivity and Psychoactive Substance Use Disorders', *Hospital and Community Psychiatry*, **45**, (5), 421–3, 435.

Wilens, T.E., Prince, J.B., Biederman, J., Spencer, T.J. and Frances, R.J. (1995), 'Attention-deficit Hyperactivity Disorder and Comorbid Substance Use Disorders in Adults', *Psychiatric Services*, **46**, (8), 761–3, 765.

14 Issues in assessing the nature and extent of local drug misuse

Martin Frischer and Avril Taylor

Introduction

In this chapter we concentrate on the practical aspects of determining the nature and extent of drug misuse at a local level, giving examples from urban and rural areas. In the UK, with considerable public funding for medical and social responses to drug misuse, 'future service development must be based on a systematic and comprehensive assessment of the nature, extent and distribution of need' (Scottish Office Ministerial Drugs Task Force Report, 1994). While there is increasing information about national levels of drug misuse in the UK (Institute for the Study of Drug Dependence, 1997), the type of information available is more suited to strategic policy making than practical interventions, particularly in relation to treatment for drug use. It is well recognised that population surveys yield useful information on recreational use, while the Home Office Notification Index and the new regional drug misuse databases give some idea of the number of drug users in treatment. It is, however, the grey area between these two levels of drug use – what might be called 'potential problem drug use' – which needs to be addressed locally. This term denotes drug-taking which may involve users coming into contact with one or more agencies such as the police, medical practitioners and/or social services drug treatment agencies.

While the Task Force document stated that service development should be grounded in an assessment of the extent and pattern of drug use, previous experience in the UK and the US indicates that this strategy is often hindered by two factors. First, information on drug use hitherto has not linked into the policy making process and second, policy makers may attach little credibility to prevalence estimates (Hartnoll, 1991; Reuter, 1993). However *Tackling Drugs Together* (Home Office, 1995) and *Drugs in Scotland: Meeting the Challenge* (Scottish Office, 1994) have created a new climate in the UK and there are now a number of initiatives to use prevalence estimates and behavioural data to influence service development. In recent years, as local prevalence estimates have become more reliable (Frischer et al., 1993; Hay and McKeganey, 1996), there are opportunities to use this information as suggested in the Task Force report in the areas of resource allocation, targeting sub-populations and evaluating interventions.

Techniques for estimating drug use prevalence

The most basic question to which policy makers often seek an answer is 'How many drug users are there in my area?' Prevalence can be estimated using either direct or indirect methods. Additionally, it is also useful to have complementary information on drug users' attitudes and behaviour, for example, with regard to use of and attitudes towards services. Whichever approach is adopted, however, it should be noted that no single prevalence study is likely to cover the entire spectrum of drug use. A large number of substances are taken by various routes (e.g., orally, intravenously, nasally) to achieve psychic effects. The 1994 Scottish Drugs Misuse Bulletin, for example, reports 22 substances or combinations (excluding alcohol) taken by the 4 772 people reported to the Scottish Drugs Misuse Database by medical practitioners and treatment agencies in 1993/4 (Information and Statistics Division, 1994). In practice, prevalence studies focus on groups, such as opiate users or injectors, who are of concern at a particular time in a specific location. Accordingly, when drawing up the specification for a local prevalence (and/or behavioural study), a number of factors need to be considered (Table 1).

Direct methods of drug use prevalence estimation

This group of methods refers to either enumerating the number of people recorded by agencies who have contact with drug users or asking people directly, e.g., in a survey, about their use of drugs.

Enumeration of known users

The first stage of any local study will usually involve specifying a geographical area and the case definition for the type(s) of drug use of interest.

Table 14.1   Factors to consider for estimating drug use prevalence

Locale	Urban, rural
Population	Total, young adults, school children, people in need of treatment/services
Types of drug use	Illicit use of prescribed drugs, illegal use of controlled drugs, experimental use, 'problematic use'
Information required	Prevalence, incidence, frequency of use, trends, user characteristics
Resources available	Money, researchers, statutory data, statistical support

Once this is done, a count (enumeration) of the number of known drug users from one or more sources can be made. If identifier information is available and ethical consent obtained, it will then be possible to take into account people who are counted more than once. It is worth noting at this point that obtaining identifier information can be costly and time-consuming but, as will be seen below, is vital for many forms of prevalence estimation.

The simplest form of enumeration consists of collecting identifier information from all agencies in a given location which come into contact with users who meet a specified case definition. Parker and colleagues identified 1 848 cases (1 305 individuals) from 10 sources in the Wirral area of Merseyside in 1984–85 (Parker et al., 1988). Their case definition was simply problem drug use as evidenced by the involvement of official agencies. In Glasgow, an attempt to enumerate known drug-injecting during 1990 was more problematic because many agencies did not have information on injecting status and their definitions of drug use were tailored to their own requirements (Frischer, in press). For example, police data on drug use consists primarily of information on people arrested under the Misuse of Drugs Act. There is no way of ascertaining whether such people are injectors or even drug users. Other offences, e.g., those committed by drug users to finance the purchase of drugs, are not recorded as being drug-related. Problems encountered in retrospective enumeration can be avoided by setting up a prospective system for data collection. A prospective system has the advantage of ensuring standardised case definitions and reporting procedures. In practice this is likely to meet with resistance since agencies usually have good reasons for their in-house systems of data collection.

One drawback of prospective schemes is ensuring that all participants apply the same criteria in recording contact information.

The key source for enumeration information on problematic drug use in the UK are the Regional Drugs Misuse Databases (Institute for the Study of Drug Dependency). These contain information from a wide range of medical and non-medical agencies dealing with drug users. The validity of UK regional databases as a direct measure of prevalence has been questioned because: a) they reflect only the uptake of treatment services and b) identified users are likely to be unrepresentative of the general drug-using population (Sutton and Maynard, 1992). If the databases were used in isolation, the real size of the problem would be unknown, changes in trends and statistics would be difficult to interpret, and policy makers would be presented with an atypical picture of drug users. However, as a source of enumeration information, and when used in conjunction with other data sources, the regional databases are of considerable value (see the section on capture–recapture later in this chapter).

Needs assessments

In many situations, enumeration may form part of a needs assessment. As ascertaining drug users' needs is usually involved in quantifying the resources required to meet them, prevalence is bound to be, at least informally, specified during such a procedure. This view is endorsed in the Scottish Office Ministerial Drugs Task Force Report which recognised that, 'for effective policy development and service planning, needs assessments and prevalence estimates should be combined'. Needs assessment has been defined as 'looking at a representative sample of the drug misusing population, to ascertain social and healthcare needs'. However, it is unclear how a representative sample can be drawn without knowledge of prevalence.

Several needs assessments have been conducted in recent years by the Scottish Drugs Forum. Assessments usually take three to six months, during which time a field-worker will work with local people to identify needs and formulate appropriate responses. In 1992, for example, a needs assessment was conducted in East Lothian with the operational aim of providing statistical and qualitative data on problem drug use in order to 'facilitate the development of a local strategy to guide development and prioritisation of services' (McKenna, 1993). Four methods were used:

1   Collation of data from document sources.
2   Semi-structured interview and questionnaires to workers coming into contact with drug users (e.g., social workers, health visitors, general practitioners).

3   Survey of 100 people aged 13–18 attending youth clubs.
4   Survey of 47 problem drug users.

Multi source enumeration (method 1) was judged to be of limited value, although identifier information was not obtained. The survey of young people (method 3) gave some idea of prevalence: there were indications of increasing experimentation with drugs towards the younger end of the age spectrum. Overall, the needs assessment approach provides a general overview of known drug misuse, which for many purposes may be sufficient. However, most assessments do not really enumerate the extent of the hidden population of potentially problematic users who may require services.

Population surveys

Whereas needs assessments usually interview convenience samples, population surveys generally aim to interview representative samples of the population of interest. As mentioned in the introduction, general population surveys are increasingly seen as valid instruments for assessing casual or recreational drug use. For example, the 1994 British Crime Survey found that 28 per cent of the 10 000 16–59-year-olds who self-completed a questionnaire about drug use admitted to lifetime use (Ramsay and Percy, 1996). These findings were broadly in line with the Drug Use and Drug Prevalence Study (Leitner et al., 1993) carried out two years earlier. This was a household survey of 5 000 respondents aged 16 years and over from four cities in England and Scotland. Each city provided a representative sample of approximately 1 000 people from the general population along with a 'booster' sample of 250 young people thought to be most at risk from drug misuse.

Large scale population surveys are useful for providing information about drug use prevalence at the national level and for allowing comparison between geographic areas (Ramsay and Percy, 1997). By the inclusion of demographic and lifestyle questions, another major advantage of surveys lies in their ability to provide information about the characteristics and lifestyle factors associated with drug misuse.

Like other approaches to estimating drug use prevalence, however, large scale or household surveys have limitations. Whereas the face validity of enumeration is high, it is more difficult to assess in a survey whether people can accurately recall past events and, further, that they then truthfully report their behaviour. Responses may also depend on respondent/interviewer characteristics and the way in which information is obtained. For example, a self-completion questionnaire within the context of a face-to-face interview on crime may suggest that researchers perceive drug use as bad. In self-completion questionnaires, some respondents may misunderstand the procedure or tick the wrong boxes by mistake (although the use of lap-top computers for self-completion appears to reduce this type of error (Ramsay and Percy, 1997). Household surveys also tend to ignore other settings such as prisons and homeless units where high-risk groups may be more likely to be found.

General population studies are particularly problematic at a local level as very large samples are required for problematic drug use (e.g., injecting) to be identified. For example, in the 1993 Scottish Crime Survey, questionnaires on drug use were completed by 3 197 people aged 16–59 (Hammersley, 1994). With 15 health board areas in Scotland, sample sizes in individual health boards are of limited utility in determining the scale of local drug use. Of course, local samples can be higher when total geographical coverage is not required. One of the centres included in the 1992 Drug Use and Drug Prevalence Study was the city of Glasgow, where a representative sample of 972 people aged 16 and over were interviewed (response rate: 71 per cent) together with a 'booster' sample of 258 people aged 16–25 living in areas of social deprivation (Leitner et al., 1993).

Figure 14.1 shows that almost 20 per cent of the main sample and over 50 per cent of the booster sample had 'ever used' an illicit substance. However,

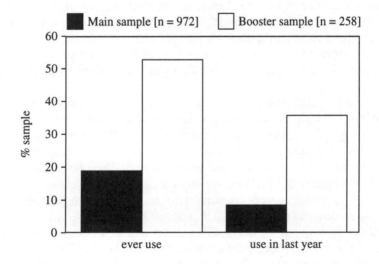

Figure 14.1   Drug use and drug prevention survey conducted in Glasgow, 1992: Use of controlled or unprescribed drugs

rates of reported injecting were only one per cent among regular drug users (those who had used drugs in the last year) in the main sample and two per cent in the booster sample. These percentages, extrapolated to Glasgow, suggest that the number of current injectors was about 2 000 in 1990, although this is based on self-reported injecting from only three individuals. If even one or two of these respondents ticked the box incorrectly or misunderstood the question, the estimate would be considerably different. Conversely, if one or two injectors did not report, for whatever reason, that they had injected in the previous year, prevalence would be underestimated.

Another factor which needs to be considered is non-response. Detailed studies of non-responders in the USA (Turner et al., 1992) indicate that a proportion of non-responders do not differ from responders with respect to the use of cannabis or cocaine (neutral non-responders). However, some non-responders (18 per cent in the American study) were more likely to be taking these drugs. This group is referred to as critical non-responders. If we apply the same critical non-responder correction factor as was used in a recent German study (Institut für Therapieforschung, 1994) to the Drug Use and Drug Prevalence Study, the estimate would increase to 14 000!

At the aggregate level of ever used drugs, the impact of critical non-responders is probably minimal and therefore the prevalence of 'ever use' found in the 1993 Scottish Crime Survey (Hammersley, 1994) is probably within the confidence limits shown in Figure 14.2. However, the figure also illustrates the wider confidence intervals for selected health board areas. Should these regional differences be used, for example, in determining resource allocation for education and prevention?

School surveys

School surveys are utilised to calculate prevalence of drug use among school-age children, who are often excluded from or inadequately represented in general population surveys. One of the most comprehensive British surveys of schoolchildren has recently been conducted by Miller and Plant (1996). More than 7 000 pupils aged 15–16 years from 69 schools throughout the UK completed a questionnaire on substance use. Lifetime use of an illicit substance was reported by 40.6 per cent of pupils. The results also indicated regional differences, with Scottish pupils most likely to have used drugs. Schools surveys are prone to the same limitations as general population surveys, however. Additionally, pupils absent without leave may be more likely to be drug users.

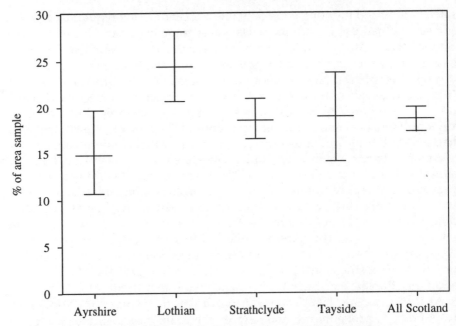

Figure 14.2　Selected regional comparisons of drug use from the 1993 Scottish Crime Survey (estimated prevalence and 95% CI for 'over' use of controlled drugs among adults aged 15–59)

Indirect methods of prevalence estimation

The limitations of direct prevalence estimation have led to the development of indirect methods which usually take as their starting point some form of direct enumeration. The indirect methods generally require considerable fieldwork and/or statistical sophistication. It is, therefore, important to understand the assumptions on which the models are based and the limitations of resultant estimates.

Capture–recapture method

The capture–recapture method (CRM) is often perceived as having the greatest scientific credibility for estimating the prevalence of drug use. The method is worth considering is some detail as it provides insight into the many factors which can affect prevalence estimation. CRM refers to a technique developed over a century ago to estimate wild animal populations. The method involves 'capturing' a random sample, who are then marked and returned to their habitat. Subsequently a second random sample is 'recaptured' and the number of marked animals from the first sample is recorded. The ratio of marked animals to the recaptured sample is assumed to be the same as the ratio of the first sample to the total population. Thus, if a 'capture' sample of 200 animals are marked and released and a 'recapture' sample of 100 contains ten animals which are marked, the estimate for the total population would be 2 000 (i.e., 10:100=200:2 000). Begon (1979) provides justification for this method and an interesting overview of the many variants of CRM. Laporte (1994) regards CRM of such importance that it could 'bring about a paradigm shift in how counting is done in all the disciplines that assess human populations'.

For this method to produce a reliable population estimate, certain criteria must be met and assumptions made. All individuals should have the same defining characteristics and be uniquely identified. Identification of a case in a sample should not change that individual's behaviour with respect to another sample. All individuals must have the same probability of being sampled. Unobserved (i.e., 'hidden') individuals must behave in a similar way to observed individuals. While the animal population estimates are based on sequential samples, in the case of human beings it is feasible (and often more practicable) to use simultaneous samples. Instead of identifying marks, identifier information is obtained from different sources which record contacts with the population of interest.

The capture–recapture method – an illustrative example using data from Ayrshire

Although the 1993 Scottish Crime Survey indicated that the prevalence of ever drug use in Ayrshire was lower than the Scottish average (see Figure 2), there were differing perceptions as to the extent of problematic drug use in the area. Ayrshire and Arran Health Board (AAHB) commissioned research in order to assess the prevalence and nature of drug use (Frischer et al., 1997a; Taylor et al., 1997a).

CRM analyses were conducted using 1995 data firstly for potentially problematic drug use by any mode of administration including injecting and secondly, only injecting (not presented here, see Frischer et al., 1997a for further details). Ethical approval was obtained to collect partial identifier information from the four sources shown in Table 14.2. This information was only used to match cases; thereafter absolutely no use was made of identifier information.

The CRM analysis began with simple two-samples estimates (see Table 3). Three of the estimates are fairly similar (2320–2930) while a further two involving sample 3 (police) are considerably higher (5870–6235). In view of

Table 14.2   Sources of information on drug users used in Ayrshire CRM analysis

Source	Source details and number of cases	Sample used to estimate users	Sample used to estimate injectors
1 Voluntary named HIV-test	Risk category, injecting drug user = 32	32	32
2 Treatment for drug use	Scottish morbidity records: SMR 1 (general hospital) = 189 SMR 4 (psychiatric hospital) = 68 SMR 22/23 (medical/non-medical drug treatment agencies) =175	364 (SMR 1 and SMR 22/23)	66 (injected last month – SMR 22/3)
3 Police arrests under Misuse of Drugs Act	amphetamine = 116, heroin = 2, cocaine = 2, LSD = 2, unprescribed painkilliers = 13, others = 14	129 (amphetamine and painkillers)	129
4 Behavioural interview study	29 current injectors, 116 current users	145	29

Table 14.3 **Preliminary estimates of the number of drug users and injectors in Ayrshire based on two sources and assuming independence**

Samples (S)	$S_A \times S_B/$ overlaps between S_A and S_B)	Estimated population	95% confidence interval
1/2	(32 × 364)/5	2330	430–4230
1/4	(32 × 145)/2	2320	0–5470
2/3	(364 × 129)/8	5870	1890–9840
2/4	(364 × 145)/18	2930	1670–4190
3/4	(129 × 145)/3	6235	0–13270

Samples: S1 = HIV test, S2 = treatment for drug use, S3 = police arrests under Misuse of Drugs Act, S4 = behavioural interview study

this disparity it seems very likely that individuals in the police sample are drawn from a larger group of recreational or casual drug users.

Based on the information gained from the two samples estimates, three samples estimates were obtained by linear modelling. This is a standard method which involves using the information on sample size and overlap between samples to estimate the number of unobserved drug users and injectors. The results are shown in Table 4. The stability of estimates when stratified for age or gender, adds confidence to their reliability.

Although stratification is a form of internal validation, it was also possible to verify the estimates from a concurrent study of drug users' behaviour in Ayrshire (Taylor et al., 1997a) (see combined methods section later in this chapter for further details). Of the estimated 2 800 potentially problematic drug users in Ayrshire, 425 were known to have received treatment for drug use. The ratio of known to unknown users of approximately 1:6 is fairly similar to the proportion of those in the behavioural study who had received treatment for drug use in the last year (26/119, approximately 1 in 5). In Glasgow it was possible to validate the CRM estimate of 8 500 injectors in 1990 using HIV data. The HIV prevalence rate among 503 injectors tested in a multi-site survey was 1.4 per cent. Combining these figures resulted in a projected 119 HIV positive current injectors in Glasgow. Data to the end of December 1990 showed that there were 100 known HIV positive injectors from Glasgow, of whom 12 had died. As there are likely to have been several unknown HIV positive injectors (either to themselves or

Table 14.4   Estimated number of drug users in Ayrshire, 1995

	Number of known users	Percentage of total estimate	Estimated total number of users	95% confidence interval	Prevalence (%)
All cases	519	19	2765	1949–4069	2.1 [1.5–3.1]
Males	387	15	2628	1767–4287	4.0 [2.7–6.6]
Females	126	33	381	246–676	0.6 [0.4–1.0]
15–24	275	21	1568	1025–2675	2.7 [2.1–5.6]
25–39	207	30	905	577–1607	0.9 [0.7–1.9]

the register), the comparison provided some validation of the drug injecting prevalence estimate.

As mentioned above, the 1992 Drug Use and Drug Prevention Survey (DUDP) estimated 2 000 current injectors (Leitner et al., 1993), which is obviously much lower than the 1990 CRM estimate. There are many reasons for exercising caution in comparing the two estimates. The DUDP estimates are based on the positive reports of three individuals, whereas the CRM estimates are based on 2 866 known drug users. (As discussed above, it was not possible to ascertain whether they were all injectors). Recent research also indicates that prevalence has been declining since 1990 (Frischer et al., 1997b). Finally, these arguments are inverted if a correction factor for critical non-responders is applied which, as discussed above, increases the DUDP estimate to 14 000.

Network analysis

Whereas CRM attempts to gauge the extent of the hidden population by statistical projection from two or more samples of known users, network analysis involves direct contact with small samples of users who provide information on their peers. The success of network analysis depends on the selection of informants and there are a number of common sense steps which should be taken during their selection. They should be firmly established within a drug-using network and should have good rapport with the field worker. There are obvious dangers in using either peripheral or encyclopedic informants whose referrals may produce biased data. Peripheral informants are likely to have minimal contact with other drug users, while with encyclopedic informants there is a danger that they have extensive contact with a sub-group of drug users. Unlike CRM, there has been little theoretical work to statistically underpin the validity of prevalence estimates resulting from network analysis.

One of the most comprehensive network analyses was conducted in the Wirral area of Merseyside in 1986 by Howard Parker and colleagues (1988). The Wirral has a population of about 340 000 which consists of 48 townships with populations ranging from 1 300 to 10 000. Four townships were chosen with varying levels of known heroin use. In each of the four townships, a field worker with extensive local knowledge and contacts selected one known drug user as a respondent who then introduced further respondents by means of a referral chain. Fifteen referrals were interviewed by the field worker in each area. Four methods were then employed to estimate prevalence of opiate use.

1   *Snowball ratio*   The 60 referrals were asked if they had been in contact with (specified) agencies in the Wirral; their identifier information was then compared with known user lists from these agencies. The main problem with this method is that with only 15 cases in each township, the ratios of unknown to known are very sensitive to fluctuations in a small number of cases.

2   *Nominee peer group*   The 60 referrals were then asked how many of their five closest friends (of the same sex and living in the same township) regularly used heroin during the previous year and, of these, how many had received treatment or been arrested for drugs offences during this period. Identifier information for nominated peers was used to establish an unknown to known ratio for each township.

3   *Triangulation*   The 60 referrals were asked to provide initials and gender for up to ten people who they knew to have taken heroin regularly in 1986. Seven people would not provide identifier information. The 53 remaining interviewees nominated 297 other persons. Removal of duplicates (same initials and gender) left 163 unique cases – of these 66 were identified as known users and 97 as hidden. The lack of identifier information may have eliminated persons who should have been included.

4   *Snowball-recapture*   The population size was estimated using two-sample CRM. The first sample consisted of the 60 referrals produced by the snowball method and the second of the 237 people 'known' to agencies in the four townships. The results of the four methods are shown in Figure 14.3 below.

The application of four methods which produce fairly similar unknown to known ratios within townships suggests that each of the methods used are

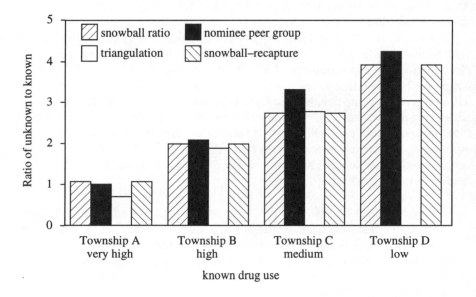

Figure 14.3   Four methods used to estimate the ratio of unknown to known opiate users in the Wirral, 1985

valid. However, it must be stressed that both methods and results cannot be separated from the context, and there is no guarantee that the same pattern of findings would be found in other locations. One drawback of nomination techniques is the requirement for supplying identifier information for friends or acquaintances. There may be communities where people would not be willing to give such information. One option is to ask nomination type questions but not request identifier information. This method was applied in the Ayrshire prevalence and behavioural study (Frischer et al., 1997a).

Ratio-estimation method

This method relies on responses to a series of simple questions and works as follows. Respondents in area Y are asked, how many people do you personally know who use drugs in Y and, of these (the nominees), how many have been in treatment in Y in the last year? Interviewee and nominee characteristics can then be related to known aggregate statistics (e.g., the number of people known to be in treatment or the number of arrests for drugs offences). Assume that the proportion of interviewees in/out of treatment is 1:2. This proportion is then applied to the total number of drug users known to be in treatment in area Y. Thus, with 70 known drug users in treatment, there are an estimated 140 drug users not in treatment. If the proportion among interviewees reflects the drug-using population, the estimate of unknown users will be accurate. The same principles apply to the nominee–ratio method but, whereas the number of unique cases is known in the interviewee–ratio method, nominees could refer to the same person. However, the accuracy of the nominee–ratio depends not on absolute numbers of nominees but the proportions of the numerator (nominees in treatment) and the denominator (nominees out of treatment) which are unique. If the proportions are similar, the estimate of unknown users will be accurate. If, however, the proportion of unique cases in the numerator is, for example, lower than in the denominator, the number of unknown users will be underestimated. As with the other network techniques, the nominee–ratio method is subject to uncontrollable sources of error and estimates depend on the plausibility of the assumptions.

Between October 1995 to January 1996, 149 current drug users (of whom 30 were injectors) were interviewed in a wide range of settings in Ayrshire (Taylor et al., 1997a) (see Combined methods section below). From the

Table 14.5   Ratio estimation for current injectors in Ayrshire, 1995

Interviewee–ratio method	N	Nominee–ratio method	N
Injector-interviewees	30	Nominated injectors	578
Injector-interviewees in treatment in AAHB	21	Nominee injectors reported to be in treatment	299
Injector-interviewees not in treatment AAHB	9	Nominee injectors out of treatment	279
Known injectors in treatment in AAHB	211	Total known in treatment	211
Estimated unknown injectors not in treatment in AAHB	90	Estimated not in treatment	197
Estimated total number of injectors	301	Estimated number of injectors	408

responses to questions on treatment and drug offences, eight ratio estimates were made; six for injectors and two for users. Table 5 gives examples of the interviewee– and nominee–ratio methods for drug injectors.

The number of 'known' injectors is actually an estimate based on returns from drug treatment agencies to the Scottish Drugs Misuse Database. Of the 175 people reported during 1995, 40 per cent had injected in the previous month and 60 per cent in the last year. The figure of 211 in Table 4 represents 50 per cent of all those known to be receiving treatment for drug use in Ayrshire. If this figure is reasonable, then the estimated number of unknown injectors based on the ratio-estimation methods is 90–197, which suggests that a considerable proportion of injectors are not in touch with services.

Combined methods

One of the disadvantages of indirect methods of prevalence estimation is that they provide little information about the characteristics and behaviours of the individuals counted in the estimation, or about their needs with regard to drug treatment services. To counter this limitation, health boards in Scotland have commissioned studies which combine indirect methods with survey methodology (Frischer et al., 1997a; Taylor et al., 1997a; Taylor et al., 1997b; Taylor and Farquhar, 1997).

In Ayrshire, for example, in addition to the capture–recapture and ratio–estimation techniques, 149 drug users were interviewed between October 1995 and January 1996 about a wide range of topics related to drug use, including patterns of drug use and service utilisation (Frischer et al., 1997b). In order to ensure that a representative sample was recruited, rather than focussing exclusively on problematic drug users, a multi-site sampling strategy was employed with drug users interviewed in both in-treatment and out-of-treatment settings. All the sample had used an illicit drug in the six months prior to interview, and a fifth of those interviewed were current drug injectors. The responses to the questionnaire provided policy makers with information about the levels of satisfaction among drug users about current service provision, along with an indication of the types of problems most commonly experienced by drug users in the area.

Summary and future developments

In a recent survey of Scottish drug action teams, most respondents indicated that they expected drug misuse to increase in their area over the next five years. With some exceptions, they also felt that existing surveillance and research did not provide a sound basis for planning services to drug users. Against this pessimistic background there are, however, some encouraging signs. Many areas are now conducting prevalence and/or behavioural studies on drug use and there is the will to use the results in formulating policy. The examples given in this chapter illustrate some of the potential for assessing local needs.

In the wider context, the European Drug Monitoring Centre for Drugs and Drug Addiction (EMCDDA), discussed in the chapter on European Policy, has recognised the need to improve prevalence estimation throughout Europe, and considerable resources are being devoted to achieving this aim. However, this will not result in a cook-book which researchers can apply in their area, but rather a refinement of the type of methods discussed in this chapter. In so far as problematic drug use is illicit and illegal, difficulties will always remain in determining the nature and extent of the phenomena and policy makers need to accept a degree of uncertainty accompanying prevalence estimates.

References

Begon, M. (1979), *Investigating Animal Abundance: Capture-recapture for Biologists*, London: Edward Arnold.

Frischer, M., Leyland, A., Cormack, R., Goldberg, D., Bloor, M., Green, S., Taylor, A., Covell, R., McKeganey, N. and Platt, S. (1993), 'Estimating Population Prevalence of Injection Drug Use and HIV Infection Among Injection Drug Users in Glasgow', *American Journal of Epidemiology*, **138**, (3), 170–81.

Frischer, M., Taylor, A. and Barr, C. (1997a), *Estimates of Drug Use Prevalence in Ayrshire and Arran*, Glasgow: Scottish Centre for Infection and Environmental Health.

Frischer, M., Goldberg, D., Taylor, A. and Bloor, M. (1997b), 'Estimating the Incidence and Prevalence of Injecting Drug Use in Glasgow', *Addiction Research*, **5**, (4), 307–15.

Frischer, M. (in press), 'More Complex Capture–Recapture Models: An Illustrative Case Study Using Data From Glasgow, Scotland', in G. Stimson (ed.), *Estimating the Prevalence of Drug Misuse in Europe*, Strasbourg: Council of Europe.

Hammersley, R. (1994), *Use of Controlled Drugs in Scotland: Findings from the 1993 Scottish Crime Survey*, Edinburgh: Scottish Office Central Research Unit.

Hartnoll, R. (1991), 'Epidemiological Approaches to Drug Misuse in Britain', *Journal of Addictive Diseases*, **11**, (1), 47–60.

Hay, G. and McKeganey, N. (1996), 'Estimating the Prevalence of Drug Misuse in Dundee, Scotland: An Application of Capture–Recapture Methods', *Journal of Epidemiology and Community Health,* **50**, (4), 469–72.

Home Office (1994), *Tackling Drugs Together: A Consultation Document on a Strategy for England, 1995–1998,* London: HMSO.

Information and Statistics Division of the Common Services Agency for the National Health Service in Scotland (1994), *Scottish Drugs Misuse Database Bulletin 1994,* Edinburgh: ISD Publications.

Institut für Therapieforschung (1994), *Report on the Methods of Estimating the Extent of the Drug Problems in Germany,* Munich: IFT.

Institute for the Study of Drug Dependence (1997), *Drug Misuse in Britain 1996,* London: ISDD.

Laporte, R. (1994), 'Assessing the Human Condition: Capture–Recapture Techniques', *British Medical Journal,* **308**, 5–6.

Leitner, M., Shapland, J. and Wiles, P. (1993), *Drug Usage and Drug Prevention: The Views and Habits of the General Public,* London: HMSO.

McKenna, C. (1993), *Problem Drug Use and Related Needs in East Lothian,* Glasgow: Scottish Drugs Forum.

Miller, P. McC. and Plant, M. (1996), 'Drinking, Smoking and Illicit Drug Use Among 15 and 16 Year-olds in the United Kingdom', *British Medical Journal,* **313**, 394–7.

Parker, H., Bakx, K. and Newcombe, R. (1988), *Living with Heroin,* Milton Keynes: Open University Press.

Ramsay, M. and Percy, A. (1996), *Drug Misuse Declared: Results of the 1994 British Crime Survey,* London: Home Office.

Ramsay, M. and Percy, A. (1997), 'A National Household Survey of Drug Misuse in Britain: A Decade of Development', *Addiction,* **92**, (8), 931–7.

Reuter, P. (1993), 'Prevalence Estimation and Policy Formulation', *Journal of Drug Issues,* **23**, (2), 167–84.

Scottish Office Ministerial Drugs Task Force (1994), *Drugs in Scotland: Meeting the Challenge,* Edinburgh: The Scottish Office Home and Health Department.

Sutton, M. and Maynard, M. (1992), *What is the Size and Nature of the 'Drug' Problem in the UK?,* York: Centre for Health Economics.

Taylor, A., Frischer, M. and Farquhar, D. (1997a), *Rural Patterns of Illicit Substance Users in Ayrshire and Arran,* Glasgow: Scottish Centre for Infection and Environmental Health.

Taylor, A., Hutchinson, S.J., Frischer, M. and Barr, C. (1997b), *Estimating the Population Prevalence of Drug Use and Injecting Drug Use in Argyll and Clyde in 1995,* Glasgow: Scottish Centre for Infection and Environmental Health.

Taylor, A. and Farquhar, D. (1997), *Behavioural Patterns of Illicit Substance Users in Argyll and Clyde Health Board Area,* Glasgow: Scottish Centre for Infection and Environmental Health.

Turner, C.F., Lessler, J.T. and Gfroerer, J.C. (eds) (1992), *Survey Measurement of Drug Use: Methodological Studies,* Maryland: US Department of Health and Human Studies.

15 Creating a local strategy
Cameron Stark and Brian A. Kidd

Nothing is more dangerous than an idea, when it's the only one you've got.

E. Charter

Introduction

Earlier chapters in this book provide an overview of important aspects of drug misuse. This chapter differs from the others in that it does not provide new information, but rather tries to provide a framework within which to think about local strategy development. It argues that a strategic approach is an asset to an area and that flexibility and local adaptation are essential for success.

Do strategic approaches matter? In relation to drug use, an example of the importance of a concerted approach lies in HIV infection. The United Kingdom has been extraordinarily successful in preventing an epidemic of HIV infection in injecting drug users and curtailing it where it has already occurred (Stimson, 1995, 1996; Wodak, 1996). Brazil provides an example of a system which started with similar conditions, but where no organised attempt at HIV prevention was made (Dunn and Laranjeira, 1996). In mid-1995, Brazil, with three times the population of the UK, had 22 times the UK's cumulative number of people with AIDS whose main risk factor was injecting drug use. This is a striking example of integrated policy in drug use and, moreover, such responses to injecting will be required to combat Hepatitis C infection, which is far easier to contract than HIV. The problems associated with illicit drug use are not confined to infectious illnesses, however, and a wider response is needed to make the best use of resources invested in drug treatment, enforcement and prevention.

Strategic plans

Taken with the other material available on drug misuse – local and national reports, information from services and from drug users and their families, academic journals, newspaper reports and other textbooks – the volume of information and advice for people developing local strategies is overwhelming. How can all this material be converted into a local strategy and plan of action?

A strategic plan describes where an organisation – in this case, usually a collection of organisations in a Drug Action Team (DAT) – wants to go. It also sets out the actions or steps needed to achieve this (Hicks and Gullett, 1981). Strategic planning is much criticised. This is partly because of some catastrophic failures of strategic planning in business settings, but also because the environment in which organisations function changes so quickly. Strategic plans are often regarded as huge, distant creations, which are as difficult to slow down, stop and change direction as are oil tankers lumbering across the Atlantic. Front-line workers are disillusioned by years of consecutive strategic plans abandoned after only a few years, and replaced by others which are, in some cases, quite different from those which went before. Others cite difficulties in having uncomfortable information acknowledged. Data which do not fit in the strategic plan are often ignored. Common complaints about strategic planning are listed below (adapted from Irwin, 1978). Does it have to be this way?

- We don't have time to plan – we're too busy worrying about today
- Change in the drug field is too rapid – it doesn't make sense trying to plan for something we can't predict
- Planning will limit our flexibility and make it hard to respond to new demands
- Information on local drug use is poor and evidence on the effectiveness of interventions is limited – we would be basing plans on flawed or even downright wrong information
- We plan all the time, but nothing happens – it is only to keep managers happy, it does not change anything, so why waste our time in it?

There are variations of strategic planning theory, but most recognise that all planning is based on limited information, and that modification is inevitable as circumstances change. Effective planning involves five elements (adapted from Boyle, 1988):

1 *Visible commitment* The people at the top – Directors of Social Work, Chief Executives of NHS Trusts, Chairmen of Health Authorities and the like – must show that they are committed to joint planning. This must include devoting appropriate resources to planning and implementation. If this step is not in place, or it is obvious to others that only lip-service is being paid, then the process is made much more difficult or even impossible.

2 *Removal of organisational barriers* Drug services were established as individual entities. They do not lend themselves easily to joint planning. Reaching a stage where battles over territorial control are prevented, or at least recognised and tackled head on, is difficult but important. In some cases, individuals have long-held views on drug misuse which are not in line with a new plan (e.g., objection to harm minimisation when it has been adopted as a cornerstone of the local strategy). These objections will have to be acknowledged and addressed by the parent organisation. This may require transferring responsibilities to others, or making it clear to an individual that they must function within the new policy framework.

3 *Ownership* People working within services, or involved in other ways, have to have a reasonable understanding of the nature of the overall strategic approach. People need the opportunity to have their views heard during strategy development, and to understand how decisions have been reached.

4 *Clear, rapid feedback on progress* Strategies gather dust. For people in direct contact with clients, this week's strategy may be next week's scrap paper. Everyone needs to know how the process is developing, and to see how new developments or altered services fit into the overall picture. Where there are problems in making changes to services, it is important that people are aware of the nature of the difficulty, and what is being done to address it.

5 *Problem solving during implementation* Nothing goes smoothly. An enormous amount of work is required for strategic plans to convert into effective action. In some cases problems can be addressed easily, while in others they will be complex inter-organisational problems which will need to be acknowledged and tackled.

Nature of local strategy development

Strategic planning is often presented as a cycle (Figure 15.1). When this type of model is used, the feedback is often intended only to tell the parent strategy group where there are deviations from the long-term plan. In other circumstances (the barrier indicated as 'A' in Figure 15.1), the strategy group has ceased to exist, and the strategic plan has taken on a life of its own as an unquestionable central doctrine.

In real life, planning will often function as in Figure 15.2, and it is as well to accept this at the outset and to establish a mechanism which can accommodate this. Illegal drug use changes. Hall (1997) has likened drug treatment services in the UK to generals preparing to fight the last war, in that many are targeted at opiate use, rather than new patterns of recreational drug use. New information regarding ideal services or unmet need appears frequently. If a strategic plan is to retain credibility, it is important that it can adapt and

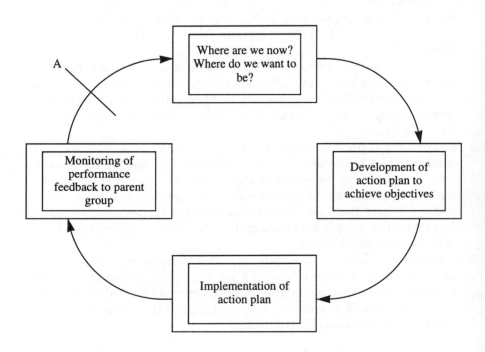

Figure 15.1   Traditional strategic planning model

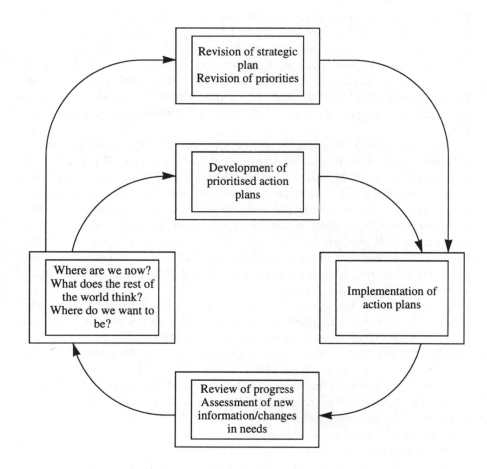

Figure 15.2   Real-life strategic planning model

remain a living plan, and not a dead, dusty snapshot. The needs assessment stage discussed below should be seen in this context.

Assessing need

People spend a great deal of time and effort in worrying about the right methods to obtain information on need. Many drug strategy groups have debated the rights and wrongs of extending epidemiological prevalence estimates to their area, of the relative merits of surveys, focus groups, collated data or individual needs assessments. The differences in approach are real, but combining a range of methods is likely to provide the best picture of overall need in an area (McKeganey, 1995; Social Work Services Inspectorate, 1996). Frischer and Taylor review information gathering methods in Chapter 14. A useful example of a combined qualitative and quantitative approach can be found in McGourty and Hotchkiss (1994). Examples of information sources can be found in the ISDD document 'Tackling Drugs Informatively' (ISDD, 1996), and the Health Education Board for Scotland publication, 'Drugs in Scotland: Informing the Challenge' (Agyako et al., 1997).

In general, much information on overall levels of illegal drug use can be obtained from population surveys into health and lifestyle. This is information which is available already in most areas, and which often includes surveys in schools. The prevalence of use of heroin, for example, is likely to be low in the general population and will not be readily identified in large-scale surveys. Often small focused pieces of work are required to examine needs in special groups. The method will vary from area to area according to what information is already available, but Table 15.1 shows some examples. All will provide some information, but together they help to make strategy development more responsive.

Some groups of people are difficult to access. In Chapter 12, Paton describes some of the difficulties involved in contacting sex workers who use drugs. Similar challenges are encountered with ethnic minority groups, in which drug use may be even more stigmatised than in the general population. In addition some groups will feel, often with justification, that services have let them down in the past, and that no effort has been made to tailor services to their needs. Strongly held views like these can make it difficult to obtain relevant information, but also make it even more important that adequate assessment is carried out. In other cases, groups of people require attention not because of their number, but because of the special nature of their need. Pregnant drug users, for example, while small in number at any one time, need special attention if their wants and needs are to be addressed. Local work is essential if such needs are to be identified and addressed. These issues relating to particular groups or situations are covered in more detail in the 'specialist' Chapters 7 to 12 which focus on rural areas, women, prisons, clubs, sex-workers and drug users with co-morbid illnesses.

Developing a framework

The structure of this book lends itself to use as a means of considering need. The main division of the UK policy documents – into prevention, treatment and enforcement – offers an obvious structure. Experience suggests that this misses many of the complexities that local strategies will want to ad-

Table 15.1 Examples of information sources in strategy development

Group	Information sought	Method/information sources
General population	Overall drug use	Population lifestyle surveys
School children	Drug use	School surveys Police information Hospital treatment, e.g. for volatile substance use
	Trends over time	Sequential surveys using similar methods
	Children's views	Structured discussions
	Parent's levels of information	Focus groups
Clubbers	Number	Snapshot surveys in clubs on particular nights Snowball sampling
	Views	Focus groups Informal discussion at clubs
Injecting drug users	Number	Needle exchange use Specialist service information – e.g. prescribing information, drug service attendances Police figures Capture–recapture estimates
	Risk factors	Surveys of people identified as injecting drugs Statistical estimates used to supply information on people not in contact with services
	Hepatitis B/C, HIV prevalence	Results of tests where injecting drug use known to be a risk factor Small-scale local surveys Testing of anonymous blood samples
	Views of services	Opinions from service users groups Personal interviews with people who have left services

dress. Many areas now use a 'settings' and client group approach. For example, there are pronounced overlaps between client groups (such as young people) and settings (such as schools). Young people, like everybody else, are part of wider community groups and are influenced by the media and by popular attitudes. Some young people do not attend school and cannot be accessed there. Groups such as people attending independent schools may be missed. Schools, therefore, cannot be considered as the only, or even the best way, of contacting this particular age group and other settings are also important. Few settings are 'pure' with regard to the relevant client group. In schools, for example, it is not only the young but also teachers and parents who need information and support. Moreover, not only information-giving tasks will be necessary. Schools will also need means of obtaining access to services when required, and will require policies and training on issues such as drug seizures, drug testing of pupils or dealing with drug-related medical emergencies.

Local frameworks need to consider not only need, but capacity to benefit. Needs assessment work will find many gaps in services, and many unmet needs. Agencies cannot tackle everything at once. Evidence of the effectiveness of interventions is limited in the drug field. In general, as earlier chapters indicate, it is better to do something than to do nothing (Task Force to Review Services for Drug Misusers, 1996). There is controversy about the degree of evidence which is required of drug-related treatments (Miller and Sanchez-Craig, 1996; Moos, 1997; Hall, 1997). Evaluation of expensive programmes has sometimes identified little or no effect from the intervention (Hawthorne, 1996). Local strategy development needs to consider the number of people likely to benefit from an initiative, the gain expected from the intervention (be it prevention, treatment or enforcement) and the cost of the change compared to alternative uses of the same resource. All interventions require evaluation, although this will often be based on comparing processes with other, successful projects, rather than a formal research evaluation.

Rush (1996) offers a model with which to consider both service structure from the point of view of a client, and overall coordination of services and interventions. A simplified version is shown in Figure 15.3 (see p. 233). This continuum of response stresses the interaction of the various stages, and the importance of evaluation and review, as discussed above. Rush also stresses the importance of taking the local context into account. This is an essential consideration and relates to the discussion above regarding the steps required to make strategic plans work.

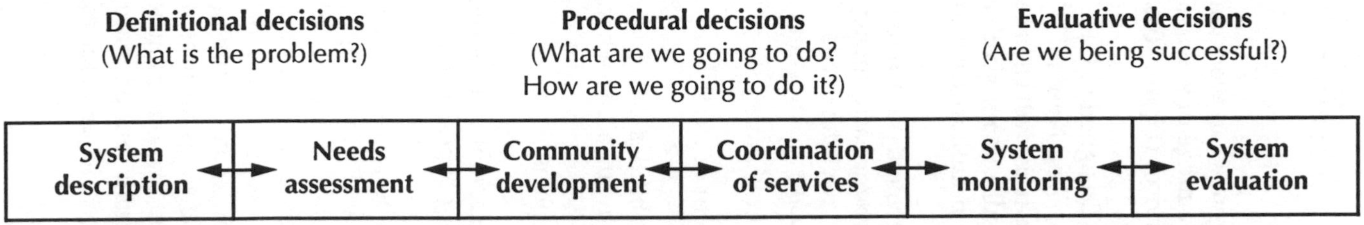

Definitional decisions (What is the problem?)		Procedural decisions (What are we going to do? How are we going to do it?)		Evaluative decisions (Are we being successful?)	
System description	Needs assessment	Community development	Coordination of services	System monitoring	System evaluation

From Rush, 1996.

Figure 15.3 Framework for drug strategy development

Sharing information	Sharing resources	Joint-commissioning	Consortium	Merger
e.g. needs assessment information, service specifications	e.g. staff, facilities, equipment, inspection unit	Agreed purchasing plan Pool finance for some, or all services	One agency commissions, but each commissioner remains an independent entity	New single commissioning body (e.g. Unitary Authority)

From Ovretveit, 1994.

Figure 15.4 Types of collaboration on commissioning

233

Joint commissioning

Previous chapters make it clear that no one group or agency can work on drug misuse without cooperating with others. There are a range of ways in which organisations can cooperate in commissioning services (Figure 15.4, see p. 233).

The contrasts in the Scottish White Paper on the NHS, 'Designed to Care' (Scottish Office, 1997) and that for England and Wales, 'The New NHS' (Department of Health, 1997) mean that differences in structures will emerge over time. Despite this, the principles of cooperation will remain similar with a need to integrate plans from health services, local authorities and voluntary agencies.

Ovretveit (1994) defined joint commissioning as 'arrangements and agreements between agencies for commissioning services, where each agency has a partial responsibility for commissioning services to meet the needs of a client group or population'. He suggests that the purposes of joint commissioning are (Ovretveit, 1994):

- To share assessments of need from different perspectives
- To align plans or forge a common plan
- To agree priorities and shared and separate responsibilities
- To avoid the duplication or gaps in services which can occur when each agency commissions services in isolation
- To ensure that contracting decisions further agreed plans.

Generally, the aim is to strengthen the commissioner's capability to meet the needs of the population at the lowest cost by pooling experience and knowledge, and agreeing joint strategies, for example by encouraging the involvement of new providers. The nature of cooperation between agencies on a DAT will be different for each area with which they deal. For example, enforcement issues will be the responsibility of the police and criminal justice services. Other areas will be less clear cut. In schools, education staff, health service staff and police may all play a role, with responsibility remaining with the education department and other agencies contributing resources in line with education policy. In other circumstances such as a counselling and treatment agency, there may be agreement that one agency will commission the service using financial resources from two or more partners. Each DAT will work this out for itself, but the matter requires explicit consideration.

Lessons learnt

The Social Policy Research Centre have produced a review of DATs in England on behalf of the Central Drugs Coordination Unit. This report provides the best source of information on implementation to date (Duke and MacGregor, 1997). A similar report has been commissioned in Scotland, but results were not available at the time of writing. Duke and MacGregor (1997) identified four stages in the development of DATs:

1 *Establishing Systems* This included examinations of existing arrangements, and the establishment of DATs and DRGs.
2 *Working Together* DATs needed to gain experience of working together. They reported mixed success on joint commissioning arrangements.
3 *Developing Strategy* This included ways of accessing information and local knowledge and setting priorities for action. The report noted that local conditions had a major affect on the way DATs and DRGs had developed in each area.
4 *Assessing Impact and Ensuring Sustainability* The authors of the review suggested that key elements on this would include access to resources, management of organisational relationships and ensuring appropriate geographical boundaries for the DAT.

Points raised by the work included differences in style between DATs where Health Authorities played an important role, and those in which Local Authorities were particularly influential. Health Authority-dominated DATs were seen to have a focus on service provision, while those with Local Authority dominance were more concerned with community safety and involving non-professional groups in discussion.

Involvement of organisations at senior level had raised the priority of drug misuse on local agendas. Agencies had increased awareness of each other's goals, and relations with the police had improved in most areas. Remaining questions included how to prioritise need, how far to focus on illegal drugs, and how to respond to tensions in providing services for injecting drug users and having to respond to the potential dangers of recreational drug use.

Conclusions

Government policy requires each area to have a strategic plan for management of drug misuse. Work in other fields suggests that high-level organsational commitment is necessary for strategy development to be effective. Barriers to the development and implementation of strategic plans are well known, and can be avoided. Each area will choose the methods which suit it best, but existing planning models can be readily adapted to suit local circumstance. A review of DATs in England suggested that they had already had an impact on local activities, but this was patchy and reflected the organisations which had taken the largest role in each area. By building on existing work, DATs can learn from the past and respond to future pressures in as efficient a way as possible. Flexibility, a willingness to learn from one another and acknowledgement that there is no one approach to drug misuse are essential.

References

Agyako, A., Inglis, J., Nettleship, H., Oates, K. and Pollard, R. (1997), 'Drugs in Scotland: Informing the Challenge', Edinburgh: Health Education Board for Scotland.

Boyle, D. (1988), 'The Strategic Planning Process', in D. Lock and N. Farrow (eds), *The Gower Handbook of Management*, (2nd edn), Aldershot: Gower.

Department of Health (1997), *The New NHS*, London: HMSO.

Duke, K. and MacGregor, S. (1997), Tackling Drugs Locally: The Implementation of Drug Action Teams in England, HMSO: London.

Dunn, J. and Laranjeira, R. (1996), 'Brazil: The Epidemic that was Allowed to Happen', *Addiction*, **91**, 1094–5.

Hall, W. (1997), 'Evidence-based Treatment for Drug Misuse: Bridging the Gap Between Aspiration and Achievement, *Addiction*, **92**, 373–4.

Hawthorne, G. (1996), 'The Social Impact of Life Education: Estimating Drug Use Prevalence Among Victorian Primary School Students and the Statewide Effect of the Life Education Programme', *Addiction*, **91**, 1151–9.

Hicks, H.G. and Gullett, C.R. (1981), *Management*, New York: McGraw-Hill.

Irwin, P.H. (1978), 'Who Really Believes in Strategic Planning?', *Managerial Planning*, Nov.–Dec., 6–9.

Institute for the Study of Drug Dependence (1996), 'Tackling Drugs Informatively', London: ISDD.

McGourty, H. and Hotchkiss, J. (1994), 'Drug Misuse and Services for Drug Users in Chester', Liverpool Public Health Observatory. Observatory Report Series No. 18, Liverpool: Liverpool Public Health Observatory.

McKeganey, N. (1995), 'Quantitative and Qualitative Research in the Addictions: An Unhelpful Divide', *Addiction*, **90**, 749–51.

Miller, W.R. and Sanchez-Craig, M. (1996), 'How to Have a High Success Rate in Treatment: Advice for Evaluators of Alcoholism Programs', *Addiction*, **91**, 779–85.

Moos, R.H. (1997), 'How to Become a True Scientist: A Guide to Minimising Pesky Treatment Effects', *Addiction*, **92**, 481–2.

Ovretveit, J. (1994), *Integrated Commissioning for Health*, London: Brunel University.

Rush, B. (1996), 'Alcohol and Other Drug Problems and Treatment Systems: A Framework for Research and Development', *Addiction*, 91, 629–42.

Scottish Office Department of Health (1997), *Designed to Care*, Edinburgh: Stationery Office.

Social Work Services Inspectorate (1996), 'Population Needs Assessment in Community Care: A Handbook for Planners and Practitioners', Edinburgh: HMSO.

Stimson, G. (1995), 'AIDS and Injecting Drug Use in the United Kingdom, 1987–1993: The Policy Response and the Prevention of the Epidemic', *Social Science and Medicine*, 41, 699–716.

Stimson, G. (1996), 'Has the United Kingdom Averted an Epidemic of HIV-1 Infection Among Drug Users?', *Addiction*, 91, 1085–8.

Task Force to Review Services for Drug Misusers (1996), 'Report of an Independent Review of Drug Treatment Services in England', London: Department of Health.

Wodak, A. (1996), 'A Stupendous Public Health Achievement', *Addiction*, 91, 1090–2.

Index

239